6 chr 263   10—
D0557100

GARCIA

By the Editors of Rolling Stone

LITTLE, BROWN AND COMPANY

BOSTON   NEW YORK   LONDON

A ROLLING STONE PRESS BOOK

EDITOR: Holly George-Warren
ASSOCIATE EDITOR: Shawn Dahl
EDITORIAL ASSISTANT: Greg Emmanuel
EDITORIAL CONTRIBUTORS:
Parke Puterbaugh, Patricia Romanowski

ART DIRECTOR: Fred Woodward
PHOTO EDITOR: Jodi Peckman
DESIGNERS: Gail Anderson, Lee Bearson,
Geraldine Hessler, Eric Siry
DESIGN ASSOCIATES: Yoomi Chong,
Amy Goldfarb, Fredrik Sundwall

COVER DESIGN: Fred Woodward
COVER PHOTOGRAPH: Herbi Greene

Copyright © 1995 ROLLING STONE PRESS

ALL RIGHTS RESERVED. No part of this
book may be reproduced in any form or
by any electronic or mechanical means,
including information storage and retrieval
systems, without the permission in writing
from the publisher, except by a reviewer who
may quote brief passages in a review.

FIRST PAPERBACK EDITION

ISBN 0-316-75449-8 (HC)
ISBN 0-316-75445-5 (PB)

Library of Congress Catalog
Card Number 95-81696

10 9 8 7 6 5 4 3 2

IM

Printed in China

The body type of this book is Hoefler Text,
designed by Jonathan Hoefler in 1991.

All Family Dog Productions posters are ©
Family Dog Productions, d.b.a. of Chester L.
Helms, 771 Bush St., San Francisco, CA 94108

TABLE OF CONTENTS

ROCK & ROLL COMMUNITY – that's a pretty apt description for the extraordinary bond the Grateful Dead and their audience have held since the Sixties. And it was in that spirit that this book was created. Editors, designers, writers and researchers – running the gamut of Deadheadness – all joined forces with a single goal. Working as a team, a family, we sought to make *Garcia* the best possible tribute we could muster, drawing upon more than a quarter century's coverage of the man and his band in ROLLING STONE. Here, then, is Jerry Garcia speaking to ROLLING STONE journalists in 1967, 1969, 1972, 1973, 1977, 1978, 1980, 1989, 1991 and 1993. We wanted a myriad of voices: An intellect and artistic vision and personality as complex as Garcia's require as many different takes on the man as possible. So we also dug up a 1976 Garcia interview previously published several years after the fact in the Deadhead 'zine *Relix* and a 1982 Q&A with Garcia from ROLLING STONE's then-sister publication, *The Record*. For a special issue of ROLLING STONE, a number of writers expressed their thoughts on the great man's passing – as did several of Garcia's contemporaries, colleagues and loved ones. Those pieces are reprinted here, as are essays written especially for *Garcia* by Ken Kesey, Jann S. Wenner and Anthony DeCurtis. ❧ PEOPLE ALL OVER the country enthusiastically offered their help, which is what really brought to fruition the book you now hold. Our deepest gratitude to Deborah Koons Garcia, Dennis McNally, Robert Hunter, David Stanford, Ken Kesey, Sterling Lord, Charles Reich, Gerard McCauley, Parke Puterbaugh, David McGee, Patricia Romanowski, Philip Bashe, Ben Fong-Torres, Jay Blakesburg, Jim Miller, Stephen Davis, John Milward, Toby Gleason, Billy Altman, David Browne, Walter Keeler, Robert Warren, Will Rigby, Greg Wustefeld, Nancy Bilyeau, Susan Richardson, Caren Gerszberg, Beth Renaud, Elizabeth Gehrman, Dave Dunton, Fredrik Sundwall, Yoomi Chong, Carolyn Zarillo, Liz Gall, Lucy Ware, Nathaniel Schiffman, Angela Ciminello, Jonathan Hoefler, David Nettles and Marianne Burke. Many thanks to the very talented writers and photographers whose work appears here. We also wish to thank our agent, Sarah Lazin, and our Little, Brown editor, Michael Pietsch, as well as LB's Clif Gaskill and Nora Krug: their support and belief in our efforts were most gratifying. We couldn't have done it without ROLLING STONE's Jann S. Wenner, Kent Brownridge, John Lagana, Fred Woodward, Jodi Peckman, Gail Anderson, Amy Goldfarb, Eric Siry, Geraldine Hessler, Lee Bearson, Fiona McDonough, Kevin Mullan, Willis Caster, Tom Worley, Eric Flaum, Chris Raymond, Chris Popkie, Denise Sfraga, Tobias Perse, Bill Van Parys, Sid Holt, Patty Cohen, Matt Hendrickson, Kara Manning, Laura Sandlin and Mary MacDonald. If not for my Rolling Stone Press staff – Shawn Dahl and Greg Emmanuel – this book would not exist. ❧ OF COURSE, the most thanks of all go to Jerry Garcia and the Grateful Dead – for your music and your message, which you have shared with so many. (For me, it began at Duke University's Cameron Indoor Stadium in 1976.) Long after this book becomes dust, your music will live on.

– Holly George-Warren
EDITOR, ROLLING STONE PRESS
OCTOBER 1995

MESSAGE TO GARCIA
BY KEN KESEY

Hey, Jerry —

What's happening? I caught your funeral. Weird. Big Steve was good. And Grisman. Sweet sounds. But what really stood out – stands out – is the thundering silence, the lack, the absence of that golden Garcia lead line, of that familiar slick lick with the uptwist at the end, that merry snake twining through the woodpile, flickering in and out of the loosely stacked chords . . . a wriggling mystery, bright and slick as fire . . . suddenly gone.

And the silence left in its wake was – is – positively earsplitting.

Now they want me to say something about that absence, Jer. Tell some backstage story, share some poignant reminiscence. But I have to tell you, man: I find myself considerably disinclined. I mean, why go against the grain of such an eloquent silence?

I remember standing out in the pearly early dawn after the Muir Beach Acid Test, leaning on the top rail of a driftwood fence with you and Lesh and Babbs, watching the world light up, talking about our glorious futures. The gig had been semisuccessful, and the air was full of exulted fantasies. Babbs whacks Phil on the back.

"Just like the big time, huh, Phil."

"It is! It is the big time! Why, we could cut a chart-busting record to-fucking-*morrow!*"

I was even more optimistic: "Hey, we taped tonight's show. We could *release* a record tomorrow."

"Yeah, right – " (holding up that digitally challenged hand the way you did when you wanted to call attention to the truth or the lack thereof) " – and a year from tomorrow be recording a 'Things Go Better With Coke' commercial."

You could be a sharp-tongued popper-of-balloons shithead when you were so inclined, you know. A real bastard. You were the sworn enemy of hot air and commercials, however righteous the cause or lucrative the product. Nobody ever heard you use that microphone as a pulpit. No antiwar rants, no hymns to peace. No odes to the trees and All Things Organic. No ego-deaths or born-againnesses. No devils denounced, no gurus glorified. No dogmatic howlings that I ever caught wind of. In fact, your steadfast denial of dogma was as close as you ever came to having a creed.

The many faces of the San Francisco scene in the Sixties: (Clockwise from top left) Jerry Garcia; Mountain Girl (a.k.a. Carolyn Adams, Garcia's second wife); Stewart Brand; Ken Kesey; Neal Cassady; Ken Babbs; Janis Joplin; (center) Kesey.

And to the very end, Old Timer, you were true to that creed. No commercials. No trendy spins. No bayings of belief. And if you did have any dogma, you surely kept it tied up under the back porch, where a smelly old hound belongs.

I guess that's what I mean about a loud silence. Like Michelangelo said about sculpting: "The statue exists inside the block of marble. All you have to do is chip away the stone you don't need." You were always chipping away at the superficial.

It was the false notes you didn't play that kept that lead line so golden pure. It was the words you didn't sing. So this is what we are left with, Jerry: this golden silence. It rings on and on without any hint of letup . . . on and on. And I expect it will still be ringing years from now.

Because you're *still* not playing falsely. Because you're *still* not singing "Things Go Better With Coke."

Ever your friend,

Keez

"My way is music. Music is me being me and trying to get higher. I've been into music so long that I'm dripping with it; it's all I ever expect to do." ~JERRY GARCIA, 1969

* * *

I HAD JUST LEFT my first Rolling Stones concert at the San Jose Civic Center and, my ears still ringing with "Satisfaction," somehow ended up at an old Victorian house by the campus of San Jose State. I opened the door to discover a hundred people my age and older wandering around with heads full of acid. A band had set up in the living room, playing electrified blues and free-form jams. I remember the music being very enchanting and very strong. During a lull I walked up to one of them – Bob Weir, I believe – and asked, "Who are you?" He answered, "The Grateful Dead." My reply: "Faarrr-out."

This was 1965. The party turned out to be one of the first of Ken Kesey's now legendary Acid Tests, unscripted multimedia happenings at which the various elements in the San Francisco scene came together in a spontaneous, psychedelic incubator. The Grateful Dead served as the house band for the Acid Tests. They were the ideal group of musicians for those formless rituals, being conversant in everything from Beat Generation literature to all kinds of indigenous American music, including folk, blues, jazz, bluegrass and rock & roll. It was this collage of music, literature, lifestyle and philosophy that laid the groundwork for the emerging hippie culture, and the Grateful Dead embodied it *in toto.*

It was a movement of such persuasive power and passion that I felt moved to document it journalistically by founding ROLLING STONE in 1967. Because the Grateful Dead were a driving force behind the San Francisco scene, they figured prominently in ROLLING STONE as well. I wrote about their drug bust at the house at 710 Ashbury in the Haight in the very first issue. My account accompanied a two-page spread of photographs that found the band cavorting on the stoop of their house, seemingly unperturbed by their legal troubles. I remember interviewing them, as it were, hanging out in the kitchen.

We wrote about the Dead before they got big because, quite simply, they were one of my favorite bands. I used to see them play almost every weekend at San Francisco's psychedelic ballrooms, and I got to know them from those shows and through mutual friends. Jerry would talk to me about what he'd like to see published in ROLLING STONE. He was very inquisitive and literary-minded, so he always wanted more interviews in the magazine. He loved to talk, to qualify and explain and describe things. Musically, I recall being struck by his versatility and skill with the guitar. Sometimes I'd stand next to him onstage or just to the side of the stage and mention a guitar player's name while he was in the middle of a performance. Without missing a beat, he'd shift into that guitar player's style.

I saw them a lot in the early years, when Pigpen was still around and they were a bit more blues based. They had a tremendous reverb sound that sounded great in the dance halls. I loved it when they did hard-core rhythm & blues like "In the Midnight Hour," "Good Lovin'," "Viola Lee Blues" and "Walkin' the Dog" and when Jerry would sing Bob Dylan

songs. I liked them as a performing band then and as a recording band circa *Workingman's Dead* and *American Beauty,* which were classics of philosophy no less than songcraft. By this time, of course, the Grateful Dead were earning extensive coverage in ROLLING STONE on their own merits, based on their popularity and significance as a band. (Incidentally, Garcia – with and without the Grateful Dead – has made eleven cover appearances, which puts him in a group that includes Bob Dylan, John Lennon, Bruce Springsteen and Mick Jagger, with and without the Stones.)

Throughout the formative years of both ROLLING STONE and the Grateful Dead, Jerry and I would compare notes on our respective organizations and try to learn from what the other was doing. The Dead were an ongoing experiment in social organization, guided by Jerry's philosophy of letting things evolve without imposing too much authority or structure. Eventually, they became the most successful touring rock band in musical history – which is undeniably ironic, coming from the perspective of San Francisco in the mid-Sixties. I don't think anyone, myself included, envisioned them as a big-time national band. The Jefferson Airplane had an early hit single, and the Steve Miller Band and a few others landed major-label contracts, but the Dead were "our band." It just seemed they were going to be resolutely on the lowest rung in terms of commercial success. They looked funky, the music was strange, and on and on.

The triumph of Jerry Garcia and the Grateful Dead is that they succeeded entirely on their own terms. A mass audience found its way to them, feeding off the Dead's music and the philosophies they espoused. Over the years, I have been constantly amazed by the Deadhead phenomenon. I think it stands for a number of things that are good and wholesome, principally a desire that the world be a gentler place or at least that there be a space in it where the Dead can play and you can go and groove with your brothers and sisters. It's really the hippie ethos, alive and well and surviving over the decades.

The last time I saw Jerry was in 1991 at Bill Graham's funeral, which was the first time I'd seen everybody from the San Francisco scene *en masse* in years. Three years later I helped induct the Grateful Dead into the Rock and Roll Hall of Fame, giving an "I'm proud to be a Deadhead" speech. I still feel very much like a Deadhead. I remain very connected to that past and my early memories of San Francisco, knowing those guys and enjoying those shows at the Fillmore and the Avalon so much. I can recollect them all clearly and feel very grounded in that place and time.

I am sure that much the same allegiance holds true for every Deadhead, regardless of the point at which he or she came aboard during the band's long history. It's a tradition that's been handed down. More than that, however, it's an environment where certain ideas and values that the Dead promulgated about life could be found and could be lived. The seeds they've sown have taken root all over, extending beyond concert settings into people's daily existences. This, as much as any notes he played, is Jerry Garcia's legacy. ☾

~JANN S. WENNER

WE NEVER decided to be the Grateful Dead. What happened was, the Grateful Dead came up as a suggestion because we were at Phil's house one day; he had a big Oxford dictionary. I opened it up, and the first thing I saw was the 'grateful dead.' It said that on the page, and it was so astonishing.

~*JERRY GARCIA, 1972*

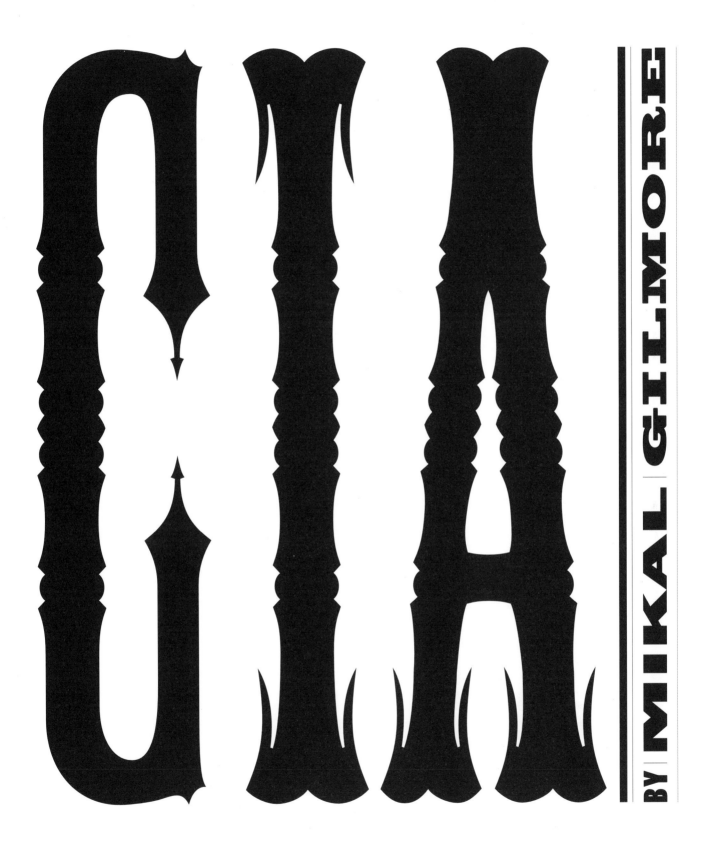

GIA

BY MIKAL GILMORE

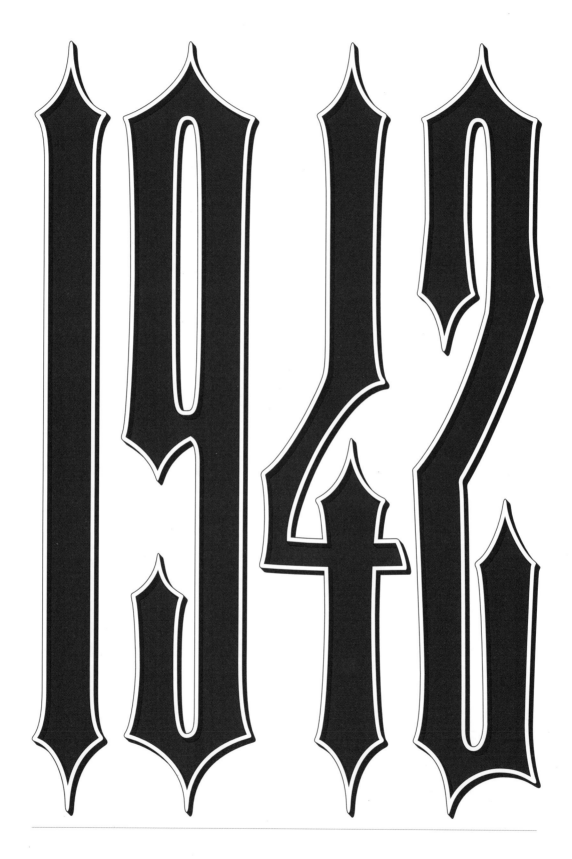

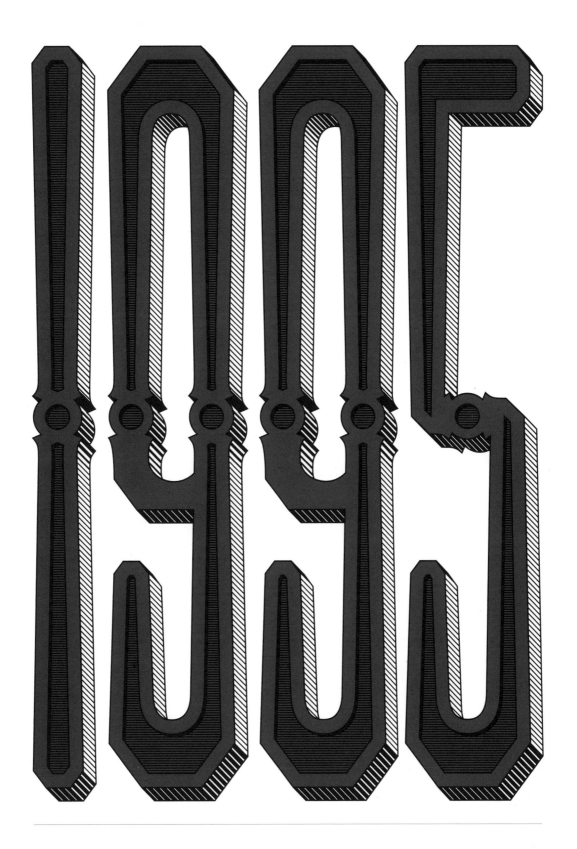

H E WAS THE UNLIKELIEST of pop stars and the most reticent of cultural icons.

Onstage he wore plain clothes – usually a sacklike T-shirt and loose jeans to fit his heavy frame – and he rarely spoke to the audience that watched his every move. Even his guitar lines – complex, lovely and rhapsodic but never flashy – as well as his strained, weatherworn vocal style had a subdued, colloquial quality about them. Offstage he kept to family and friends, and when he sat to talk with interviewers about his remarkable music, he often did so in sly-witted, self-deprecating ways. "I feel like I'm sort of stumbling along," he said once, "and a lot of people are watching me or stumbling along with me or allowing me to stumble for them." It was as if Jerry Garcia – who, as the lead guitarist and singer of the Grateful Dead, lived at the center of one of popular culture's most extraordinary epic adventures – was bemused by the circumstances of his own renown.

And yet, when he died on August 9, 1995, a week after his fifty-third birthday, at a rehabilitation clinic in Forest Knolls, California, the news of his death set off immense waves of emotional reaction. Politicians, newscasters, poets and artists eulogized the late guitarist throughout the day and night; fans of all ages gathered spontaneously in parks around the nation; and in the streets of San Francisco's Haight-Ashbury – the neighborhood where the Grateful Dead lived at the height of the hippie epoch – mourners assembled by the hundreds, singing songs, building makeshift altars, consoling one another and jamming the streets for blocks around. Across town at San Francisco City Hall, a tie-dye flag was flown on the middle flagpole, and the surrounding flags were lowered to half-mast. It was a fitting gesture from a civic government that had once feared the movement that the Grateful Dead represented but now acknowledged the band's pilgrimage across the last thirty years to be one of the most notable chapters in the city's modern history.

Chances are, Garcia himself would have been embarrassed, maybe even repelled, by all the commotion. He wasn't much given to mythologizing his own history. In some of his closing words in his last interview in this magazine, in 1993, he said: "I'm hoping to leave a clean field – nothing, not a thing. I'm hoping they burn it all with me . . . I'd rather have my immortality here while I'm alive. I don't care if it lasts beyond me at all. I'd just as soon it didn't."

Garcia's fans and friends, of course, feel differently. "I think that Garcia was a real avatar," says John Perry Barlow, who knew the late guitarist since 1967 and cowrote many of

Preceding pages: Jerome John Garcia with José and Ruth Garcia, circa 1942; Jerry Garcia photographed in Indianapolis. At left: Father and son, 1947.

the group's songs with Bob Weir. "Jerry was one of those manifestations of the energy of his times; one of those people who ends up making the history books. He wrapped up in himself a whole set of characteristics and qualities that were very appropriate to a certain cultural vector in the latter part of the twentieth century: freedom from judgment, playfulness of intellect, complete improvisation, antiauthoritarianism, self-indulgence and aesthetic development. I mean, he was truly

extraordinary. And he never really saw it himself or could feel it himself. He could only see its effect on other people, which baffled and dismayed him.

"It made me sad to see that, because I wanted him to be able to appreciate, in some detached way, his own marvel," Barlow says. "There was nothing that Garcia liked better than something that was really diverting and interesting and lively and fascinating. You know, anything that he would refer to as a 'fat trip,' which was his term for that sort of thing. And he wasn't really able to appreciate himself, which was a pity because, believe me, Jerry was the fattest trip of all. About the most he would say for himself was that he was a competent musician. But he would say that. I remember one time he started experimenting with MIDI; he was using all these MIDI-sampled trumpet sounds. And he started playing that on his guitar, and he sounded like Miles Davis, only better. I went up to him the first time I ever heard him do it, and I said, 'You could have been a great fucking trumpet player.' And he looked at me and said, 'I am a great fucking trumpet player.' So, he knew."

* * *

J EROME JOHN GARCIA was born in 1942, in San Francisco's Mission District. His father, a Spanish immigrant named José "Joe" Garcia, had been a jazz clarinetist and Dixieland bandleader in the Thirties, and he named his new son after his favorite Broadway composer, Jerome Kern. In the spring of 1948, while on a fishing trip, Garcia saw his father swept to his death in a California river.

After his father's death, Garcia spent a few years living with his mother's parents, in one of San Francisco's working-class districts. His grandmother had the habit of listening to Nashville's Grand Ole Opry radio broadcasts on Saturday nights, and it was in those hours, Garcia would later say, that he developed his fondness for country-music forms – particularly the deft, blues-inflected mandolin playing and mournful, high-lonesome vocal style of Bill Monroe, the principal founder of bluegrass. When Garcia was ten, his mother, Ruth, brought him to live with her at a sailor's hotel and bar that she ran near the city's waterfront. He spent much of his time there listening to the boozy, fanciful stories that the hotel's old tenants told, or sat alone, reading Disney and horror comics and poring through science-fiction novels.

When Garcia was fifteen, his older brother Tiff – who years earlier had accidentally lopped off Jerry's right-hand middle finger while the two were chopping wood – introduced him to early rock & roll and rhythm & blues music. Garcia was quickly drawn to the music's funky rhythms and rough-hewed textures, but what captivated him most were the lead-guitar sounds – especially the bluesy mellifluousness of players like T-Bone Walker and Chuck Berry. It was otherworldly sounding music, he later said, unlike anything he had heard before. Garcia decided he wanted to learn how to make those same sounds. He went to his mother and proclaimed that he wanted an electric guitar for his upcoming birthday.

During this same period, the Beat scene was in full swing in the Bay Area, and it held great sway at the North Beach arts school where Garcia took some courses and at the city's coffeehouses, where he heard poets like Lawrence Ferlinghetti and Kenneth Rexroth read their venturesome works.

By the early Sixties, Garcia was living in Palo Alto, California, hanging out and playing in the folk-music clubs around Stanford University. He was also working part-time at Dana Morgan's Music Store, where he met several of the musicians who would eventually dominate the San Francisco music scene. In 1963 Garcia formed a jug band, Mother McCree's Uptown Jug Champions. Its lineup included a young folk guitarist named Bob Weir and a blues aficionado, Ron McKernan, known to his friends as "Pigpen" for his often unkempt appearance. The group played a mix of blues, country and folk, and Pigpen became the frontman, singing Jimmy Reed and Lightnin' Hopkins tunes.

Then, in February 1964, the Beatles made their historic appearance on *The Ed Sullivan Show,* and virtually overnight, youth culture was imbued with a new spirit and sense of identity. Garcia understood the group's promise after seeing its first film, *A Hard Day's Night.* For the first time since Elvis Presley – and the first time for an audience that had largely rejected contemporary rock & roll as seemingly trivial and inconsequential – pop music could be seen to hold bold, significant and thoroughly exhilarating possibilities that even the ultraserious, socially aware folk scene could not offer. That became even more apparent a year later, when Bob Dylan – who had been the folk scene's reigning hero – played an assailing set of his defiant new electric music at the Newport Folk Festival.

As a result, the folky purism of Mother McCree's all-acoustic format began to seem rather limited and uninteresting to Garcia and many of the other band members, and before long the ensemble was transformed into an electric unit, the Warlocks. A couple of the jug-band members dropped out, and two new musicians joined: Bill Kreutzmann, who worked at Dana Morgan's Music Store, on drums; and on bass, a classically trained musician named Phil Lesh, who, like Garcia, had been radicalized by the music of the Beatles and Bob Dylan.

It was around this time that Garcia and some of the group's other members also began an experimentation with drugs that would forever transform the nature of the band's story. Certainly this wasn't the first time drugs had been used in music for artistic inspiration or had found their way into an American cultural movement. Many jazz and blues artists (not to mention several country & western players) had been smoking marijuana and using various narcotics to intensify their music making for several decades, and in the Fifties the Beats had extolled marijuana as an assertion of their non-conformism. But the drugs that began cropping up in the youth and music scenes in the mid-Sixties were of a much different, more exotic sort. Veterans Hospital near Stanford University had been the site of government-sanctioned experiments with LSD, a drug that induced hallucinations in those who ingested it and that, for many, also inspired something remarkably close to the patterns of a religious experience. Among those who had taken the drug at Veterans Hospital were Robert Hunter, a folksinger and poet who would later become Garcia's songwriting partner, and Ken Kesey, author of *One Flew Over the Cuckoo's Nest* and

Sometimes a Great Notion. Kesey had been working on an idea about group LSD experiments and had started a loosely knit gang of artists and rogues, called the Merry Pranksters, dedicated to this adventure. Kesey's crew included a large number of intellectual dropouts like himself and eccentric rebels like Neal Cassady (the inspiration for Dean Moriarty in Jack Kerouac's *On the Road*) and Carolyn Adams (later known as Mountain Girl), who eventually married Garcia and had two children with him.

The Pranksters had been holding parties at a house in the nearby town of La Honda, California, to see what would happen when people took LSD in a setting where there were no regulations or predetermined situations. At Kesey's invitation, the Grateful Dead – as the Warlocks were now called – became the house band for these collective drug experiments, known as the Acid Tests. The Dead would play for hours as the Pranksters filmed the goings-on – everything from freakouts to religious revelations to group sex. The Acid Tests were meant to be acts of cultural, spiritual and psychic revolt, and their importance to the development of the Grateful Dead cannot be overestimated. The Dead's music, Garcia later said, "had a real sense of proportion to the event" – which is to say that sometimes the group's playing would seem to overshadow the event, and at other times it would function as commentary or backdrop to the action of the event itself. Either way, the band did not see itself as the star of the party; if there were stars, they were formed from the union of the music and musicians with the audience and the spirit and shape of what was happening from moment to moment – which meant there was a blur between the performers, the event and the audience.

Consequently, the Acid Tests became the model for what would shortly become known as the Grateful Dead trip. In the years that followed, the Dead would never really forsake the philosophy of the Acid Tests. Right until the end, the band would encourage its audience to be involved with the music and the sense of fellowship that came from and fueled the music.

* * *

BY 1966, the spirit of the Acid Tests was spilling over into the streets and clubs of San Francisco – and well beyond. A new community of largely young people – many sharing similar ideals about drugs, music, politics and sex – had taken root in the Haight-Ashbury district, a rundown but picturesque section of the city adjacent to Golden Gate Park, where the members of the Grateful Dead now shared a house. In addition, a thriving club and dance-hall scene – dominated by Chet Helms' Avalon Ballroom and Bill Graham's Fillmore – had sprung up around the city, drawing the notice of the media, the police and various political forces.

The Grateful Dead's Victorian house at 710 Ashbury Street, 1966: Phil Lesh, Bob Weir, Bill Kreutzmann, Ron "Pigpen" McKernan and Garcia. Following pages: Mountain Girl and Garcia.

The public scrutiny would in part eventually make life in the Haight difficult and risky. But there was also a certain boon that came from all the new publicity: The music and ethos of the San Francisco scene had begun to draw the

interest of East Coast and British musicians and were starting to affect the thinking of artists like the Beatles and Bob Dylan – the same artists who only a year or two before had exerted such a major influence on groups like the Grateful Dead. For that matter, San Francisco bands were having an impact not just on pop and fashion styles but also on social mores and even the political dialogue of the times. Several other bands, of course, participated in the creation of this scene, and some – including Jefferson Airplane, Quicksilver Messenger Service and Janis Joplin with Big Brother and the Holding Company – would make music as inventive and memorable as the Dead's. In addition, nobody should underrate concert promoter Bill Graham's importance to the adventure; he was an often acerbic character, but he would emerge as an invaluable and scrupulous caretaker of the community that he served.

Still, it was the Grateful Dead who became known as the "people's band" – the band that cared about the following it played to and that often staged benefits or free shows for the common good. And long after the Haight's moment had passed, it would be the Grateful Dead – and the Dead alone among the original San Francisco groups – that would still exemplify the ideals of fraternity and compassion which most other Sixties-bred groups had long ago relinquished and many subsequent rock artists repudiated in favor of more corrosive ideals.

The San Francisco scene was remarkable while it lasted, but it couldn't endure forever. Because of its reputation as a youth haven, the Haight was soon overrun with runaways and the sort of health and shelter problems that a community of mainly white, middle-class expatriates had never had to face before. In addition, the widespread use of LSD was turning out to be a little less ideal than some folks had imagined: There were nights when so many young people seemed to be on bad trips, the emergency rooms of local hospitals could not accommodate them all. By the middle of 1967 – a season still referred to as the Summer of Love – the Haight had started to turn ugly. There were bad drugs on the streets, there were rapes and murders, and there was a surfeit of starry-eyed newcomers who had arrived in the neighborhood without any means of support and were expecting the scene to feed and nurture them. Garcia and the Dead had seen the trouble coming and tried to prompt the city to prepare for it. "You could feed large numbers of people," Garcia later said, "but only so large. You could feed one thousand, but not twenty thousand. We were unable to convince the San Francisco officials of what was going to happen. We said there would be more people in the city than the city could hold." Not long after, the Dead left the Haight for individual residences in Marin County, north of San Francisco.

By 1970, the idealism surrounding the Bay Area music scene – and much of the counterculture – had largely evaporated. The drug scene had turned fearful; much of the peace movement had given way to violent rhetoric; and the quixotic dream of a Woodstock generation, bound together by the virtues of love and music, had been irreparably damaged, first by the Manson Family murders, in the summer of 1969, and then, a few months later, by a tragic and brutal event at the Altamont Speedway, just outside San Francisco. The occasion was a free concert featuring the Rolling Stones. Following either the example or the suggestion of the Grateful Dead (there is still disagreement on this), the Stones hired the Hell's Angels as a security force. It proved to be a day of horrific violence. The Angels battered numerous people, usually for little reason, and in the evening, as the Stones performed, the bikers stabbed a young black man to death in front of the stage.

The record the band followed with, *Workingman's Dead,* was the Dead's response to that period. The album was a statement about the changing and badly frayed sense of community in America and its counterculture, and as such, it was a work by and about a group of men being tested and pressured at a time when they could have easily pulled apart from all the madness and stress and disappointment. The music reflected that struggle, particularly in songs like "Uncle John's Band," a parable about America that was also the band's confession of how it nearly fell apart, and "New Speedway Boogie," about Altamont. "One way or another, this darkness has got to give," Garcia sang in the latter song, in a voice full of fear, fragility and hard-earned courage. *Workingman's Dead* and the record that followed it, *American Beauty,* made it plain how the Grateful Dead found the heart and courage and talent to stick together and make something new and meaningful from their fraternity. "Making the record became like going to a job," Garcia said. "It was something we had to do, and it was also something we did to keep our minds off some of these problems, even if the music is about those problems."

In a conversation I had with Robert Hunter in 1989, he revealed something else that he thought had influenced Garcia's singing in that period and made it so affecting. "It wasn't only because of the gathering awareness of what we were doing," he said, "but Jerry's mother had died in an automobile accident while we were recording *American Beauty,* and there's a lot of heartbreak on that record, especially on 'Brokedown Palace,' which was, I think, his release at that time. The pathos in Jerry's voice on those songs, I think, has a lot to do with that experience. When the pathos is there, I've always thought Jerry is the best. The man can get inside some of those lines and turn them inside out, and he makes those songs entirely his. There is no emotion more appealing than the bittersweet when it's truly, truly spoken."

* * *

WITH 'WORKINGMAN'S DEAD' and *American Beauty,* the Grateful Dead hit a creative peak and turned an important corner. For one thing, the two records sold better than anything the group had issued before, and as a result the band was able to begin working its way free of many of the crushing debts it had accrued. More important, the Dead now had a body of fine new songs to perform onstage for its rapidly expanding audience. With the next album, a double live set, *Grateful Dead* (entitled *Skullfuck* until Warner Bros. balked), the band issued an invitation to its fans: "Send us your name and address, and we'll keep you informed."

It was the sort of standard fan club pitch that countless pop acts had indulged in before, but what it set in motion for the Dead would prove unprecedented: the biggest sustained fan reaction in pop-music history. (According to *The New Yorker*, there are currently 110,000 Deadheads on the band's mailing list.) Clearly the group had a devoted and far-flung following that – more than anything else – simply wanted to see the Grateful Dead live. One of the aphorisms of the time was "There's nothing like a Grateful Dead show," and though that adage sometimes backfired in unintended ways – such as those occasions when the band turned in a protracted, meandering and largely out-of-tune performance – as often as not, the claim was justified. On those nights when the group was on – propelled by the double drumming of Mickey Hart and Bill Kreutzmann, and the dizzying melodic communion of Garcia and Weir's guitars and Lesh's bass – the Grateful Dead's verve and imagination proved matchless.

It was this dedication to live performance, and a penchant for near-incessant touring, that formed the groundwork for the Dead's extraordinary success during the last twenty or so years. Even a costly failed attempt at starting the band's own autonomous record label in the early Seventies, plus the deaths of three consecutive keyboardists – McKernan, of alcohol-induced cirrhosis of the liver, in 1973; Keith Godchaux, in a car accident, in 1980, a year after leaving the band; and Brent Mydland, of a morphine and cocaine overdose in 1990 – never really deterred the Dead's momentum as a live act.

By the summer of 1987, when the group enjoyed its first and only Top Ten single ("Touch of Grey") and album (*In the Dark*), the commercial breakthrough was almost beside the fact in any objective assessment of the band's stature. The Grateful Dead had been a top concert draw in America for several years and in fact had probably played before more people over the years than any other performing act in history. But the nature of the band's success went well beyond big numbers and high finances: From the late Sixties to the mid-Nineties, the Grateful Dead enjoyed a union with their audience that was unrivaled and unshakable. Indeed, the Dead and their followers formed the only self-sustained, ongoing fellowship that pop music has ever produced – a commonwealth that lasted more than a quarter-century.

At the same time, Jerry Garcia and the other members of the Grateful Dead paid a considerable price for their singular accomplishment. By largely forswearing studio recordings after the Seventies (the band has released only two collections of all-new music in the past fifteen years) and by never returning to the sort of songwriting impetus that made works like *Workingman's Dead* and *American Beauty* so notable, the Dead lost the interest of much of the mainstream and important cutting-edge pop audiences of the last two decades. To the group's detractors, the Grateful Dead often appeared as little more than a Sixties relic, a band frozen in the sensibility of exhausted ideals, playing to a gullible cult audience that, like the group itself, was out of touch with the changing temper of the times.

Garcia and the Dead's other members heard this sort of criticism – and countless "dinosaur" jokes – plenty over the years, and it had to have cut deep into their pride. Perhaps the general pop world's disregard and outright ridicule, combined with all those years of restless touring, even took a certain toll on the spirits of the various band members. In any event, something began to wear on Garcia in the mid-Eighties, and whatever it was, it never really let up on him. By 1984, rumors were making the rounds among Deadheads – who just may be the best networked community on the planet – that Garcia's guitar playing had lost much of its wit and edge, that his singing had grown lackadaisical and that, in fact, he was suffering from drug problems. The rumors proved true. Garcia had been using cocaine and heroin for several years and had developed a serious addiction. The problem became so acute that one day in January 1985, the other members of the Grateful Dead paid Garcia a visit and told him they were afraid he was killing himself. They also reportedly issued the sort of warning they had never before issued to a band mate: Garcia would have to choose between his involvement with the band and his drug use. But before Garcia could act on the Dead's ultimatum, he was arrested in Golden Gate Park on January 18, in possession of numerous packets of heroin and cocaine. Two months later a municipal court judge allowed Garcia to enter a Marin County drug-diversion program in lieu of a jail sentence, and Garcia committed himself to overthrowing his drug habits.

The next year, though, following the Grateful Dead's 1986 summer shows with Bob Dylan and Tom Petty and the Heartbreakers, Garcia passed out at his home in San Rafael, California, and slipped into a diabetic coma. His body had simply been overwhelmed by all the years of road life and drug usage. He was in the coma for a few days, and when he recovered, it wasn't at first apparent whether he would fully regain his musical agility. But with the help of an old friend, keyboardist Merl Saunders, and with the support of the Dead, Garcia recovered his skills, and the Dead went on to enjoy a long-overdue commercial success with "Touch of Grey," a song about aging gracefully and bravely.

Unfortunately, though, Garcia's health continued to be a problem, and according to some accounts, so did his appetite for drugs. He collapsed from exhaustion in 1992, resulting in the Dead's canceling many of the performances on their tour. After his 1993 recovery, Garcia devoted himself to a regimen of diet and exercise. At first the pledge seemed to work: He shed more than sixty pounds, and he often appeared renewed and better focused onstage. There were other positive changes at work: He had become a father again in recent years and was attempting to spend more time as a parent, and in 1994 he entered into his third marriage, with filmmaker Deborah Koons. Plus, to the pleasure of numerous Deadheads, he had recently written several of his best new songs in years, with his longtime friend Robert Hunter, in preparation for a new Grateful Dead album.

These were all brave efforts for a man past fifty with considerable health problems and a troubled drug history. In the end, though, they weren't enough to carry him further. In mid-July he checked into the Betty Ford Center in Rancho Mirage, California, for one more go at overcoming his heroin use. According to one report, he wanted to be clean for the

Dead's fall tour and was planning to give away his oldest daughter, Heather, at her upcoming wedding. He checked out two weeks later so he could spend his fifty-third birthday, on August 1, with family and friends. A week later he went into a different clinic, Serenity Knolls, in Marin County. He was already clean, most sources report; he just wanted to be in sound shape. This time Jerry Garcia did not walk out and return to the loving fraternity of his band, his fans and his family. Shortly after 4:00 a.m. on Wednesday, August 9, a clinic counselor found him unconscious. In his sleep, it seems, he had suffered a fatal heart attack.

* * *

J ERRY GARCIA and the Grateful Dead were so active for so long and were so heartening for the audience that loved them that it seems somewhat astonishing to realize that the band's adventure is probably over – or that at least its most vital part is finished. Of course, anybody paying attention – anybody aware of the ups and downs in Garcia's well-being – might have seen it coming. Still, endings are always tough things to be braced for.

"He was like the boy who cried wolf," says Barlow. "He'd come so close so many times that I think people gradually stopped taking the possibility as seriously as they otherwise would have. Or maybe we felt so certain that this would happen someday that we had managed, as a group, to go into a kind of collective denial about it. I am finding that I looked at this event so many times, and shrank back from it in fear so many times, that I erected a new callous against it each time I did so. Now that I'm here at the thing itself, I hardly know what to think of it. Every deposition of every imagined version of it is now standing in the way of being able to understand and appreciate the real thing.

"But this is a very large death," says Barlow. "There are a lot of levels on which to be affected here, all the way from the fact that I'm going to miss terribly the opportunity to spend time in conversation with one of the smartest and most playful minds I've ever run up against, to the fact that there will never truly be another Grateful Dead concert . . . I never thought of myself as a Deadhead exactly . . . but that's been a pretty fundamental part of my life – of all our lives – for the past thirty years."

It is, indeed, a considerable passing. To see the Grateful Dead onstage was to see a band that clearly understood the meaning of playing together from the perspective of the long haul. Interestingly, that's something we've seen fairly little of in rock & roll, since rock is an art form, the most valuable and essential pleasures of which – including inspiration, meaning and fraternity – are founded in the knowledge that such moments cannot hold forever. The Grateful Dead, like any great rock & roll band, lived up to that ideal, but they also shattered it or at least bent it to their own purposes. At their best the Dead were capable of surprising both themselves and their audience while at the same time playing as though they had spent their whole lives learning to make music as a way of talking to one another, and as though music were the language of their fellowship and, therefore, their history. No doubt it was. What the Grateful Dead understood – probably better than any

other band in pop-music history – was that nobody in the group could succeed as well, or mean as much, outside the context of the entire group, and that the group itself could not succeed without its individuals. It was a band that needed all its members playing and thinking together to keep things inspiring. Just as important, it was a band that realized it also needed its audience to keep things significant – indeed, it would be fair to say that for the past twenty years the Dead's audience informed the group's worth as much as its music did.

In the hours after I learned of Garcia's death, I went online to the Well, the Bay Area computer conference system that has thrived in no small part due to its large contingent of Deadheads. I wanted to see how the fans were doing and what they were saying in the recognition of their loss. For the most part – at least in those first hours that I scanned the messages – what I found were well-meaning, blithe comments, people sending each other "beams" (which are like positive extrasensory wishes) and fantasies of group hugs. They were the sort of sentiments that many people I know would gag at, and, I must admit, they proved too saccharine for my own sensibility. Still, one of the things I had to recognize about the Deadheads years ago, when I did some writing about the band and its fans, was that this was a group of people for whom good cheer wasn't just a shared disposition but also an act of conscious dissent: a protest against the anger and malice that seem to characterize so much of our social and artistic temper these days. The Deadheads may sometimes seem like naifs, but I'm not convinced their vision of community is such an undesirable thing. After all, there are worse visions around. Consider, for example, the vision of today's Republican Congress.

In any event, for my tastes, I saw far too little attention paid – by both the Deadheads and the media – to just how much darkness made its way into Garcia and the Dead's music, and how strong and interesting that darkness was. For that matter, there was always a good deal more darkness in the whole Sixties adventure than many people have been comfortable acknowledging – and I don't mean simply all the drug casualties, political ruin and violence of the period. There was also a willingness to explore risky psychic terrain – a realization that your best hopes could also cost you some terrible losses – and I think that those possibilities were realized in the Dead's music and history as meaningfully as they were anywhere.

In fact, the darkness crept in early in the Dead's saga. It could be found in the insinuation of the band's name, which many fans in the early San Francisco scene cited as being too creepy and disturbing a moniker for a rock group. It could also be heard deep down in much of the band's best music – in the strange layers and swirls that made parts of *Aoxomoxoa* such a vivid and frightening aural portrayal of the psychedelic experience, and in the meditations about death and damage that the band turned into hard-boiled anthems of hope on *Workingman's Dead* and other works of that period. And, of course, there was also all the darkness in the band's history that delivered so many of its members to their deaths.

Not all darkness is negative. In fact, sometimes wonder-

ful and kind things can come from it, and if there's one thing that was apparent to everybody about Jerry Garcia, it was that he was a good-humored man with generous instincts. But there was much more to him than that, and it wasn't always obvious on the surface. In a conversation I had several years ago with Robert Hunter about Garcia, Hunter told me: "Garcia is a cheery and resilient man, but I always felt that under his warmth and friendliness there was a deep well of despair – or at least a recognition that at the heart of the world there may be more darkness, despair and absurdity than any sane and compassionate heart could stand."

In his last interview with ROLLING STONE, in 1993, Garcia had this to say about his own dark side: "I definitely have a component in my personality which is not exactly self-destructive, but it's certainly ornery . . . It's like . . . 'Try to get healthy' – 'Fuck you, man' . . . I don't know what it comes from. I've always clung to it, see, because I felt it's part of what makes me *me*. Being anarchic, having that anarchist streak, serves me on other levels – artistically, certainly. So I don't want to eliminate that aspect of my personality. But I see that on some levels it's working against me."

Garcia, of course, made his own choices, and whatever they may have cost him, I would argue that in some ways they were still brave, worthy choices. Maybe they were even essential to the wondrous creations of his life's work. His achievements, in fact, were enormous. He helped inspire and nurture a community that in some form or another has survived for thirty years and may even outlast his death; he cowrote a fine collection of songs about America's myths, pleasures and troubles; and, as the Grateful Dead's most familiar and endearing member, he accomplished something that no other rock star ever has: He attracted an active following that has only grown larger in size and devotion with each passing decade, from the Sixties to the Nineties. You would have to look to the careers of people like Louis Armstrong, Duke Ellington, Count Basie, Miles Davis and Charles Mingus to find the equivalent of Garcia's musical longevity and growth in the history of American bandleaders.

Most important, though, Garcia was a man who remained true to ideals and perceptions many of the rest of us long ago found easy to discard – and maybe in the end that is a bigger part of our loss at this point than the death of Garcia himself.

My favorite Grateful Dead song of the last decade or so is "Black Muddy River." It's about living one's life in spite of all the heartbreak and devastation that life can bring, and in its most affecting verse, Garcia sang: "When it seems like the night will last forever / And there's nothing left to do but count the years / When the strings of my heart start to sever / Stones fall from my eyes instead of tears / I will walk alone by the black muddy river / Dream me a dream of my own / I will walk alone by the black muddy river . . . and sing me a song of my own."

Those were among the last words Garcia sang at the Grateful Dead's final show with him, at Chicago's Soldier Field on July 9. Not bad as far as farewells go, and not bad, either, for a summing-up of a life lived with much grace and heart. It is a good thing, I believe, that we lived in the same time as this man did, and it is not likely that we shall see charms or skills so transcendent, and so sustained, again. ❦

THERE'S NO WAY to measure his greatness or magnitude as a person or as a player. I don't think eulogizing will do him justice. He was that great – much more than a superb musician with an uncanny ear and dexterity. He is the very spirit personified of whatever is muddy river country at its core and screams up into the spheres. He really had no equal. 🦋 TO ME he wasn't only a musician and friend, he was more like a big brother who taught and showed me more than he'll ever know. There are a lot of spaces and advances between the Carter Family, Buddy Holly and, say, Ornette Coleman, a lot of universes, but he filled them all without being a member of any school. His playing was moody, awesome, sophisticated, hypnotic and subtle. There's no way to convey the loss. It just digs down really deep.

~BOB DYLAN, 1995

END OF THE BEGINNING

BY ROBERT STONE

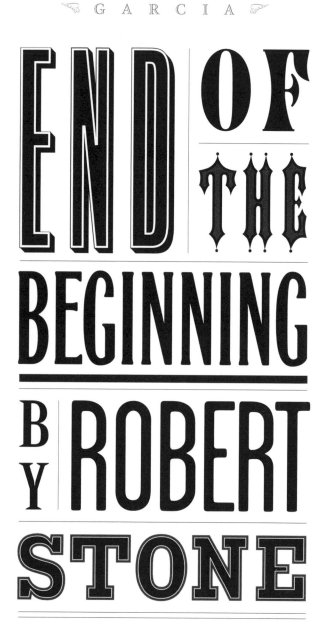

IN THE EARLY SIXTIES in Northern California, people liked to think that everything was beginning again. There was a notion that the world's sensibility was opening to new vistas. Some years later a friend of mine who was hiding from the law (a few overdue bills had come up in the meantime) sent me a telegram with those very words: "Everything is beginning again."

The statement would always somehow refer to that by then vanished period, the first time everything had begun again. For years and years thereafter, one might hear people utter variations on that motif, whether about music or good times or their love life. Everything was always beginning again.

But everyone really knew – and those of us who were there would swear to it – that things began again only once, nearly thirty years ago, in the green and golden hills around the Bay Area. There was a new consciousness and a new free-

dom and new music that would open all the secret gardens of the world, and everything would get a fresh start. We have to admit immediately that drugs played their part.

At about this time a lot of the new music was coming from England. The Beatles, the Rolling Stones and the many now-forgotten outfits that appeared tapped into American black music in an utterly unself-conscious way that afforded them great freedom of opportunity. A famous black novelist once said that no white writer should write black dialogue that he wasn't prepared to read from the stage of the Apollo Theatre, in Harlem, New York, on amateur night. The same law applied to music. Most white American musicians, no matter how good might be their rendering of Son House or Sonny Terry and Brownie McGhee, would never have dreamed of trying to perform that kind of music in public. The proximity of black America and its bitter, pissed-off readiness to mock beyond humiliation any white attempt to truly get down made such a notion unthinkable.

The English, on the other hand, didn't have to live here; to them, black America was long ago and far away. And in their smoky corner clubs they had not the slightest hesitation about emulating the Delta greats, the trills and riffs and gospel rolls of the giants of American music. It was not necessarily that the English had the talent or the soul in greater measure – they simply lacked the self-consciousness. Elvis Presley and Jerry Lee Lewis and a few other Southerners had effected a kind of appropriation of the black sound a little earlier. But the Southerners did it in a way that to some degree obscured its influences and left the public unaware of the process.

But in those green and golden hills by the Bay, self-consciousness about music was as much a bygone mode as self-consciousness about personal dignity or dressing well or being a good dancer. Everybody wore anything they wanted and dreamed up their own numbers and danced any which way. Everybody got to do whatever they wanted. That was how it was supposed to be.

As a beautiful place, a center of celebration attracting novelty and youth, the Bay Area supported a great many musicians. They were every bit as ready as the English to claim all the world's vital music as their own. They had no scruples about adding black country blues to their repertoire and turned also to bluegrass and the Texas waltz and the kind of Okie rhythms Buck Owens had recorded in Bakersfield.

On the San Francisco peninsula, where a lot of these liberated bands played, people like Ken Kesey were working up what was designed to be in the nature of a brand-new world. In one of the world's longest-running private jokes, Kesey's friends would come to be called the Merry Pranksters. Many of the bands around came to provide background music for the strange blending of literary and chemical techniques the Pranksters hoped would lead them beyond the New Beginning to some Dionysian Jerusalem. The imminent heaven that seemed to pulse just beneath California's sunny surface might be turned loose by happening on the right magic. Gratuitous grace would abound. Of course, you would need music. The bands would be there to provide the anthems.

Some great ones are gone now, unremembered, like the Anonymous Artists of America, who hung out with the Merry Pranksters for a while. All of them were equally heedless of proprietary labels or anyone's ideas about authenticity. They would switch styles and methods on a whim in the manner of those days. A pack of country-style toodlers like Mother McCree's Uptown Jug Champions might wake up one morning to discover they'd become an electric band called the Warlocks.

The Warlocks played in a place called St. Michael's Alley, in a long-vanished Palo Alto, California, neighborhood of little low-rent bungalows, overgrown gardens and live oaks where, as I remember, everyone was smart and funny and beautiful. The Warlocks included Bill Kreutzmann, who'd been taught to play drums by a friend of mine who left music for computers. They'd recruited Phil Lesh, a classically trained trumpeter with perfect pitch. There were Bob Weir and the poet/lyricist Robert Hunter and Ron "Pigpen" McKernan, a chain-smoking, overweight keyboardist with a drinking problem. And there was Jerry Garcia. Suddenly the informing word was *weird,* and the Warlocks had become the Grateful Dead, a sort of house band for the Pranksters during their phase of Acid Tests. Those tests were less a series of performances than of dark, stoned sacraments at which the customers were not unlikely to find themselves translated from mere concertgoers into something rich and strange.

For years I've gone around saying that the phrase "the grateful dead" came from a verse in the Egyptian *Book of the Dead*: "In the land of night, the ship of sun is borne by the grateful dead." Fond as I am of this piece of scholarship, people who've spent hours trying to track it down in the original Coptic tell me it simply isn't there.

Dr. Vick Lovell, the Dr. Van Helsing of such arcana, claims the name refers to a class of fairy tale, the ones in which the hero receives a gift from the hereafter for a good deed done the deceased.

Jerry Garcia has gone to join them now, the second of the original Dead to die. McKernan, who died in 1973, prefigured him in a number of ways. Like Garcia, McKernan was, as they say, a substance abuser, and he had been warned that the stuff would kill him. Unlike Garcia, McKernan never made the effort to pull out. Garcia tried, but if life was working for him again, entropy works against us all, and he seems to have waited too long.

No doubt the term "the end of an era" is going to get a workout now. But if a phrase was ever apt, this is, and now is the time for it. Deep within the event signaled by Jerry Garcia's death and the end of the era his music signifies lies a singular irony: The world isn't beginning again. Beginnings now belong to a new century that is not ours, we rough contemporaries of Jerry Garcia. Beginnings belong to the new millennium. But we'll go on listening to that music so bright and shining and rich with promise, so mellow and comforting, bringing ease to the overwrought, spirit to the weary. The art and the thought and the spirit of liberation of the Sixties flourished in their way. But of that holistic magic vision of the garden set free, the music of Jerry Garcia and the Grateful Dead is the purest single remnant. It was supposed to be an accompaniment to the New Beginning. In fact, it was the thing itself, all that remains with us. ☙

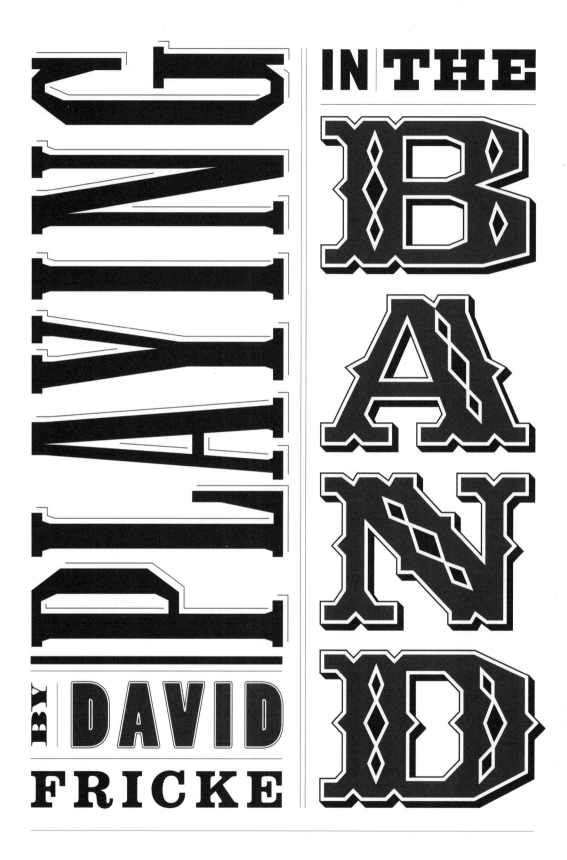

PLAYING IN THE BAND

BY DAVID FRICKE

IN ROCK & ROLL, there is Grateful Dead music – and then there is everything else. No other band has been so pure in its outlaw idealism, so resolute in its pursuit of transcendence onstage and on record and so astonishingly casual about both the hazards and rewards of its chosen, and at times truly lunatic, course. "Well, I just see us as a lot of good-time pirates," Jerry Garcia told a reporter just as the New Euphoria hit its high-noon peak in San Francisco in the mid-Sixties. "I'd like to apologize in advance to anybody who believes we're something really serious. The seriousness comes up as lightness, and I think that's the way it should be."

Garcia wasn't actually talking about his band but about the local bliss missionaries in general. But that benevolent-brigand spirit, the rare gift of turning subversion into sunlight – that was the essence of the music and the mission of the Dead. "The important thing is that everybody be comfortable," Garcia added. "Live what you have to live and be comfortable."

As a guitarist, songwriter and – given his pillar-of-salt stage presence and rather grandfatherly countenance in recent years – deceptively commanding figure in a band ostensibly made up of equals, Jerry Garcia tried to live that axiom to the fullest. "I don't think of my work as being full-time work," he declared in 1972. "What I'm doing is my work, but I'm playing! When I left the straight world at fifteen, when I got my first guitar and left everything I was doing, I was taking a vacation – I was going out to play, and I'm still playing."

Preceding page: (Clockwise from top left) Weir, Pigpen, Garcia, Lesh and Kreutzmann, 1967. "I just see us as a lot of good-time pirates."

Yet for Garcia and the other core members of the Dead, there was no life, and no comfort, without risk. No task was accomplished successfully without some attendant mess and an edifying side trip to the margins. In a music business that prefers expedience to expedition and treats even its most celebrated renegades like errant children, the Dead routinely took the longer, harder route to revelation. Some of the most enduring songs in their repertoire – "Truckin'," "Uncle John's Band," "Casey Jones," "Dark Star," John Phillips' outlaw fable "Me and My Uncle," the traditional "I Know You Rider" – are about motion, in real time and otherwise, and about the world of diversion and possibility on the road to enlightenment.

The Dead spent three decades on that road. They were in no hurry to become celebrities. And when they did become stars, the Dead were more interested in the utopian investments that wealth and the luxury of time could buy: their first misfire at starting an independent label in 1973; the huge, hideously expensive wall-of-speakers P.A. that the band dragged around on tour in '73 and '74; the heavy logistics of their historic shows under the stars at the Great Pyramid, in Egypt, in September 1978.

Musically the Grateful Dead were a product of square-root influences. The songs, the jamming – even those long twilight stretches in concert when the band would dissolve into look-Ma-no-maps quadrants of free improvisation – were born of elemental Americana: hard-bitten Mississippi blues, galloping Chicago R&B, the back-porch and campfire strains of classic country music, old-timey Appalachian bluegrass. One side of the Dead's humble indie-45 debut,

issued in 1966 on the Scorpio label, was a reading of the traditional country-blues chestnut "Stealin'." Over the past decade, as they labored at leisure over original material for their infrequent studio releases, the Dead increasingly returned to the Motown, Willie Dixon, Jimmy Reed and Bob Dylan songbooks that had been part of their source material going back to their dance-band days as the Warlocks. (Dylan's "It's All Over Now, Baby Blue" and "She Belongs to Me" were both features of the Dead's early shows.)

Yet the Dead, who were charged with a mutinous optimism and an irrepressible restlessness too often mistaken for unprofessionalism, were rarely content to leave well enough alone. Sometimes it was something as simple as adding an asymmetrical kick to "Viola Lee Blues"– a twelve-bar, 78-rpm-vintage stomper covered on the group's 1967 debut album – by cutting a half bar out of it. Or it could be as willfully trippy as 1969's *Aoxomoxoa,* an attempt to make a disciplined, song-based record that instead mutated into an unforgettable marvel of rococo psychedelia, as elegant and cryptic as Rick Griffin's mesmerizing cover art.

Even between the extremes – 1970's pair of jewels, *Workingman's Dead* and *American Beauty*; the graceful, spacey *Blues for Allah* in 1975; the unlikely 1987 chart monster, *In the Dark* – the Dead never lapsed into formula. They spent their entire career struggling to bottle on LP the living color of their stage performances. But the Dead refused to betray the substance of their music and the improbable mix of talents and personalities that fueled it.

Back in December 1967, Joe Smith – the executive at Warner Bros. Records who signed the Dead to the label – wrote a letter to the band's then manager, Danny Rifkin, complaining about, in Smith's words, the "lack of professionalism" that was hampering completion of the band's second album, *Anthem of the Sun.* "The Grateful Dead are not one of the top acts in the business yet," Smith wrote (to his subsequent chagrin). "Their attitudes and their inability to take care of business when it's time to do so would lead us to believe that they never will be truly important. No matter how talented your group is, it's going to have to put something of itself into the business before it goes anywhere."

Later, someone scrawled across the letter in big capital letters the words FUCK YOU.

* * *

I FIRST SAW the Grateful Dead at Woodstock in 1969. They sucked, albeit through no fault of their own. (The sound system wimped out on them.) But that was my first lesson in life with the Dead: Not every night is brilliant. The second lesson, as I kept going back for more, was, Don't give up so easily – the process is half the fun. The Dead could be maddeningly inconsistent in performance. They could take up the better part of an evening's first set just to get their engine turning over. A few years ago I took my wife to see the band for the first time. The Dead opened with a sluggish version of "Let the Good Times Roll" that sounded like they were barely able to make the good times *crawl.* "Pick it up, pick it up!" she exclaimed, snapping her fingers impatiently, oblivious to the startled Deadheads around her. "This is rock & roll!" But then, just as you settled back for a long haul, the

Dead could turn on a dime into the high-wire swing of "The Other One," tap the serene beauty of "Box of Rain" or leave you exhilarated with a steaming "One More Saturday Night." They were rarely better than when skating across the thin ice of a daredevil second-set medley like the one I remember from October 18, 1994, at Madison Square Garden, in New York: the aching, elegiac "He's Gone" sidewinding into the back-to-back chooglers "Smokestack Lightnin'" and "Truckin'," a slow-motion drop into the nightly free fall of "Drums"/"Space," then a pillow-soft landing onto the spooky melancholy of "The Days Between." It was the last Grateful Dead show I saw. I was blessed with one of the great ones.

The devoted "know when we have a bad night," Garcia said in '89, "and they appreciate a good try. In a way they've allowed themselves that latitude to enjoy a show for lots of different reasons. I think that's in their favor – no matter what the experience has been, they don't get burned. When a Grateful Dead show is horrible, it's interesting."

That was also true of the records. One of the most underrated LPs in the Grateful Dead canon is 1968's *Anthem of the Sun,* a twisted, lysergic dance-party record and raw sonic splat that is contagiously propulsive and, in its way, raggedly soulful. With the recent additions of Mickey Hart and keyboardist Tom Constanten – who first met Phil Lesh in the early Sixties when they registered for music classes together at the University of California at Berkeley – the Dead dared to marry acid-damaged art music (electronically treated vocals, Constanten's prepared piano, brain-fuck sound effects) with the funky snort of live rock & roll (locomotive extracts from a memorable February 1968 gig at the Carousel Ballroom).

At one point, Bob Weir literally drove the band's producer Dave Hassinger out of the studio. At a session for "Born Cross-Eyed," "the song got quiet at one point, and so I announced, 'Right here I want the sound of thick air,' " Weir recalled in *Playing in the Band,* David Gans and Peter Simon's 1985 oral and pictorial history of the Dead. "I couldn't describe it back then

At right: The post-Pigpen Dead in 1973 (clockwise from top right) Lesh, Kreutzmann, Donna Godchaux, Weir, Keith Godchaux and Garcia. Following pages: The Grateful Dead in Daly City, 1967.

because I didn't know what I was talking about. I do know now: a little bit of white noise and a little bit of compression. I was thinking about something kind of like the buzzing that you hear in your ears on a hot, sticky summer day." The Dead finished the album themselves at great expense. The recording bills, combined with those for *Aoxomoxoa,* left the band in debt to its label into the Seventies.

The Dead pulled back from the extreme precipices and

chemically enhanced detours of psychedelia after 1969's *Live Dead* (the finest official document of their late-Sixties stage prowess), finding renewed strength in the natural energy of country picking, bluesy grooves and folky harmonizing. The earth tones and sawdust charms of *Workingman's Dead* and *American Beauty* may have been descended from frontier fantasies like Bob Dylan's *John Wesley Harding* or Crosby, Stills and Nash, but the Dead came by their new direction honestly. And those two Dead albums – which set the tone for much

of their music for the next twenty-five years – threw the band's unique ensemble chemistry into sharp relief.

Bob Weir, a teenage straight arrow who fell from suburban grace into bohemia via Garcia's early bluegrass outfit, Mother McCree's Uptown Jug Champions, brought a bright, eternally boyish tenor to the Dead's vocal mix. He also matured into a strong, inventive songwriter, usually in collaboration with lyricist John Barlow, despite the long shadow cast by Garcia and his longtime friend and lyric-writing partner, Robert Hunter. ("Victim or the Crime," cowritten with actor Gerrit Graham for 1989's *Built to Last,* is a fine late-period example of Weir's writing.)

Tall, blond, inscrutable Phil Lesh arrived at rock & roll via the trumpet and deep studies in contemporary classical music, electronic composition and avant jazz. (The only recorded evidence of his horn playing with the Dead is the Spanish-flavored flourish in "Born Cross-Eyed.") But as a bassist, Lesh was the

the sweet glide of his pedal steel guitar on "Teach Your Children," by Crosby, Stills, Nash and Young, is probably his finest moment as a sessionman – an artful touch of Nashville poignancy with a bracing Bay Area breeze blowing through it.

"The thing that propels me through music is the emotional reality of it," Garcia said in 1993. "And as I get older, I surrender more to that. I trust that intuition."

* * *

M AYBE GARCIA didn't trust it enough. During the last ten years of his life, he divided his time between music – the Dead; the Jerry Garcia Acoustic Band; a two-week solo residency on Broadway in 1987; a 1993 children's album cut with mandolinist David Grisman – and a hard drug habit that challenged a body already overburdened by diabetes, a chronic weight problem and chain-smoking. But the tragedy of Garcia's death is not in the circumstances that surely led to it. Given his recent close calls (his diabetic coma in '86, his collapse from exhaustion during a 1992 tour), Garcia enjoyed a few extensions in his lease on life.

The sadness is in the dark narcotic haze that – for some people – will obscure the weight of Garcia's musical achievement and in the fact that Garcia couldn't find quite enough salvation in the music he played or in the joy it brought to others. It's easy in retrospect to read more into the music than Garcia intended, but his performance of the traditional country lament "I'm Troubled," on *Almost Acoustic,* the live 1988 CD by the Jerry Garcia Acoustic Band, has a few new chills to it: the delicate picking, the tender vocal harmonies, the seemingly prophetic chorus ("I'm troubled / I'm troubled / I'm troubled in mind / If trouble don't kill me / Lord, I'll live a long time").

Garcia and the Grateful Dead could have hung up their rock & roll shoes years ago, content in the knowledge that the band had set a working standard for aesthetic integrity and social responsibility in rock & roll. The Dead established a nation-state of fans who were not mere consumers or devotees but true citizens of the *Zeitgeist.* And they inspired several generations of bands – from Sixties peers like the Allman Brothers Band to successful youngsters like Phish – who absorbed and recycled that family vibe, not just the musical notes.

But the broader impact of Garcia's passing and the probable end of the Dead as a touring and recording unit should not be underestimated. "It's an adventure you can still have in America, just like Neal [Cassady] on the road," Garcia said of life with the Dead. "You can't hop the freights anymore, but you can chase the Grateful Dead around. You can have all your tires blow out in some weird town in the Midwest, and you can get hell from strangers. You can have something that lasts throughout your life as adventures, the times you took chances. I think that's essential in anybody's life, and it's harder and harder to do in America."

With the death of Jerry Garcia, it just got a little harder. ❦

Above: The Dead in 1979, Garcia, Weir, Brent Mydland, Lesh, Kreutzmann, Hart. At right: The Dead with short-lived keyboardist Tom Constanten (left), 1969. Following pages: The Grateful Dead's Haight-Ashbury street party, March 3, 1968.

unshakable anchor of the Dead's rhythmic foundation, while the intuitive fluidity of Bill Kreutzmann and Mickey Hart's tandem drumming elevated the band's heartbeat drive into a dynamic form of percussive communion.

Pigpen, whose gentle manner belied his nickname, carried himself onstage with a crusty charisma that the Dead respectfully declined to replace after his death. During their respective passages through the group, keyboardists Keith Godchaux (with vocalist and wife Donna), Brent Mydland, Vince Welnick and frequent guest Bruce Hornsby all brought a more tempered, lyrical glow to the Dead's otherwise rough-hewed populism.

But it was Jerry Garcia's surprisingly fragile singing and the articulate glass-blade stab of his guitar that through the Seventies and Eighties characterized the genial vulnerability and bright, contagious energy of the Dead's retooled-roots sound. As a songwriter framing Hunter's singular blend of gravelly realism and metaphoric reverie, Garcia was equally adept at evergreen country-blues portraiture ("Uncle John's Band"), roadhouse romanticism ("Sugaree") or anthemic celebration ("Touch of Grey"). "Wharf Rat" – a bittersweet ballad about a down-but-not-quite-out alcoholic captured with a startling chamber-group intimacy on the 1971 live album Skull and Roses (so nicknamed after Alton Kelley's cover art) – is quintessential Garcia. His voice gently shivers with spiritual remorse and dogged hopefulness; by the song's end, the achingly slow, bluesy tempo and the skeletal chiming of Garcia's guitar have taken on a warm, churchy glow.

As a solo artist and a frequent picker on other artists' records, Garcia always took a piece of the Dead's aesthetic with him wherever he went. The 1991 live double CD *Jerry Garcia Band* is a fine reflection of his interpretive powers as he settles comfortably into the elasticized grooves of songs as diverse as Bruce Cockburn's "Waiting for a Miracle," the Beatles' "Dear Prudence" and Bob Dylan's "Señor (Tales of Yankee Power)." The cracker-barrel purity of Garcia's banjo plucking is still a joy to behold on the 1975 live album he cut with the one-shot bluegrass group Old and In the Way. And

YOU KNOW, *I think the Grateful Dead is, like, one dumb guy instead of five, you know... dumb guys.*

* * *

I'M NOT the leader of the Grateful Dead or anything like that. There isn't any fuckin' leader, I mean, because I can bullshit you guys real easy, but I can't bullshit Phil or Pigpen and them guys watchin' me go through my changes all these years, and we've had so many weird times together . . . I know in front, the leader thing doesn't work because you don't need one. ~*1972*

ONE OF THE THINGS about us was that we never had the glamour flash that the Airplane had or Moby Grape or whatever. They were always sort of glamorous and sellable, and we never had that thing, that glossy image. They would see Pigpen and just say *forget* it.

~*JERRY GARCIA, 1976*

THE DEAD

BY BEN FONG-TORRES

WHEN IN THE MID-SIXTIES San Francisco came to represent nothing left to lose, there was a handful of identifiable pioneers who changed the face, the sound and the style of pop culture. The changers included the concert promoters Bill Graham and Chet Helms, poster and light-show artists, hosts and alchemists like Ken Kesey and Augustus Owsley Stanley, radio pioneer Tom Donahue, jazz critic Ralph J. Gleason and – yes – ROLLING STONE.

At the epicenter, of course, were the musicians. Early on, the Grateful Dead, along with a few others, played free concerts as often as paying gigs. Extending their songs into jazz-like improvisatory jams, they broke down the lines between artist and audience.

Back then we – ROLLING STONE and the Grateful Dead – were brothers in arms. The Dead did it onstage; we watched and listened, reported, ranted and raved. For our very first issue – published in November 1967 – we lucked, journalistically speaking, into a story for the ages: The Grateful Dead getting busted at their Haight-Ashbury digs.

The band and the magazine always had a special relationship, despite the occasional negative album review or report on an unpleasant incident or ROLLING STONE's move to New York in 1977. Our common roots transcended trivia; our love of great music kept us bonded.

One day in early '70 we got an impromptu visit from the management and various members of the Dead. The band had just wrapped up recording *Workingman's Dead;* they knew the album was something special, and the band wanted to share it right away. Magazine staffers gathered in the only sizable office (Jann's, of course) and listened in awe to pedal-steel licks and tight, pretty country harmonies – from the Dead! – on "Uncle John's Band," "Dire Wolf" and "Casey Jones." Our minds, as someone would later say, were young and blown.

In later years I had occasion to interview Garcia and profile the Dead. Every five years it seemed there would be an anniversary of some sort, and the Dead were always there. And Garcia was always there – was always present – for you. Even his most offhand remarks rang true, like the best of Robert Hunter's lyrics.

It was a Saturday afternoon in late November 1975, and we were preparing for a special issue on the tenth anniversary of the San Francisco scene. Garcia greeted some scruffy press at His Master's Wheels, a studio in an alley off Market Street, and I asked him about the warping of time.

"It seems like hundreds of years," Garcia said, "and it also seems like not too much time at all. I don't know. Time, you know. Some things haven't changed at all, really. And the world has changed." Perhaps not enough, but in his own quiet, unassuming, different-beat way, Jerry Garcia

did his best to change it – or at least to loosen it up a little.

In his successes, in his failures and in the way he addressed them both, with candor, humility and beatific good humor, he was quintessentially San Franciscan. We were his, and he was ours.

Along with names forgotten by all but the most avid poster collectors – those of the Marbles, the Mystery Trend, Frumious Bandersnatch, Chocolate Watch Band – the Grateful Dead were at the vanguard of what became known as the San Francisco Scene, the Summer of Love, the Sixties. But of all the bands – including Jefferson Airplane, Big Brother and the Holding Company, Country Joe and the Fish, Quicksilver

Messenger Service, the Charlatans, Moby Grape, the Steve Miller Blues Band – it was the Dead that remained intact (more than less) and carried the San Francisco banner for three decades.

Sure, the Dead moved out of their Haight-Ashbury digs shortly after that bust in fall of '67, but they were forever tied to San Francisco and the Sixties, and they never resisted or disavowed those bonds. It wasn't just that the Dead were born in the city. It was that the city was reborn with the Dead. San Francisco, as Ralph Gleason put it, was suddenly "the Liverpool of the West."

And in the spirit of a restless town in restless times, the Dead rolled on, breaking and making up rules as they went, eschewing recordings as a stepping-stone to riches and relying on concerts instead. But as far from home as the road took them, they returned to punctuate their tour schedule with New Year's Eve concerts in Oakland or San Francisco, year-end runs that took Bay Area Deadheads to Mardi Gras, Halloween, Chinese New Year and Acid Test all at once.

"Jerry was a true San Franciscan," says Deborah Koons Garcia, his wife of a year and a half, by way of explaining why any memorial event, any celebration of Jerry Garcia's life, would have to be in San Francisco. And so it was, in the Polo Field of Golden Gate Park, where the Dead played the

Garcia: "Hey, Jann, have you ever had anybody say anything to you about what you print, man?" Jann: "Yes, indeed." Garcia: "Far-out. It must be weird." Preceding pages: The infamous bust press conference (from left) Phil Lesh, managers Rock Scully and Danny Rifkin, Bob Weir and Garcia. At left and right: Pigpen, Garcia.

Human Be-In in 1967 and, most recently, the memorial concert for Bill Graham in 1991. This time, the Dead's music was on tape, and the band members were there to address the crowd.

Bob Weir, his arms raised to the heavens, said that Garcia "filled this world full of clouds of joy. Just take a little bit of that and reflect it back up to him." And they did – fifty thousand arms lifted to the sky, holding imaginary mirrors and sending a bit of San Francisco to wherever he might be. ℮

BUSTED!
THE DEAD DID GET IT

BY JANN S. WENNER

"THAT'S WHAT YA GET for dealing the killer weed," laughed narcotics agent Jerry Van Ramm at the members of the Grateful Dead household he and his agents had rounded up into the Dead's kitchen.

The Good Ole Grateful Dead had gotten it. Eight narcotics agents, followed by a dozen reporters and television crews, raided the Dead's house at 710 Ashbury Street on October 2. A little after 3:30 in the afternoon, two members of the band, Pigpen and Bob Weir; their two managers, Rock Scully and Danny Rifkin; their equipment manager, Bob Matthews; and six friends had been busted on dope charges.

The cops carried no warrant and broke in the front door even after being denied entry. Danny and Rock weren't in the house but were yanked from the porch when they came strolling by after the reporters had arrived. As well as members of the band, the police confiscated the files, money and phone books of the band and of the Haight-Ashbury Legal Organization, whose offices are in the Dead's house.

While the narcs did their work, a rooting section gathered on the sidewalk across the street from the house and, like a Greek chorus, filled the air with a running commentary on the proceedings.

Jerry Garcia and Mountain Girl weren't home at the time of the bust. Bill Kreutzmann and Phil Lesh live elsewhere, but Phil's old lady, Florence, was at 710 and was handcuffed to Weir on the way to the Hall of Justice.

After six hours in jail, the dastardly eleven were released on bail. On October 23 they return to the Hall of Justice for a preliminary hearing. Their chances look good. In the meantime, they showed up at their bail-bondsman's office the cold morning after the arrest, were arraigned in court (where Rock was arrested again on the additional charge of maintaining a house where narcotics are used) and had a press conference.

The press conference was held in the Dead's living room, filled to capacity with a tangle of microphones, television cameras, lights, wires, notepads, soundmen, reporters and photographers. Danny opened it with a statement:

"The arrests were made under a law that classifies smoking marijuana, along with murder, rape and armed robbery, as a felony. Yet almost anyone who has ever studied marijuana seriously and objectively has agreed that marijuana is the least harmful chemical used for pleasure and life enhancement.

"The law contains an even greater evil. It encourages the most outrageously discriminatory type of law enforcement. If the lawyers, doctors, advertising men, teachers and political officeholders who use marijuana were arrested today, the law might well be off the books before Thanksgiving. The law creates a mythical danger and calls it a felony. The people who enforce the law use it almost exclusively against individuals who threaten their ideas of the way people should look and act.

"Behind all the myths is the reality. The Grateful Dead are people engaged in constructive, creative effort in the musical field, and this house is where we work as well as our residence. Because the police fear and misinterpret us, our effort is now interrupted as we deal with the consequences of a harassing arrest."

Questions and answers followed, much like a Beatles press conference. In response to "How long did it take you to grow your hair that long, Danny?" Rifkin said, "We've always figured that if we ever held a press conference, the first reporter who asked a stupid question would get a cream pie in his face, and you're him."

A huge bowl of whipped cream was ceremoniously produced, to everyone's obvious delight, including all the reporters – except the one. He cringed, and Danny, taking pity, spared him. After the conference was finished, cookies, coffee and cake were served, and the predictable jokes were made.

ROLLING STONE didn't leave. We adjourned to the porch to take a few pictures of one of the most beautiful bands in the world.

Notice all the rifles. Pigpen has a big collection. If he had been thinking quick, he would have been prepared for all eventualities.

Dig Jerry: He's Big Man on Campus. Who else has a shirt like that? Jerry said that *One of the photos that ran with this on-the-scene report in 'Rolling Stone,' Issue Number One: (Clockwise from top left) Garcia, Pigpen, Weir, Lesh, Rifkin, Scully and Kreutzmann.* if they put out a warrant for his arrest – which so far they haven't – he would beat them to it and go down to the Hall of Justice voluntarily to surrender, carrying a white flag. ☾

DEAD ZONE

ZONE

BY MICHAEL LYDON

THE DEAD DIDN'T GET IT GOING Wednesday night at Winterland, and that was too bad. The gig was a bail fund benefit for the People's Park in Berkeley, and the giant ice-skating cavern was packed with heads. The whole park hassle – the benefit was for the four hundred fifty busted a few days before – had been a Berkeley political trip all the way down, but the issue was a good-timey park, so the crowd, though older and more radical than most San Francisco rock crowds, was a fine one in a good dancing mood, watery mouths waiting for the groove to come. The Airplane were on the bill too; so were Santana and a righteous range of others – a San Francisco all-star night, the bands making homegrown music for homegrown folks gathered for a homegrown cause.

But the Dead stumbled that night. They led off with a warm-up tune that they did neatly enough, and the crowd, swarmed in luminescent darkness, sent up "good old Grateful Dead, we're so glad you're here" vibrations. The band didn't catch them. Maybe they were a bit tired of being taken for granted as surefire deliverers of good vibes – drained by constant expectations. Or they might have been cynical – a benefit for those Berkeley dudes who finally learned what a park is but are still hung up on confrontation and cops and bricks and spokesmen giving TV interviews and all that bullshit. The Dead were glad to do it, but it was one more benefit to bail out the politicos.

Maybe they were too stoned on one of the Bear's custom-brewed elixirs, or the long meeting that afternoon with the usual fights about salaries and debt priorities and travel plans for the upcoming tour that they'd be making without a road manager, and all the work of being, in the end, a rock & roll band, may have left them pissed off. After abortive stabs at "Doin' That Rag" and "St. Stephen," they fell into "Turn On Your Love Light" as a last resort, putting Pigpen out in front to lay on his special brand of oily rag pig-ism while they funked around behind. It usually works, but not that night. Mickey Hart and Bill Kreutzmann couldn't find anything to settle on, and the others kept trying ways out of the mess, only to create new tangles of bumpy rhythms and dislocated melodies. For the briefest of seconds a nice phrase would pop out, and the crowd would cheer, thinking maybe this was it, but before the cheer died, the moment had also perished. After about twenty minutes they decided to call it quits, ending with a long, building crescendo, and topping that with a belching cannon blast (which fell right on the beat, the only luck they found that night), and split the stage.

The Warlocks in 1965: (Clockwise from left) Garcia, Weir, Lesh, Pigpen and Kreutzmann. "We got a regular job at a Belmont club and developed a whole malicious thing, playing songs longer and weirder, and louder, man. It was loud, and for a bar it was ridiculous. People had to scream at each other, and pretty soon we had driven out all the regular clientele. They'd run out clutching their ears."

"But, y'know, I dug it, man," said Jerry Garcia the next night. "I can get behind falling to pieces before an audience sometimes. We're not *performers;* we are who we are for those moments we're before the public, and that's not always at the peak." He was backstage at the Robertson Gymnasium at the University of California at Santa Barbara, backstage being a curtained-off quarter of the gym, the other three quarters being stage and crowd. His red solid-body Gibson with its RED, WHITE, AND BLUE POWER sticker was in place across his belly, and he caressed/played it without stopping. Rock Scully, the manager, was scrunched in a corner dispensing tequila complete with salt and lemon to the band and all comers, particularly bassist Phil Lesh, who left his Eurasian groupie alone and forlorn every time he dashed back to the bottle.

"Sure, I'll fuck up for an audience," said Mickey from behind his sardonic beard, bowing. "My pleasure. We'll take you as low and mean as you want to go."

"See, it's like good and evil," Jerry went on, his yellow glasses glinting above his eager smile. "They exist together in their little game, each with its special place and special humors. I dig 'em both. What is life but being conscious? And good and evil are manifestations of consciousness. If you reject one, you're not getting the whole thing that's there to be had. So I had a good time last night. Getting in trouble can be a trip, too."

His good humor was enormous, even though it had been a bitch of a day. The travel agent had given them the wrong flight time and, being the day before Memorial Day weekend, there was no space on any other flight for all fourteen of them. So they had hustled over to National Rent-a-Car, gotten two matched Pontiacs and driven the 350 miles down the coast. Phil drove one and, because he didn't have his license and had six stoned backseat drivers for company, he had gotten pretty paranoid. The promoter, a slick Hollywood type, had told them at five in the afternoon that he wouldn't let them set up their own P.A. "It's good enough for Lee Michaels, it's good enough for you," he said, and they were too tired to fight it.

The Bear, who handles the sound system as well as the chemicals, was out of it anyway. When the band got to the gym, he was flat on his back, curled up among the drum cases. Phil shook him to his feet and asked if there was anything he could do, but Bear's pale eyes were as sightless as fog. By that time the MC was announcing them. With a final "Oh, fuck it, man," they trouped up to the stage through the massed groupies.

Robertson Gym stank like every gym in history. The light show, the big-name band and the hippie ambience faded before that smell, unchanged since the days when the student council hung a few million paper snowflakes from the ceiling and tried to pass it off as Winter Wonderland. Now it was Psychedelic Wonderland, but the potent spirits of the long-departed sweat socks still owned the place. That was okay; another rock & roll dance in the old school gym. They brought out "Love Light" again; this time the groove was there, and for forty minutes they laid it down, working hard and getting that bob-and-weave interplay of seven-man improvisation that can take you right out of your head. But Jerry kept looking more and more pained, then suddenly signaled to bring it to a close. They did, abruptly, and Jerry stepped to a mike.

"Sorry!" he shouted. "But we're gonna split for a while and set up our own P.A. so we can hear what the fuck is happening." He ripped his cord out of his amp and walked off. Rock took charge.

"The Dead will be back, folks, so everybody go outside, take off your clothes, cool down and come back. This was just an introduction."

Backstage was a brawl. "We should give the money back if we don't do it righteous!" Jerry was shouting. "Where's Bear?"

Bear wandered over, still lost in some intercerebral space.

"Listen, man, are you in this group, are you one of us?" Jerry screamed. "Are you gonna set up that P.A.? Their monitors suck, I can't hear a goddamn thing out there. How can I play if I can't hear the drums?"

Bear mumbled something about taking two hours to set up the P.A., then wandered off. Rock was explaining to the knot of curious onlookers.

"This is the *Grateful Dead,* man. We play with *twice* the intensity of anybody else, we *gotta* have our own system. The promoter screwed us, and we tried to make it, but we just can't. It's gotta be *our* way, man."

Ramrod and the other quippies were already dismantling the original P.A.

"Let's just go ahead," said Pigpen. "I can fake it."

"I can't," said Jerry.

"It's your decision," said Pig.

"Yeah," said Phil, "if you and nobody else gives a good goddamn."

But it was all over. Bear had disappeared, the original P.A. was gone, someone had turned up the houselights and the audience was melting away. A good night, a potentially great night, had been shot by a combination of promoter burn and Dead incompetence, and at 1:00 a.m. it didn't matter who was to blame or where it had started to go wrong. It was too far gone to save that night.

"We're really sorry," Phil kept saying to the few who still lingered by the gym's back door. "We burned you of a night of music, and we'll come back and make it up."

"If we dare show our faces in this town again," said rhythm guitarist Bob Weir as they walked to the cars. The others laughed, but it wasn't really funny.

They rode back to the Ocean Palms Motel in near silence.

"When we missed that plane, we should have known," said Bill Kreutzmann. "An ill-advised trip."

Jerry said it was more than that. They took the date because their new manager, Lenny Hart, Mickey's father, while new at the job, had accepted it from Bill Graham. The group had already decided to leave Millard, Graham's booking agency, and didn't want any more of his jobs but took it rather than making Hart go back on his word. "That's the lesson: Take a gig to save face, and you end up with a shitty P.A. and a well-burned audience."

"Show biz, that's what it was tonight," Mickey Hart said softly. "And show biz is the shits."

The others nodded, and the car fell silent. Road markers flicked by the car in solemn procession as the mist rolled in off the muffled ocean.

* * *

IT'S NOW ALMOST FOUR YEARS since the Acid Tests, the first Family Dog dances, the Mime troupe benefits and the Trips Festival; almost the same since Donovan sang about flying Jefferson Airplane and a London discotheque called Sibylla's became the "in" club because it had the first light show in Europe; two and a half since the Human Be-In, since *Newsweek* and then the nation discovered the Haight-Ashbury hippies and the "San Francisco Sound." The Monterey Pop Festival, which confirmed and culminated that insanely explosive spring of 1967, is now two years gone by. The biggest rock & roll event of its time, that three-day weekend marked the beginning of a new era. The Beatles (who sent their regards), the Stones, Dylan, even the Beach Boys – the giants who had opened things up from '63 to '67 – were all absent, and the stage was open for the first generation of the still-continuing rock profusion. Monterey was a watershed, and the one to follow it has not yet come. Though it was, significantly, conceived in and directed from Los Angeles, its inspiration, style and much of its substance were San Francisco's. The quantum of energy that pushed rock & roll to the level on which it now resides came from San Francisco.

Since then, what San Francisco started has become so diffuse, copied, extended, exploited, rebelled against and simply accepted that it has become nearly invisible. One can't say "acid rock" now without embarrassed quotations. The city, once absurdly overrated, is now underrated. The process of absorption has been so smoothly quick that it is hard to remember when it was all new, when Wes Wilson posters were appearing fresh every week, when Owsley acid was not just a legend or mythical standard, when only real freaks had hair down past their shoulders, when forty-minute songs were revolutionary, and when a dance was not a concert but a stoned-out bacchanal. But it was real; had it not been so vital, it would not have been so quickly universalized. Since 1966, rock & roll has come to San Francisco like the mountain to Mohammed.

Rock & roll, in fact, has always been regional music on the lower levels, but success, as much for the Beatles and Dylan as for Elvis or James Brown, always meant going to the big city, to the music industry machine. That machine, whether in London, New York or Los Angeles, dictated that the rock & roll life was a remote one of stardom, which – with a complex structure of fan mags and fan clubs, personal aides, publicity men, limited tours and carefully spaced singles – controlled the stars' availability to the public for maximum titillation and maximum profit. The fan identified with his stars (idols), but across an uncrossable void. The machine also tended either to downplay the regional characteristics of a style or to exaggerate them into a gimmick. A lucky or tough artist might keep his musical roots intact, but few were able to transfer the closeness they had with their first audience to their mass audience. To be a rock & roll star, went the unwritten law, you had to go downtown.

San Francisco's major contribution to rock was the flaunting of that rule. The Beatles had really started it; on one hand the most isolated and revered group, they were also the most personal: You knew the image – of course, not the real them – but the image was lively and changing. The same is true for Dylan, but San Francisco made it real. The early days at the Fillmore and Avalon were not unlike the months that the Rolling Stones played the Crawdaddy Club in Richmond,

but for the first time there was the hope, if not assumption, that those days would never have to end. The one-to-one performer-audience relationship was what the music was about. San Francisco's secret was not the dancing, the light shows, the posters, the long sets or the complete lack of stage act, but the idea that all of them together were the creation and re-creation of a community. Everybody did their thing, and all things were equal. The city had a hip community, one of bizarrely various people who all on their own had decided that they'd have to find their own way through the universe and that the old ways wouldn't do no more. In that community everybody looked like a rock star, and rock stars began to look and act and live like people, not gods on the make. The way to go big-time was to encourage more people to join the community or to make their own – not to enlarge oneself out of it and into the machine's big time. San Francisco said that rock & roll could be making your own music for your friends – folk music in a special sense.

Sort of; because it didn't really work. Dances did become concerts, groups eagerly signed with big record companies from L.A. to New York, did do long tours, did get promo men, secluded retreats, Top Forty singles and did become stars. Thousands took up the trappings of community with none of its spirit; the community itself lost hope and direction, fought bitterly within itself and fragmented. San Francisco was not deserted for the machine as Liverpool had been, but the machine managed to make San Francisco an outpost, however funky, of itself. Janis Joplin is still the city's one superstar, but the unity of the musical-social community has effectively been broken; musicians play for pay, audiences pay to listen. There is now a rock musician's community that is international, and it is closer to the audience community than ever before in rock's history. But the San Francisco vision has died (or at least hibernated) unfulfilled. There are many reasons: bad and/or greedy management, the swamping effect of sudden success, desperation, lack of viable alternatives and the combined flatteries of fame, money and ridiculous adulation of young egos.

But the central reason is that rock is not folk music in that special sense. The machine, with all its flashy fraudulences, is not a foreign growth on rock, but its very essence. One cannot be a good rock musician and, either psychically or in fact, be an amateur, because professionalism is part of the term's definition. Rock & roll, rather than some other art, became the prime expression of that community because it was rock, machine and all, the miracle beauty of American mass production, a mythic past, a global fantasy, an instantaneous communications network and a maker of superheroes. There's no way to combine wanting that and wanting "just folks" too. The excitement of San Francisco was the attempt to synthesize these two contradictory positions. To pull it off would have been a revolution; at best, San Francisco made a reform. In the long haul, its creators, tired of fighting the paradox, chose modified rock over folk music.

All except the Grateful Dead, who've been battling it out with that mother of a paradox for years. Sometimes they lose, sometimes they win.

The Grateful Dead are not the original San Francisco

band – the Charlatans, the Great Society and the Airplane all predate them, even in their Warlocks stage – and whether they are the best, whatever that would mean, is irrelevant. Probably they are the loudest; someone once described them as "living thunder." Certainly they are the weirdest – black satanic weird and white archangel weird. As weird as anything you can imagine, like some horror comic monster who, besides being green and slimy, happens also to have seven different heads, a 190 IQ, countless decibels of liquid fire noise communication and is coming right down to where you are to gobble you up. But if you can dig the monster – bammo – he's a giant puppy to play with. Grateful Dead weird, ultimately, and what an image that name is. John Lennon joked about the flaming hand that made them Beatles, but Jerry Garcia is serious:

"Back in the late days of the Acid Tests, we were looking for a name. We'd abandoned the Warlocks; it didn't fit anymore. One day we were all over at Phil's house, smoking DMT. He had a big Oxford dictionary, opened it, and there was 'grateful dead,' those words juxtaposed. It was one of those moments, y'know, like everything else on the page went blank, diffuse, just sorta *oozed* away, and there was *grateful dead. Big* black letters *edged* all around in gold, man, blasting out at me, such a stunning combination. So I said, 'How about Grateful Dead?' and that was it."

The image still resonates for the Dead: They are, or desire to become, the Grateful Dead. Grateful Dead may mean whatever you like it to mean: life-in-death, ego death, reincarnation, the joy of the mystic vision. Maybe it is Rick Griffin's grinning skull balancing on the axis of an organic universe that is the cover of *Aoxomoxoa,* their latest record. It doesn't matter how you read it, for the Dead – as people, musicians and a group – are in that place where the meanings of a name or event can be as infinite as the imagination and yet mean precisely what they are and no more.

In their first beginning they were nothing spectacular, just another rock & roll band made up of suburban ex-folkies who, in '64 and '65 – with Kennedy dead, the civil rights movement split into black and white, Vietnam taking over from Ban the Bomb, with the Beatles, Stones and Dylan – were finding out that the sit-and-pluck number had run its course. Jerry had gone the whole route: digging rock in the mid-Fifties, dropping into folk by the early Sixties, getting deep into traditional country music as a purist scholar, reemerging as a brilliant bluegrass banjo player and then, in 1964, starting Mother McCree's Uptown Jug Champions with Pigpen and Bob Weir. Weir, who had skipped from boarding school to boarding school before quitting entirely, got his real education doing folk gigs and lying about his age. "I was seventeen," he says, "looked fifteen and said I was twenty-one." Pigpen, né Ron McKernan, is the son of an early white rhythm & blues DJ, and from his early teens had made the spade scene, playing harp and piano at parties, digging Lightnin' Hopkins and nursing a remarkable talent for spinning out juiced blues raps. All three were misfits: Jerry had dropped out of high school, too, to join the army, which kicked him out after a few months as unfit for service. "How true, how true," he says now.

But the Jug Champions couldn't get any gigs, and when a

Palo Alto music store owner offered to front them with equipment to start a rock band, they said yes. Bill Kreutzmann, then Bill Sommers to fit his fake ID, became the drummer. A fan of R&B stylists, he was the only one with rock experience. At first the music store cat was the bass player, but concurrently Phil Lesh, an old friend of Jerry's, was coming to a similar dead end in formal electronic music, finding less and less to say and fewer people to say it to. A child violinist, then Stan Kenton–style jazz trumpeter and arranger, he went to a Warlocks gig on impulse, and the group knocked him out. "Jerry came over to where I was sitting and said, 'Guess what, you're gonna be our bass player.' I had never played bass, but I learned, sort of, and in July 1965 the five of us played our first gig – some club in Fremont."

For about six months the Warlocks were a straight rock & roll band. No longer. "The only scene then was the Hollywood hype scene, booking agents in flashy suits, gigs in booze clubs, six nights a week, five sets a night, doing all the R&B-rock standards. We did it all," Jerry recalls. "Then we got a regular job at a Belmont club and developed a whole malicious thing, playing songs longer and weirder, and louder, man. For *those* days it was loud, and for a bar it was ridiculous. People had to scream at each other to talk, and pretty soon we had driven out all the regular clientele. They'd run out clutching their ears. We isolated them, put 'em through a real number, yeah."

The only people who dug it were the heads around Ken Kesey up at his place in La Honda. All the Warlocks had taken acid ("We were already on the crazy-eyed fanatic trip," says Bob Weir), and, given dozens of mutual friends, it was inevitable that the Warlocks would play at La Honda. There they began again.

"One day the idea was there: 'Why don't we have a big party, and you guys bring your instruments and play, and us Pranksters will set up all our tape recorders and bullshit, and we'll all get stoned.' That was the first Acid Test. The idea was of its essence formless. There was nothin' going *on.* We'd just go up there and make something of it. Right away we dropped completely out of the straight music scene and just played the Tests. Six months: San Francisco, Muir Beach, Trips Festival, then L.A."

Jerry strains to describe what those days were like, because, just like it says in Tom Wolfe's *Electric Kool-Aid Acid Test,* the Dead got on the bus, made that irrevocable decision that the only place to go is further into the land of infinite recession that acid opened up. They were not to be psychedelic dabblers painting pretty pictures, but true explorers.

Jerry continues: "What the Kesey thing was depended on who you were when *you* were there. It was open, a tapestry, a mandala – it was whatever you made it. Okay, so you take LSD, and suddenly you are aware of another

At left: Captain Trips strolls the streets of San Francisco, 1966. Following pages: A Dead rehearsal in 1966 at the Sausalito heliport.

plane, or several other planes, and the quest is to extend that limit, to go as far as you can go. In the Acid Tests that meant to do away with old forms, with old ideas, try something *new.* Nobody was doing *something,* y'know, it was everybody doing bits and pieces of something, the result of which was something else.

"When it was moving right, you could dig that there was something that it was getting toward, something like ordered chaos, or some *region* of chaos. The Test would start off and then there would be chaos. Everybody would be high and flashing and going through insane changes during which everything would be *demolished,* man, and spilled and broken and affected, and after that, another thing would happen, maybe smoothing out the chaos, then another, and it'd go all night 'til morning.

"Just people being there, and being responsive. Like, there were microphones all over. If you were wandering around, there would be a mike you could talk into. And there would be somebody somewhere else in the building at the end of some wire with a tape recorder and a mixing board and earphones listening in on the mikes, and all of a sudden something would come in and he'd turn it up because it seemed appropriate at *that* moment.

"What you said might come out a minute later on a tape loop in some other part of the place. So there would be this odd interchange going on, electro-neural connections of weird sorts. And it was people, just *people,* doing it all. Kesey would be writing messages about what he was seeing on an opaque projector, and they'd be projected up on the wall, and someone would comment about it on a mike somewhere and that would be singing out of a speaker somewhere else.

"When we were playing, we were playing. When we weren't, we'd be doing other stuff. There were no sets; sometimes we'd get up and play for two hours, three hours, sometimes we'd play for ten minutes and all freak out and split. We'd just do it however it would happen. It wasn't a *gig,* it was the Acid Tests, where anything was okay. Thousands of people, man, all helplessly stoned, all finding themselves in a roomful of other thousands of people, none of whom any of them were afraid of.

"It was magic, far-out, beautiful magic."

* * *

Since then the search for that magic has been as important for the Dead as music, or rather, music for the Dead has to capture that magic. All of them share the vision to one degree or another, but its source is essentially Jerry Garcia. "Fellowship with man" stresses the need of "a persevering and enlightened leader . . . a man with clear, convincing and inspired aims, and the strength to carry them out." Some call Jerry a guru, but that doesn't mean much; he is just one of those extraordinary human beings who looks you right in the eyes, smiles encouragement and waits for you to become yourself. However complex, he is entirely open and unenigmatic. He can be vain, self-assertive and even pompous, but he doesn't fool around with false apology. More than anything else, he is cheery – mordant and ironic at times, but undauntedly optimistic. He's been through thinking life is but a joke, but it's still a game to be played with relish and passionately enjoyed. Probably really ugly as a kid – lumpy, fat-faced and frizzy-haired – he is now beautiful, his trimmed hair and beard a dense, black aureole around his beaming eyes. His body has an even grace, his face a restless eagerness, and a gentleness not to be confused with "niceness" is his manner.

His intelligence is quick and precise, and he can be devastatingly articulate, his dancing hands playing perfect accompaniment to his words.

Phil Lesh, Jerry's more explosive and dogmatic other half, comes right out and says that the Grateful Dead "are trying to save the world," but Jerry is more cautious. "We are trying to make things groovier for everybody so more people can feel better more often, to advance the trip, to get higher, however you want to say it. But we're musicians, and there's just no way to put that idea, 'save the world,' into music; you can only *be* that idea, or at least make manifest that idea as it appears to you and hope that maybe others follow. And that idea comes to you only moment by moment, so what we're going after is no farther away than the end of our noses. We're just trying to be right behind our noses.

"My way is music. Music is me being me and trying to get higher. I've been into music so long that I'm dripping with it; it's all I ever expect to do. I can't do anything else. Music is a yoga, something you really do when you're doing it. Thinking about what it means comes after the fact and isn't very interesting. Truth is something you stumble into when you think you're going someplace else, like those moments when you're playing and the whole room becomes one being – precious moments, man. But you can't *look* for them and they can't be repeated. Being alive means to continue to change, never to be where I was before. Music is the timeless experience of constant change."

Musical idioms and styles are important to Jerry as suggestive modes and historical and personal fact, but they are not music, and he sees no need for them to be limiting to the modern musician or listener. "You have to get past the idea that music *has* to be *one* thing. To be alive in America is to hear all kinds of music constantly – radio, records, churches, cats on the street, everywhere music, man. And with records, the whole history of music is open to everyone who wants to hear it. Maybe Chuck Berry was the first rock musician because he was one of the first blues cats to listen to records, so he wasn't locked into the blues idiom. Nobody has to fool around with musty old scores, weird notation and scholarship bullshit. You can just go into a record store and pick a century, pick a country, pick *anything,* and dig it, make it a part of you, add it to the stuff you carry around and see that it's all music."

The Dead hanging out on San Francisco's Potrero Hill, 1968. "We're trying to make things groovier for everybody so more people can feel better more often."

The Dead, like many modern groups, live that synthesis, but the breadth of idioms encompassed by the members' previous experience is probably unmatched by any other comparable band. Electronic music of all sorts, accidental music, classical music, Indian music, jazz, folk, country & western, blues and rock itself – one or all of the Dead have worked in all those forms. In mixing them they make Grateful Dead music, which, being their own creation, is their own greatest influence. It is music beyond idiom, which makes it difficult for some whose criteria for musical greatness allow only individual expression developed through disciplined understanding of a single accepted

idiom. But a Dead song is likely to include Jerry's country & western guitar licks over Bill and Mickey's 11/4 time, with the others making more muted solo statements – the whole thing subtly orchestrated by an extended, almost symphonic, blending of themes. Whatever it is, Jerry doesn't like to call it rock & roll – "a label," he says – but it is rock: free, daring music that makes the good times roll, that can, if you listen, deliver you from the days of old.

It works because the Dead are, like few bands, a group tried and true. Five have been performing together for four years; Tom Constanten, though he joined the group full time only last year because of an air force hitch, has been with them from the beginning. Mickey, a jazz drummer leading the straight life until two years ago, joined because Dead music was his music. After meeting Bill and jamming with him twice, he asked to join a set at the Straight Theatre. "We played 'Alligator' for two hours, man, and my mind was blown. When we finished and the crowd went wild, Jerry came over and embraced me, and I embraced him, and it's been like that ever since."

The Dead have had endless personal crises; Pigpen and Bob Weir have particularly resisted the others. Pig because he is not primarily a musician, and Bob because of an oddly stubborn pride. Yet they have always been a fellowship: "Our crises come and go in ways that seem more governed by the stars than by personalities," says Bob. A year ago Bob and Pigpen were on the verge of leaving. Now the Dead, says Phil, "have passed the point where breaking up exists as a possible solution to any problem. The Dead, we all know, is bigger than all of us."

In life as well as in music; as with the magic, life for the Dead has to be music, and vice versa. When the Acid Tests stopped in February 1966 and Kesey went to Mexico, the Dead got off the bus and started their own (metaphorical) bus. For roughly three months they lived with Augustus Owsley Stanley III, the media's and legend's "Acid King," on the northern edge of Watts in L.A., as he built them a huge and complex sound system. The system was no good, say some, adding that Owsley did the group nothing but harm. Owsley was weird all right, "insistent about his trip," says Bob, keeping nothing but meat and milk to eat, forbidding all vegetables as poisons, talking like a TV set you couldn't turn off, and wired into a logic that was always bizarre and often perversely paranoid, if not downright evil. But what others thought or think of Owsley has never affected the Dead; he is Owsley, and they follow their own changes with him, everything from hatred to awe to laughing at him as absurd. If you're going further, your wagon is hitched to a star; other people's opinions of the trip's validity are like flies to be brushed aside.

Their life, too, is without any idiom but their own. They returned to San Francisco in June 1966 and after a few stops moved to 710 Ashbury, in the middle of the Haight. It was the first time they actually lived in the city as a group, and they became an institution. "Happy families are all alike," Tolstoy said, but the happy family at 710 was different from most, a sliding assortment of madmen who came and went in mysterious tidal patterns, staying for days or weeks or just mellow afternoons on the steps bordered with nasturtiums. A strange black wing decorated an upper window, and occasional passersby would be jolted by sonic blasts from deep in the house's entralia. Like the Psychedelic Shop, the Panhandle or the Oracle office, it was another bus, an energy center as well as a model, a Brook Farm for new transcendentalists.

With all the other groups in the city, they did become a band, an economic entity in an expanding market. They did well; since the demise of Big Brother, they are second only to the Airplane of the San Francisco groups and are one of the biggest draws in the business. But the Dead were always different. Their managers, Rock Scully and Danny Rifkin, were of the family: stoned, ten-thumbed inefficiency. While other groups were fighting for recognition, more and bigger gigs, the Dead played mostly for free. Monterey was a godsend of exposure to most groups, but the Dead bitched about it, arguing that it should be free or, if not, the profits should go to the Diggers; refusing to sign releases for the film that became *Monterey Pop!* and finally organizing a free festival on a nearby campus and stealing banks of amps and speakers for an all-night jam (they were, eventually, returned).

But, of course, they did go; maybe Monterey was an "L.A. pseudo-hip fraud," but the Dead were a rock band as well as a psychedelic musical commune, and they knew it. The problem was combining the two. The spirit that had energized the early days was changing and becoming harder to sustain. The formlessness was becoming formalized; artifacts, whether posters, clothes, drugs or even the entire lifestyle, became more important than the art of their creation.

"The Acid Tests have come down to playing in a hall and having a light show," Jerry says. "You sit down and watch and of course the lights are behind the band so you can see the band *and* the lights. It's watching television – loud, large television. That form, so rigid, started as a misapprehension anyway. Like Bill Graham, he was at the Trips Festival, and all he saw was a light show and a band. Take the two and you got a formula. It is stuck, man, hasn't blown a new mind in years. What *was* happening at the Trips Festival was not a rock & roll show and lights, but that other thing. But if you were hustling tickets and trying to get a *production* on, to put some of the *old* order to the chaos, you couldn't feel it. It was a sensitive trip, and it's been lost."

Yet in trying to combine their own music-lifestyle with the rock & roll business, they have missed living the best of either. Their dealings with the business world have been disastrous. Money slips through their fingers, bills pile up, instruments are repossessed and salaries aren't paid. The group is $60,000 in debt, and those debts have meant harm to dozens of innocent people. "I remember times we've said, 'That cat's straight, let's burn him for a bill,'" says Phil Lesh.

They have never gotten along with Warner Bros., reacting distrustfully to all attempts at guidance. The first record, *The Grateful Dead,* was a largely unsuccessful attempt to get a live sound in the studio. The second, *Anthem of the Sun,* was recorded in four studios and at eighteen live performances; halfway through they got rid of producer Dave Hassinger and finished it themselves months behind schedule. *Aoxomoxoa* was delivered as a finished product to Warners, cover and all; the company did little more than press and distribute it. All the records have fine moments, snatches of lyric Garcia melodies and driving ensemble passages. *Aoxomoxoa* (more a mystic palindrome than a word, by the way) is in many ways brilliant; precisely mixed by Jerry and Phil, it is a record composition, not a recording of anything, and its flow is obliquely powerful. But none of them are as open and vital as the Dead live, even accounting for the change in medium. "The man in the street isn't ready for our records," says Jerry. But that also means that, fearful of being commercial, the Dead have discarded the value of immediate musical communication in making records; the baby, unfortunately, has gone out with the bathwater. A double-record album of live performances, though, is planned.

* * *

IT IS NOT THAT THEY can't be commercially successful. Their basic sound is hard rock/white R&B slightly freaked – not very different from Steppenwolf's, Creedence Clearwater's or the Sir Douglas Quintet's. "The Golden Road (to Unlimited Devotion)," their 1967 single, could quite easily be a hit single today. They would have been happy had success come to them; unsought success, a gift of self-amplification, is a logical extension of electrifying instruments. But they just won't and can't accept even the machine's most permissive limits. Their basic sound is just that, something to build from, and they know intuitively, if to their own frustration, that to accept the system, however easy a panacea it might seem, would to them be fatal.

They see themselves, with more than a touch of self-dramatization, as keepers of the flame. Smoking grass onstage, bringing acid to concerts, purposely ignoring time limits for sets, telling audiences to screw the rules and ushers and dance – those are just tokens. In late 1967 they set up the Great Northwestern Tour with the Quicksilver Messenger Service and Jerry Abrams' Headlights, completely handling a series of dates in Northern California, Oregon and Washington. "No middlemen, no bullshit," says Rock Scully. "We did it all, posters, tickets, promo, setting up the halls. All the things promoters say you can't do, we did, man, and 'cause we weren't dependent, we felt free and everybody did. That told us that however hard it gets, *it can be done,* you don't have to go along."

Out of that energy came the Carousel Ballroom. The Dead, helped by the Airplane, leased a huge Irish dance hall in downtown San Francisco and started a series of dances that were a throwback to the good old days. But running a good dance hall means taking care of business and keeping a straight head. The Carousel's managers did neither. They made absurdly bad deals, beginning with an outlandish rent, and succumbed to a destructive fear of Bill Graham. Graham, in the smaller Fillmore, smack in the center of an increasingly unfriendly ghetto, was vulnerable and ready to be cooperative. But to the Dead and their friends he was big bad Bill Graham. Graham moved swiftly, took up the lease and

renamed it the Fillmore West. The Dead were on the street again, licking their wounds, self-inflicted and otherwise.

A year later they are still in the street; they are not quite failures by accepted business terms but certainly have been stagnated by their own stubborn yearning. A bust in the fall of 1967 and the increasing deterioration of the Haight finally drove them from 710 in 1968; similar hassles may drive the remnants of the family from their ranch in Novato. And the band members now all live in separate houses scattered over San Francisco and Marin County. Financial necessity forced them to sign with Graham's booking agency in early 1969, though they will soon leave it. They are still talking of making a music caravan, traveling from town to town in buses like a circus. They know a new form has to be found; the "psychedelic dance-concert" is washed up, but what is next? Maybe a rock & roll rodeo, maybe something else that will just happen when the time comes. They don't know, but they are determined to find it. It is hard to get your thing together if your thing is paradise on earth. "We're tired of jerking off," says Jerry. "We want to start fucking again."

* * *

SEVEN O'CLOCK FRIDAY MORNING, Santa Barbara was deep in pearly mist, and Jerry Garcia was pacing back and forth in an alley behind the motel, quietly turning on. One by one, yawning and grunting, the others appeared and clambered into the Pontiacs. It was the start of a long day: 8:00 a.m. flight into San Francisco, change planes for Portland, crash in the motel until the gig, play, then get to bed and on to Eugene the next day. There was neither time nor energy for postmortems; the thing to do was to get on with it.

At 7:30 Lenny Hart was fuming. The Bear was late again. Where was he? No one knew. Lenny, square-faced and serious, drummed on the steering wheel. "We gotta go, can't wait for him. What's so special about Bear that he can't get here like everyone else?" Phil started back to the motel to find him, but then out Bear came, sleepy but dapper in a black leather shirt and vest, pale blue pants and blue suede boots. Lenny's eyes caught Bear's for an instant, then he peeled out.

No one missed the confrontation: Lenny and the Bear, like two selves of the Dead at war, with the Dead themselves sitting as judges. Lenny, a minister who has chosen the Dead as his mission, is the latest person they've trusted to get them out of the financial pit. The Bear, says Jerry, is "Satan in our midst," friend, chemist, psychedelic legend and electronic genius; not a leader, but a moon with gravitational pull. He is the prince of inefficiency, the essence at its most perverse of what the Dead refuse to give up. They are natural enemies, but somehow they have to coexist for the Dead to survive. Their skirmishing has just begun.

At the airport, the jet rests before the little stucco terminal. It is ten minutes after takeoff time, and the passengers wait in two clumps. Clump One, the big one, is ordinary Santa Barbara human beings: clean, tanned businessmen, housewives, college girls going away for the holiday, an elderly couple or two, a few ten-year-olds in shorts. They are quiet and a bit strained. Clump Two is the Dead: manic, dirty, hairy, noisy, a bunch of drunken Visigoths in cowboy

hats and greasy suede. Pigpen has just lit Bob Weir's paper on fire, and the cinders blow around their feet. Phil is at his twitchiest, his face stroboscopically switching grotesque leers. The Bear putters in his mysterious belted bags, Jerry discards cigarette butts as if the world were his ashtray, and Tom, one sock bright green, the other vile orange, gazes beatifically (he's a Grade Four Release in Scientology) over it all and puns under his breath.

Over on the left in the cargo area, a huge rented truck pulls up with the Dead's equipment, ninety pieces of extra luggage. Like clowns from a car, amp after amp after drum case is loaded onto dollies and wheeled to the jet's belly. It dawns on Clump One all at once that it is those arrogant heathens with all their outrageous gear that are making the plane late and keeping them, good American citizens, shivering out in the morning mist. It dawns on the heathens, too, but they dig it, shouting to the quippies to tote that amp, lift that organ. Just about that time Phil, reading what's left of the paper, sees a story about People's Park in Berkeley and how the police treated the demonstrators "like the Viet Cong." "But that's just what we are, man, the American National Liberation Front!" he shouts, baring his teeth at Clump One.

Ticket takers talk politely of "Mr. Ramrod" and "Mr. Bear"; in San Francisco Airport a pudgy waitress, "Marla" stamped on the plastic nameplate pinned to her right udder, leaves her station starry-eyed and says she's so glad to see them because she came to work stoned on acid and it's been a freak-out until she saw them like angel horsemen galloping through her plastic hell; Tom, his mustachioed face effortlessly sincere, gives a beginning lecture on the joys of Scientology, explaining that he hopes someday to be an Operating Thetan (O.T.) and thus be able to levitate the group while they're playing – and of course they won't ever have to plug in.

Pig glowers beneath his corduroy hat, grunting, "Ahhh, fork!" whenever the spirit moves, and the Bear starts a long, involved rap about how the Hell's Angels really have it down, man, like this cat who can use a whip like a stiletto, could slice open your nostrils, first the right, then the left, neat as you please, and everyone agrees that the Angels are righteously ugly.

They miss their San Francisco connection and have to hang around the airport for a couple of hours, but that somehow means that they arrive first-class, free drinks and all. With lunch polished off, Mickey Hart needs some refreshment, so he calls across the aisle to Ramrod, then holds his fingers to his nose significantly. Ramrod tosses over a small vial of cocaine and a jackknife, and Mickey, all the while carrying on an intense discussion about drumming, sniffs up like he was lighting an after-dinner cigar: "Earth music is what I'm after" – sniff – "the rhythm of the earth, like I get riding a horse" – sniff sniff – "and Bill feeds that to me, I play off of it, and he responds. When we're into it, it's like a drummer with two minds, eight arms, and one soul" – final snort, and then the vial and jackknife go the rounds. Multiple felonies in the first-class compartment, but the stewardesses are without eyes to see. The Dead, in the very grossness of their visibility, are invisible.

The plane lands in Portland. "Maybe it'll happen today," says Jerry waiting to get off, "the first rock & roll assassination. Favorite fantasy. Sometime we'll land, and when we're all on the stairs, a fleet of black cars will rush the plane like killer beetles. Machine guns will pop from the roofs and mow us down. Paranoid, huh? But, fuck, in a way I wouldn't blame 'em." No black cars, though, that day anyway.

Lenny has done some figuring on the plane. "Things are looking up," he says. "We ought to have the prepaid tickets for this trip paid by the end of next week." Jerry says that's boss, and the Bear makes a point of showing off the alarm clock he got in San Francisco. Lenny takes it as a joke and says just be ready next time or he'll be left behind. Danny Rifkin brings the good news that they have a tank of nitrous oxide for the gig. Everybody goes to sleep.

The dance is at Springer's Inn, about ten miles out of town, and they start out about 9:30. A mile from the place there is a huge traffic jam on the narrow country road, and they stick the cars in a ditch and walk, a few fragments in the flow to Springer's under a full yellow moon. The last time they played Portland they were at a ballroom with a sprung floor that made dancing inevitable, but Springer's is just as nice. It's a country & western place, walls all knotty pine, and beside the stage the Nashville stars of the past thirty years grin glossily from autographed photos: "Your's sincerely, Marty Robbins," "Love to Ya'll, Norma Jean," "Warmest regards, Jim Reeves."

"You got a bigger crowd than even Buck Owens," says the promoter, and Jerry grins. It is sardine, ass-to-ass packed and drippingly hot inside.

The band stands around the equipment truck waiting for the Bear to finish his preparations. Someone donates some Cokes and they make the rounds. "Anyone for a lube job?" Bill calls to the hangers-on. "Dosed to a turn," says Phil. Jerry, already speechlessly spaced on gas, drinks deep. They are all ready.

It seems preordained to be a great night. But preordination is not fate; it comes to the elect and the elect have to work to be ready for it. So the Dead start out working; elation will come later. "Morning Dew" opens the set, an old tune done slow and steady. It is the evening's foundation stone, and they carefully mortise it into place, no smiles, no frills. Phil's bass is sure and steady, Bill and Mickey play almost in unison. Then Bob sings "Me and My Uncle," a John Phillips tune with a country-rocking beat. They all like the song, and Bob sings it well, friendly and ingenuous. Back to the groove with "Doin' That Rag," but a little looser this time. Jerry's guitar begins to sing, and over the steady drumming of Bill, Mickey

Preceding pages: Danny Rifkin and a friend trip the light fantastic at a free Grateful Dead show in San Francisco's Panhandle, 1967. At right: Waitin' to catch that plane at the Seattle airport, 1968.

lays scattered runs, little kicks and sudden attacks. Phil begins to thunder, then pulls back. Patience, he seems to be saying, and he's right: Jerry broke a string in his haste, so they pull back to unison and end the song. But Jerry wants it bad and is a little angry.

"I broke a string!" he shouts at the crowd. "So why don't you wait a minute and talk to each other. Or maybe talk to

yourself, to your various selves" – he cocks his head with a glint of malice in his eyes – "can *you* talk to your *self*? Do you even know you have selves to talk to?"

The questions, involute and unanswerable, push the crowd back – who is this guy asking us riddles, what does he *want* from us anyway? But the band is into "King Bee" by that time. They haven't played that for a while, but it works, another building block and a good way to work Pig into the center, to seduce him into giving his all instead of just waiting around for "Love Light." It is like the Stones but muddier – Pigpen isn't Mick Jagger, after all. Jerry buzzes awhile right on schedule, and the crowd eases up, thinking they're going to get some nice blues. The preceding band was a good imitation B.B. King, so maybe it will be a blues night. Wrong again.

"Play the blues!" shouts someone in a phony half-swoon.

"Fuck you, man!" Mickey shouts back. "Go hear a blues band if you want that, go dig Mike Bloomfield."

Another punch in the mouth, but the moment is there, and the audience's stunned silence just makes the opening gong of "Dark Star" more ominous. In that silence music begins, steady and pulsing. Jerry, as always, takes the lead, feeling his way for melodies like paths up the mountain. Jerry, says Phil, is the heart of the Dead, its central sun; while they all connect to each other, the strongest bonds are to him. Standing there, eyes closed, chin bobbing forward, his guitar in close under his arm, he seems pure energy, a quality like but distinct from sexuality, which, while radiating itself outward unceasingly and unselfishly, is as unceasingly and unselfishly replenished by those whose strengths have been awakened by his.

He finds a way, a few high twanging notes that are in themselves a song, and then the others are there, too, and suddenly the music is not notes or a tune, but what those seven people are *exactly:* The music is an aural holograph of the Grateful Dead. All their fibers, nuances, histories, desires, beings are clear: Jerry and his questing; Phil the loyal comrade; Tom drifting beside them both on a cloud; Pig staying stubbornly down to earth; Mickey working out furious complexities, trying to understand how Bill is so simple; and Bob succumbing inevitably to Jerry and Phil and joining them. And that is just the beginning, because at each note, at each phrase, the balances change, each testing, feeding, mocking and finally driving each other on, further and further on.

Some balances last longer than others, moments of realization that seem to sum up many moments, and then a solid groove of "Yes, that is the way it is" flows out, and the crowd begins to move. Each time it is Jerry who leads them out, his guitar singing and dancing joy. And his joy finds new levels, and the work of exploration begins again.

Jerry often talks of music as coming from a place and creating a place, a place where strife is gone, where the struggle to understand ends and knowledge is as evident as light. That is the place they are in at Springer's. However hard it is to get there, once there, you want to cry tears of ease and never leave.

The music goes fast and slow, driving and serene, loud and soft. Mickey switches from gong to drums to claves to handclapping to xylophone to a tin slide whistle. Then Bob grabs that away and steps to the mike and blows the whistle as hard as he can, flicking away insanely high and screeching notes. The band digs it and lays down a building rhythm. The crowd begins to pant, shake, and then suddenly right on the exact moment with the band, the crowd, the band, everything in the whole goddamn place begins to scream. Not scream like at the Beatles, but scream like beasts, twisting their faces, trying out every possible animal yowl that lies deep in their hearts.

And Jerry, melodies flowing from him in endless arabesques, leads it away again, the crowd and himself ecstatic rats to some Pied Piper. The tune changes from "Dark Star" to "St. Stephen," the song with a beat like bouncing boulders, and out of the din comes Jerry's wavering voice, "Another man gathers what another man spills," and everyone knows that means that there's nothing to fear, brothers will help each other with their loads, and suddenly there is peace in the hall. Phil, Bob and Bill form a trio and play a new and quiet song before Mickey's sudden roll opens it out to the group, and "St. Stephen" crashes to an end with the cannon shot and clouds of sulphurous smoke.

Out of the fire and brimstone emerges the Pig singing "Love Light," and everyone is through the mind and down into the body. Pigpen doesn't sing; Pigpen never sings. He is just Pig being Pig doing "Love Light," spitting out of the side of his mouth between phrases, starting the clapping, telling everybody to get their hands out of their pockets and into somebody else's pocket, and, like laughter, the band comes in with rock-it-to-'em choruses. The crowd is jumping up and down in witness by this time, and one couple falls onstage, their bodies and tongues entwined in mad ritual embrace. They don't make love, but in acting it out, they perform for and with the crowd, and so everyone is acting out sexual unison, with Pigpen as the master of ceremonies. The place, one body, built in music, fucks until it comes, the cannon goes off one final time, and Mickey leaps to the gong, bashing it with a mallet set

At right and following pages: Deadmates in '69, Garcia; Weir; Kreutzmann; Hart; Pigpen. "To be alive in America is to hear all kinds of music constantly: radio, records, churches, cats on the street, everywhere music, man."

afire by the cannon, and it makes a trail of flame and then sparks when it hits the gong, the gong itself radiating waves of sonic energy. Bill flails at the drums, Phil keeps playing the same figure over and over, faster and faster, and Jerry and Bob build up to one note just below the tonic, hold it until, with one ultimate chord, it all comes home. The crowd erupts in cheers as the band, sodden with sweat, stumble off the stage.

"We'll be back, folks," says Jerry. "We'll be back after a break."

Bob laughs as he hears Jerry's announcement. "It's really something when you have to lie to get off the stage."

Because it's over, gone, wiped out. They gather by the equipment van, and all but Tom, still cool and unruffled, are steaming in the chill night air. The moon has gone down, the stars are out, and there is nothing more to be done that night. ☙

THE
1ST
THE ROLLING STONE INTERVIEW
BY JANN S. WENNER *AND* CHARLES REICH
WITH JERRY GARCIA & MOUNTAIN GIRL

THE INTERVIEW WITH GARCIA was always one of those things we put off into some indefinite future because Jerry was always around and, of course, we'd do it sooner or later. What finally brought it on was a meeting with Charles Reich, the postfortyish law professor from Yale who wrote *The Greening of America*.

It turned out he was a Grateful Dead freak, and he hit me with the question "How come you haven't done an interview with Garcia yet?" I thought his enthusiasm a little . . . naive, but, what the hell, he suggested that we do an interview with Jerry together: I'd do the interview itself, and he'd come along and ask one or two questions of his own. It sounded okay to me; Reich was obviously very up on the band, knew all the lyrics and could quote them and speak intelligently about the band and its history. It would be a good combination, and, God knows, Charles "Consciousness Three" Reich Meets Jerry "Captain Trips" Garcia could turn into something of its own.

Garcia lives near Mount Tamalpais overlooking the Pacific Ocean, in a casual Fifties suburban house with his old lady, Mountain Girl (once of the Merry Pranksters and a close friend of Ken Kesey's in those days), and their little girl, Sunshine. The house is surrounded by eucalyptus trees, huge shrubs and six-foot rosebushes (beyond which is a magnificent view of the Pacific and the Far East, as far as the imagination can take you).

On the front lawn, which looks onto that magnificent view, Reich, myself, Mountain Girl and Garcia sat on a sunny afternoon and turned the tape recorder on. Five hours later, I packed up the machine and headed back to the city, not entirely sure I could drive too well and not entirely sure at all what had just gone down. Reich was wandering around somewhere in back of the house, remarking on the vibrancy of the trees (never found out exactly when and how he left that day), and Jerry had to be somewhere at 7:00 for a gig.

I received the transcriptions of the tapes about three weeks later. What had happened was one interview that I did with Jerry, based on an old familiarity, best described as the good old Grateful Dead trip; and there was a whole other interview that Reich was trying to do: Garcia as spokesman, teacher, philosopher. If I played participant and historian, Reich was the true fan and amazed adult. [Reich's name appears next to his questions.]

* * *

REICH: START US *at the beginning.*
Which beginning?
Reich: Your beginning – the day you were born.
My father was a musician. He played in jazz bands in the places that I play in San Francisco, the same ballrooms. He played clarinet, saxophone, reeds, woodwinds. He was an immigrant who, with his whole family, moved out in the Twenties or the Teens from Spain. My mother was born in San Francisco. Her mother is a Swedish lady, and her father is Irish, gold-rush-days people, who came to San Francisco then. My mother met my father somewhere back then in the Thirties, something like that; he a musician, she a nurse.

Then the Depression came along, and my father couldn't get work as a musician. I understand there was some hassle: He was blackballed by the union or something 'cause he was working two jobs or something like that, some musician's union trip, so he wasn't able to remain a professional musician, and he became a bartender, bought a bar, a little bar like a lot of guys do. He died when I was real young, and my mother took over that business.

All through this time there were always instruments around the house because of my father, and my mother played piano a little, and I had lots and lots of abortive piano lessons, you know . . . I can't read, I couldn't learn how to read music, but I could play by ear. My family was a singing family, on the Spanish side; every time there was a party everybody sang. My brother and my cousin and I when we were pretty young did a lot of street corner harmonizing . . . rock & roll . . . good old rhythm & blues, that kind of stuff, pop songs, all that.

And then my mother remarried when I was about ten or eleven or so, and she decided to get the kids out of the city, go down to the Peninsula, and we moved down to Menlo Park for about three years, and I went to school down there.

Somewhere before that, when I was in the third grade in San Francisco, I had a lady teacher who was a bohemian, you know. She was colorful and pretty and energetic and vivacious, and she wasn't like one of those dust-covered crones that characterize oldtime public school people; she was really lively. She had everybody in the class, all the kids in this sort of homogeneous school, making things out of ceramics and papier-mâché. It was an art thing, and that was more or less my guiding interest from that time on. I was going to be a painter and I really was taken with it. I got into art history and all of it. It was finally something for me to do.

When we went down to the Peninsula, I fell in with a teacher who turned me on to the intellectual world. I was eleven or twelve. He said, "Here, read this." It was *1984*. And all of a sudden it was a whole new – that was like when I was turning on, so to speak, or became aware of a whole other world that was other than the thing you got in school, that you got in the movies and all that; something very different. And so right away I was really a long way from school at that point . . . there was two or three of us that got into that because of this teacher, who ultimately got fired that same year because of being too controversial – got the kids stirred up and all that – all the classic things.

We moved back to the city when I was about thirteen or so, and I started going to Denman, a good old San Francisco rowdy roughneck school. I became a hoodlum, survival thing; you had

Preceding page: Family portrait 1968, Garcia, Mountain Girl and Sunshine. At right: Garcia and Mountain Girl at their SF home before moving to Marin, 1967.

to be a hoodlum, otherwise you walk down the street and somebody beat you up. I had my friends, and we were hoodlums, and we went out on the weekends and did a lot of drinkin' and all that. And meanwhile I was still reading and buying books and going to San Francisco Art Institute on the weekends and just sort of leading this whole secret life.

I was fifteen when I got turned on to marijuana. Finally

there was marijuana: Wow! Marijuana! Me and a friend of mine went up into the hills with two joints, the San Francisco foothills, and smoked these joints and just got so high and laughed and roared and went skipping down the streets doing funny things and just having a helluva time. It was great, it was just what I wanted, it was the perfect, it was – and that wine thing was so awful, and this marijuana was so perfect.

So what's happening to music all this time?

Nothing much, I'm goofing around, I'm trying to play rock & roll piano and stuff like that, but I'm not settled in with my mother particularly, I'm sort of living with my grandmother and I don't really have any instruments. I want really badly a guitar during this time – about three years – I want a guitar so bad it hurts. I go down to the pawnshops on Market Street and Third Street and wander around the record stores, the music stores, and look at the electric guitars, and my mouth's watering. God, I want that so bad! And on my fifteenth birthday my mother gave me an accordion. I looked at this accordion and I said, "God, I don't want this accordion. I want an electric guitar."

So we took it down to a pawnshop, and I got this little Danelectro, an electric guitar with a tiny little amplifier, and man, I was just in heaven. Everything! I stopped everything I was doing at the time. I tuned it to an open tuning that sort of sounded right to me, and I started picking at it and playing at it. I spent about six or eight months on it, just working things out. It was unknown at the time, there were no guitar players around. And I was getting pretty good, and finally I ran into somebody at school that played guitar.

Reich: Can I ask for the date?

August first – let's see, I was born in '42 – Christ, man, arithmetic, school, I was fifteen – '57. Yeah, '57, there you go, it was a good year, Chuck Berry, all that stuff.

Reich: I wanted to get a historic date like that.

Yeah, well, that's what it was, August first, 1957, I got my first guitar. And that was it. Somebody showed me some chords on the guitar, and that was the end of everything that I'd been doing until that time. We moved out of town up to Cazadero, which is up by the Russian River, and I went to a high school for about a year, did really badly, finally quit and joined the army. I decided I was going to get away from everything. Yeah, seventeen. I joined the army, smuggled my guitar in.

Reich: In joining the army, it was probably time to leave home.

Well, it was the time to leave it all. I wanted to just be someplace completely different. Home wasn't working out really for me, and school was ridiculous and – I just wasn't working out. I had to do something. At that time the only really available alternative was to join the army, so I did that.

Reich: Do you have any brothers and sisters?

I have an older brother. Circumstances made me a different guy from my brother, made it always – it was difficult for me to communicate with my brother. He was in the marines for four years. All that's evened out since he's gone kind of through a straight trip and . . . sort of fell out the other side of it, and now he's a head and living in the new

world, so to speak, so now we can communicate, whereas it used to be that we couldn't.

I lasted nine months in the army. I was at Fort Ord for basic training and then they transferred me to the Presidio in San Francisco, Fort Winfield Scott, a beautiful, lovely spot overlooking the water and the Golden Gate Bridge and all that, and these neat old barracks and almost nothing to do. It started me into the acoustic guitar; up until that time I had been mostly into electric guitar, rock & roll and stuff.

I was stuck because I just didn't know anybody that played guitar, and that was probably the greatest hindrance of all to learning the guitar. I just didn't know anybody. I used to do things like look at pictures of guitar players and look at their hands and try to make the chords they were doing, anything, any little thing. I couldn't take lessons – I knew I couldn't take lessons for the piano – so I had to learn it by myself and I just worked with my ear.

When I got out of the army, I went down to Palo Alto and rejoined some of my old friends down there who were kind of living off the fat of the land, so to speak, a sort of hand-to-mouth existence. Some were living off their parents; most of 'em, most people were living off people who were living off *their* parents.

Reich: This was the beginning of the dropout world?

Yeah, yeah, well, we were – well, like, that's the period of time I met [Robert] Hunter. Immediately after I got out of the army. Hunter – who is, like, a really good friend of mine all this time, he'd just gotten out of the army – he had an old car and I had an old car when I got out of the army, and we were in East Palo Alto sort of coincidentally. There was a coffeehouse – 'cause of Stanford, university town and all that – and we were hanging out at the coffeehouse and ran into each other.

We had our two cars in an empty lot in East Palo Alto, where they were both broken. Neither of them ran anymore, but we were living in them. Hunter had these big tins of crushed pineapple that he'd gotten from the army, like five or six big tins, and I had this glove compartment full of plastic spoons, and we had this little cooperative scene, eating this crushed pineapple day after day and sleeping in the cars and walking around.

Garcia, Pigpen, Lesh, Weir and Kreutzmann, 1967. "I think of the Grateful Dead as being a crossroads or a pointer sign, and what we're pointing to is that there's a whole lot of experience available."

He played a little guitar; we started singin' and playin' together just for something to do. And then we played our first professional gig. We got five bucks apiece.

Who are some of the people you met on the coffeehouse circuit?

I didn't get into playing the coffeehouses until a little bit later than that, really playing coffeehouses. Most of that time before that, I was learning to play well enough to play anywhere. Sixty-one or '62, I started playing coffeehouses, and the guys who were playing around then up in San Francisco at the Fox and Hounds, Nick Gravenites was around then, Nick the Greek, they called him. Pete Stampfel from the Holy Modal Rounders, he was playing around there then. Let's see . . . in Berkeley there was Jorma

[Kaukonen] playing coffeehouses about the same time that I was, and Janis [Joplin]. And Paul Kantner was playing around. Let's see . . . a lot of the people that are around now, that are still doing stuff now.

Were you making enough money to support yourself?

Nah . . . I was either not making money and mostly living off my wits, which was pretty easy to do in Palo Alto – things are very well fed – or else I was teaching guitar in record stores.

Hunter and I were still more or less together; at this time we're mostly living at this place called the Chateau in Palo Alto, and me and Hunter, and Phil is there a lot, Phil Lesh and Pigpen and all these . . . my fellow freaks.

Where did they turn up?

The old Palo Alto Peace Center was a great place for social trips. The Peace Center was the place where the sons and daughters of the Stanford professors would hang out and discuss things. And we, the opportunist wolf pack, the beatnik hordes, you know, would be there preying on their young minds and their refrigerators. And there would be all of these various people turning up in these scenes, and it just got to be very good, really high.

How did they come along?

Phil was from Berkeley and he had spent . . . his reason for being anywhere on the Peninsula was that he had done some time at San Mateo Junior College playing in their jazz band. Now, Phil, who I met down there at the Peace Center, was at that time composing twelve-tone and serial things. He'd also been a jazz trumpet player. We were in two totally different worlds musically. But somehow he was working at KPFA as an engineer, and I was up there at a folk-music thing or something like that, and Burt Corena, who ran the folk-music show there, wanted me to do a show for KPFA as a folksinger, so Phil and I got together at a party. He put together a tape of me playing in the kitchen, and it sounded pretty good to us. He took it up there and played it for them; they dug it, so I went up to the studio, and he engineered my little performance.

Whose idea was it to have a band?

See, what happened was, I got into oldtime country music, oldtime string-band music, and in order to play string-band music, you have to have a band; you can't play it by yourself. So I would be out recruiting musicians. One of the musicians I used to play with in those days was Dave Nelson, who plays guitar for the New Riders, so that's another germ, and me and Nelson were playing oldtime music, and we got into bluegrass music, playing around at coffeehouses. And Bobby Weir was really a young kid at that time, learning how to play the guitar. And he used to go hang around in the music store and he used to hang around at the coffeehouse.

Bob came from Atherton – he's from that really upper-class trip, his folks are really wealthy and all that; he was like the Atherton kid who was just too weird for anybody. He didn't make it in school, and people were beatin' up on him, and he was getting kicked out of schools all over the place. His trip was he wanted to learn to play the guitar and have a good old time, and so he'd hang around the music store . . . I met him when I was working at a music store. He was one of the king-pin pickers – on the town – I always played at the coffee-house, and Weir would come and hear me play, and so it was that kind of thing.

At that time he was like fifteen or something, really young. He's the kid guitar player. And the band thing kept happening various ways. Bluegrass bands are hard to put together because you have to have good bluegrass musicians to play, and in Palo Alto there wasn't really very many of them – not enough to keep a band going all the time.

Now, Bill Kreutzmann was working at the music store at the same time I was. My first encounter with Kreutzmann was when I bought a banjo from him way back in '61 or '62. He was just a kid then, playing rock & roll. He was in high school. I may have even played a gig with him once when I was playing electric bass in a rock & roll band on weekends.

Since I always liked playing, whether it was bluegrass music or not, I decided to put together a jug band, because you could have a jug band with guys that could hardly play at all or play very well or anything like that. So we put together the jug band, and Weir finally had his chance to play because Weir had this uncanny ability to really play the jug and play it really well, and he was the only guy around and so he of course was the natural candidate. And Pigpen, who was mostly into playin' Lightnin' Hopkins stuff and harmonica.

Where'd he come from?

He was another one of the kids from around there, he was like the Elvis Presley soul and hoodlum kid. His father was a disc jockey . . . he heard the blues, he wanted to play the blues, and I was, like, the guitar player in town who could play the blues, so he used to hang around. That's how I got to know him. He took up harmonica and got pretty good at it for those days, when nobody could play any of that stuff.

So we had the jug band with Pigpen and Weir and Bob Matthews, who's now the head guy at Alembic, and Marmaduke [of New Riders] even played with the jug band for a while, I believe.

The jug band we're talking about is pretty recent, that's like '63 . . . '63 or '64 . . . Phil's back from '61 or '60.

And you ran around and played the –

Played anyplace that would hire a jug band, which was almost no place, and that's the whole reason we finally got into electric stuff.

Whose idea was that?

Well, Pigpen, as a matter of fact; it was Pigpen's idea. He'd been pestering me for a while, he wanted me to start up an electric blues band. That was his trip . . . because in the jug-band scene, we used to do blues numbers like Jimmy Reed tunes and even played a couple of rock & roll tunes, and it was just the next step.

And the Beatles . . . and all of a sudden there were the Beatles, and that, wow, the Beatles, you know. *Hard Day's Night,* the movie and everything. Hey, great, that really looks like fun.

So Pig fronts the blues band . . .

Yeah, well . . . theoretically it's a blues band, but the minute we get electric instruments it's a rock & roll band. Because, wow, playin' rock & roll, it's fun. Pigpen, because he could play some blues piano and stuff like that, we put him on organ immediately, and the harmonica was a natural, and he was doin' most of the lead vocals at the time. We had a really rough sound, and the bass player was the guy who owned this music store that I had been workin' in, which was convenient, because he gave us all the equipment; we didn't have to go out and hassle to raise money to buy equipment.

But then, we were playing at this pizza parlor. This is, like, our first gig; we were the Warlocks, with the music store owner playing bass and Bobby and me and Pigpen . . . and Bill. And so we went and played. We played three gigs at that pizza parlor.

What was your repertoire?

We did . . . we stole a lot of . . . well, at that time, the Kinks, and the Rolling Stones' "King Bee," "Red Rooster," "Walkin' the Dog" and all that shit, we were just doing hard, simple rock & roll stuff, old Chuck Berry stuff – "Promised Land," "Johnny B. Goode" – a couple of songs that I sort of adapted from jug-band material. "Stealin' " was one of those and that tune called "Don't Ease Me In" – it was our first single, an old ragtime pop Texas song.

That first gig . . .

That first night at the pizza place, nobody was there. The next week, when we played there again, it was on a Wednesday night, there was a lot of kids there, and then the third night there was three, four hundred people . . . all up from the high schools, and in there, man, in there was this rock & roll band . . . we were playing, people were freaking out.

Phil came down from San Francisco with some friends because they heard we had a rock & roll band, and he wanted to hear what our rock & roll band was like, and it was a flash to see Phil because he had a Beatles haircut, and he'd been working for the post office and livin' in the Haight-Ashbury. He wasn't playin' any music, though, and he wasn't writing or composing or anything, and I said, "Hey, listen, man, why don't you play bass with us because I know how musical you are; I know you've got absolute pitch and it wouldn't take you too long, and I could show you some stuff to get you started." He said, "Yeah, well, that'd be far-out." So we got him an old guitar to practice on and borrowed a bass for him, and about two weeks later we rehearsed for a week, and we went out and started playing together.

We never decided to be the Grateful Dead. What happened was the Grateful Dead came up as a suggestion because we were at Phil's house one day; he had a big Oxford dictionary, I opened it up, and the first thing I saw was the Grateful Dead. It said that on the page and it was so astonishing. It was truly weird, a truly weird moment.

I didn't like it really, I just found it to be really powerful. Weir didn't like it, Kreutzmann didn't like it, and nobody really wanted to hear about it. But then people started calling us that, and it just started, it just got out, Grateful Dead, Grateful Dead . . . We sort of became the Grateful Dead because we heard there was another band called Warlocks. We had about two or three months of no name, and we were trying things out, different names, and nothing quite fit.

Reich: I'd like to know about your life outside of playing. What kind of scene was that?

Well, I got married back there somewhere, and it was one of those things where she got into trouble, you know, in the classic way. "I want to have the baby," "Well, okay, let's get married." We got married, and the parents thing and all that, and it was like I was tryin' to be straight, kinda. I was working in the music store, in earnest now, and our baby was born, and it was okay and all that, but it wasn't really workin'. I was really playin' music, I was playin' music during the day at the music store practicing, and at nights I would go out and gig.

Reich: Were you interested in anything besides music?

Yeah, I was interested in everything besides music. Drugs, of course.

Reich: Okay. Let's talk for a minute about that; how they came in at that time . . . it was an old story.

I'd been getting high for a long time, but marijuana turned up in the folk-music world, and there was speed. The thing about speed in those days was that you stayed up and raved all night, or played. *The Doors of Perception* and stuff like that, we were talking about. And there was mescaline; we could not find mescaline, but we could find peyote. That was the only psychedelic around at that time.

Reich: Poetry, literature, stuff like that?

All that, all of that, and on all levels. That was like a continuing thing, but then along came LSD, and that was the end of that whole world. The whole world just went kablooey.

Reich: What's the date of that?

Let's see, LSD came around to our scene I guess around – it all was sort of happening at the same time, around '64, I guess. We started hearing about it in '63 and started getting it about in '64.

When we were living at the Chateau, even earlier, like '61, '62, I guess, or '63, the government was running a series of drug tests over at Stanford, and Hunter was one of the participants in these. They gave him mescaline and psilocybin and LSD and a whole bunch of others and put him in a little white room and watched him. And there were other people on the scene that were into that. Kesey. And as soon as those people had had those drugs, they were immediately trying to get them, trying to find some way to cop 'em or anything, but there was no illicit drug market at that time.

Reich: Two questions together: How did it change your life? And how did it change your music?

Well, it just changed everything, you know. It was just – ah, first of all, for me personally, it freed me, you know; the effect was that it freed me, because I suddenly realized that my little attempt at having a straight life and doing that was really a fiction and [it] just wasn't going to work out. Luckily, I wasn't far enough into it for it to be shattering or anything; it was like a realization that just made me feel immensely relieved; I just felt good, and it was the same with my wife. At that time it sort of freed us to be able to go ahead and live our lives rather than having to live out an unfortunate social circumstance, which is what the whole thing is about.

Reich: In what sense did it free you?

In making it all right to have or not have. That is, I think the first lesson that LSD taught me in sort of a graphic way was . . . just . . . it's okay to have something, and it's also okay to not have it.

When was the first time you played music on LSD?

Uh, when we were, let's see . . . we . . . oh, we were the Warlocks and we were playing in a bar in Belmont. We were playing this straight bar, and we would do five sets a night, forty-five on and fifteen off, and we'd be sneaking out in the cars, smoking joints between each set and so forth. One of those days we took it. We got high and goofed around in the mountains and ran around and did all kinds of stuff, and I remembered we had to work that night. We went to the gig and we were all a little high, and it was all a little strange. It was so weird playing in a bar being high on acid. It was just too weird; it definitely wasn't appropriate.

The first time that music and LSD interacted in a way that really came to life for us as a band was one day when we went out and got extremely high on some of that early dynamite LSD, and we went that night to the Lovin' Spoonful – remember that thing, the Lovin' Spoonful, the Charlatans and whoever else down at the Family Dog, Longshoreman's Hall, it was one of the first ones – and we went there, and we were stoned on acid watching these bands play.

That day – the Grateful Dead guys, our scene – we went out, took acid and came up to Marin County and hung out somewhere around Fairfax or Lagunitas or one of those places up in the woods and just went crazy. We ended up going into that rock & roll dance, and it was just really fine to see that whole scene – where there was just nobody there but heads and this strange rock & roll music playing in this weird building. It was just what we wanted to see.

It was just truly fantastic. We began to see that vision of a truly fantastic thing. It became clear to us that working in bars was not going to be right for us to be able to expand into this new idea. And about that time the Acid Test was just starting to happen.

How did the music change? You're still playing country music and you're playing blues and . . .

Well, we got more into wanting to go . . . to take it farther. In the nightclubs, in bars, mostly what they want to hear is short, fast stuff, umm . . . and we were always trying to play a little, stretch out a little . . .

Mountain Girl: More . . . loud.

Jerry: So our trip with the Acid Test was to be able to go play long and loud. Man, we can play long and loud, as long and loud as we wanted, and nobody would stop us.

Mountain Girl: Oh, God . . .

Reich: So, like, would you take something you'd played before and just make it longer and longer and louder and louder? And you were improvising?

Of course, we were improvising cosmically, too. Because being high, each note, you know, is like a whole universe. And each silence. And the quality of the sound and the degree of emotional . . . when you're playing and you're high on acid in these scenes, it is like the most important thing in the world. It's truly, phew, cosmic . . .

Our consciousness concerning music is opening up more, so the music is becoming . . . is having more facets than it seemed to, having more dimensions . . . and we've also seen the effect of all of a sudden we find a certain kind of feeling or a certain kind of rhythm, and the whole place is like a sea and it goes boom . . . boom . . . boom. It's like magic, and it's like that something you discover on LSD and you discover that another kind of sound will, like, create a whole other, you know . . .

When did you meet Kesey, and how?

The Chateau, where we were all livin' several years earlier, was situated physically about two or three blocks from Kesey's place, and there were people from Kesey's that were over at our scene and so on. We didn't hang out down there too much because at the time it was a college trip, you know, they were college people kind of, and it was – it made us self-conscious to be there, we were so, you know . . . undesirable, they didn't really want us, nobody wanted us hangin' out.

But then, years later, here we are a rock & roll band. They were hearin' about us up at Kesey's place from our friends who are stayin' up there and gettin' high and comin' down and gettin' high with us.

There was this interaction goin' on. Just like there was interaction between our scene down on the Peninsula and the San Francisco scene . . . the San Francisco scene, all these little networks of one or two guys that go back and forth; sometimes it's dealers, sometimes it's musicians, you know, that was, like, the old line of communication.

So it became obvious, because you guys are a band, and we're right up here in La Honda and we're having these parties, we want to move the parties out into the world a little bit and just see what happens. So they had this first one down in San Jose, we took our stuff down there and . . .

Had you met Kesey?

No, I had never met Kesey. It was Page, John Page Browning, he was sort of the messenger. I don't think there was any . . . ever any real decision, just sort of a loose thing.

It was in a house . . . right after the Stones concert, the same night, the same night. We went there and played, but – you know, shit, our equipment filled the room, damn near, and we were like really loud and people were just, ah . . . There were guys freakin' out and stuff, and there were hundreds and hundreds of people all around in this residential neighborhood, swarming out of this guy's house.

We just decided to keep on doing it; that was the gist of it. We had all these people at this house that wasn't adequate, but the idea was then to move it to a different location, and then the idea was to move it to a different location *each week*.

They had film and endless kinds of weird tape-recorder hookups and mystery speaker trips and all . . . just all sorts of really strange . . . it always seemed as though the equipment was able to respond in its own way. I mean it . . . there were always magical things happening. Voices coming out of things that weren't plugged in and, God . . . it was just totally mind-boggling to wander around this maze of wires and stuff like that. Sometimes they were, like, writhing and squirming. Truly amazing.

That was the Acid Test, and the Acid Test was the prototype for our whole basic trip. But nothing has ever come up to the level of the way the Acid Test was. It's just never been equaled really, or the basic hit of it never developed out.

What happened was light shows and rock & roll came out of it, and that's, like, the thing that we've seen go out.

* * *

REICH: YOU HAVE a reputation that during the Haight-Ashbury time and later, that you were the sort of spiritual advisor to the whole rock scene.

That's a crock of shit, quite frankly.

Jefferson Airplane says that on their first or second album.

I know. That's because at that time, they were making their second record, and they were concerned about it; they didn't want it to be like their first record. And RCA had given them the producer, and he was, like, this straight producer who used to produce André Kostelanetz or somebody like that, and he didn't really know what they wanted to do, how they wanted to sound or how they wanted their thing to be. The Airplane thought it would be helpful to have somebody there who could communicate to their producer who they could communicate to, and since they all knew me and I understood their music and understood what they were doing pretty much at the time, it would be far-out. I went down there and hung out and was a sort of go-between between them and their producer and helped out with some arrangements and stuff like that; I just hung out.

Reich: But that's a big difference from being the "guru" of the whole scene.

Here's the thing: I would like to preface this whole interview by saying I'm one of those guys who's a compulsive question answerer. But that doesn't necessarily mean I'm right or anything. That's just one of the things I can do. It's kinda like having a trick memory. I can answer any question. I'm just the guy who found myself in the place of doing the talking every time there was an interview with the Grateful Dead.

How about among the musicians themselves?

I've played with nearly all the musicians around, and we all get along okay. But the whole music scene is very groovy. Here there's very little competition, very few ego games. Everybody knows what it takes to make music pretty good around here. It's that thing of being high and playing. I think it's the scene this area has that makes it attractive for musicians, and that's why a lot of them moved here. That freedom, that lack of competition, the fact that you aren't always having to battle and you can really get into what playing music is all about. But as for coming to me for advice and shit like that, that's ridiculous. That's like "Captain Trips." That's bullshit.

* * *

HOW DID YOU AVOID the music business taking over your lives? Because nobody wanted it?

Yeah . . . that's a good part of it. And with us, we've never really been successful in the music business; we've never had a super-big hit album or a hit single or anything like that. Grateful Dead freaks are our audience, you know . . . We're not mass market or anything like that, which I think is super-great. I think that we've been really lucky because we haven't had to put up with all the celebrity stuff, or star stuff. At

Mountain Girl and Garcia at Party Central, 710 Ashbury Street, June 1967.

the same time, it's been somewhat of a struggle to survive, but we're doing good, we're doing okay . . . so it worked out okay.

Do you think you could cope with a Crosby, Stills, Nash and Young–type of success?

I might be able to cope with it, but I don't think that I could be really that comfortable with it, you know, because I . . . the place where I get strung out is . . . is . . . I'd like to be fair, you know, I want to be fair, so I don't like to pull the thing of having somebody at the door that says, "No, fuck you, you can't see Garcia, you know, you're not going in no matter what, no matter how good your rap is."

Our backstage scene and all that is real open. We try to let as much stuff as possible come by, and I've just gotten into the thing of being able to move around pretty fast so I don't have to get hung up into anything, but I like to let it flow rather than stop it. I think that if there's more pressure along that line, it's getting now to where maybe fifty or one hundred or two hundred people backstage is getting kinda outrageous, and if we were, like, super-popular it would be that many more, and that – I'm thinking in purely physical terms – would start to get to be a problem . . . somewhere in there, if we get much more famous.

That's why I feel pretty good about finishing up our Warner Bros. thing, stopping being part of that mainstream and just kinda fallin' back so that we can continue to relate to our audience in a groovy, intelligent way without having to be part of a thing that . . . Really, that other world of the higher-up celebrity thing really doesn't seem to want us too badly, so, you know, we're able to avoid it. We're really not that good, I mean star kinda good or big-selling records good.

Do you think it'll go on for a long time . . . the band?

Uh, I don't see why not. Barring everybody dying or complete disinterest or something like that. As long as it's groovy and the music is happening . . . I don't see why it shouldn't just keep on going. We don't have any *real* plans, but we're committed to this thing . . . we're following it, we're not directing it. It's kinda like saying, "Okay, now I want to be here, now I want to go there," in a way. Nobody's making any real central decisions or anything. Everything's just kinda hashed out. It stumbles. It stumbles, then it creeps, then it flies with one wing and bumps into trees, and shit, you know. We're committed to it by now, after six years. What the fuck? It's still groovy for us. It's kinda like why break up the thing when it's working, when it seems to be working good and everybody's getting off.

What's the scene with Pigpen now?

He's pretty sick. But he's living. He was really, really *extremely* sick. I don't really know *how* sick, because I never hung out at the hospital that much, although I did give him a pint of blood. We all did. He was really fucked up; his liver was full of holes and then he had some kind of perforated ulcer . . . just all kinds of bum trips from juicing all these years. And he's a young dude, man, he's only twenty-six. I think he might even be younger than that.

From juicing! It's incredible, but he survived it, and he isn't dead. He survived it, and now he's got the option of being a juicer or not being a juicer. To be a juicer means to

die, so now he's being able to choose whether to live or die. And if I know Pigpen, he'll choose to live. That's pretty much where he's at. For the time being, he's too sick, too weak to go on the road, and I wouldn't want to expose him to that world. I don't think it's good for him at this point. It would be groovy if he could take as long as it takes to get him to feelin' right, and then to work on his solo album and get himself together in terms of becoming . . . It's sorta, like, stepping out of the blues story, 'cause Pigpen is a sort of guy who's, like, been a victim of the whole blues trip – it's like Janis exactly – in which you must die. That's what the script says. So Pigpen went up to the line, and he's seen it now, so the question is how he's going to choose.

* * *

*W*HAT'S THE CREATIVE PART *of making your music? Do you make it as you go along on the road, or do you make it when you're settled back in San Francisco, or do you make it all the time?*

I'd say we make it all the time. Because we've all pretty much decided after a long time that we're in fact musicians and . . . it's just something you do, it's in your head, musical pieces and records and all that. As a band, for the last two years, our music has been evolving as we play it. We haven't been rehearsing, because we haven't had a place to rehearse, like, that's a whole other school of problems, rock & roll rehearsal spots.

Reich: How does a song come into being, and how does it grow from its beginnings into what you might hear eventually on the record?

They're all different. Sometimes I'll start out with a set of chord changes that're just attractive to my ear. And then I'll hear a sketch of a melody over it. Then I'll just sort of let that be around my head, for however long it is there, for three or four weeks. I won't . . . I never try to work on stuff, you know, like sit down and labor it. But pretty soon there'll be more adjoining pieces to any one phrase, a melodic phrase, say. Then I hum it to myself for a long time and kind of play it on the guitar for everybody who's around, and then I'll get together with Hunter, who writes our lyrics, and we'll go through what he's got. If he's got lyrics already written that he likes, I'll see if anything fits, or else we'll start working on something from scratch. But the whole thing is completely organic – there isn't . . . I don't have any scheme . . .

Reich: It comes from somewhere outside.

For sure. And what happens is that you're lucky enough to remember a little of it as it's going by. And then what it turns into after it's become a song in your head is it turns into a piece of material for the band – everybody plays an equal role in that part of it – and that's the way it finally evolves as a song on a record or something like that. If it's one of my songs, it's never what I originally heard, it's always something that includes more than I might have conceived myself.

Do you alter the words when you write with Hunter?

Many times, yeah . . . sometimes I use pieces of three or four of his different songs and put them together. I also adjust the phrasing. I sort of edit . . . to make the things more singable usually. But he's gotten to be really a craftsman at it lately. In the last year or so, he's gotten to really understand what it is to sing words, and just the technique, that vowels sing a certain way and consonants sing a certain way and what you have to do. Certain things you can sing real gracefully, and other things you can't sing to save your soul.

"Truckin'" seems to be the story of the Dead.

When Hunter first started writing words for us . . . originally he was on his own trip and he was a poet. He was into the magical thing of words, definitely far-out, definitely amazing. The early stuff he wrote that we tried to set to music was stiff because it wasn't really meant to be sung. After he got further and further into it, his craft improved, and then he started going out on the road with us, coming out to see what life was like, to be able to have more of that viewpoint in the music, for the words to be more Grateful Dead words. "Truckin'" is the result of that sort of thing. "Truckin'" is a song that we assembled, it didn't . . . it wasn't natural, and it didn't flow, and it wasn't easy, and we really labored over the bastard . . . all of us together.

Reich: How has your music changed from one record to another?

The first one was called *The Grateful Dead.* At that time we had no real *record* consciousness. We were just going to go down to L.A. and make a record. We were completely naive about it. We had a producer whom we had chosen – Dave Hassinger – and we were impressed by him because he'd been the engineer on a couple of Rolling Stones records that we liked the sound of; that was as much as we were into record making.

So we went down there and, what was it we had . . . Dexamyl? Some sort of diet watcher's speed, and pot and stuff like that. So in three nights we played some hyperactive music. That's what's embarrassing about that record now: The tempo was way too fast. We were all so speedy at the time. It has its sort of crude energy, but obviously it's difficult for me to listen to it; I can't enjoy it really. I just plain cannot enjoy it, just because even as soon as we'd finished it, there were things that we could hear . . .

Mountain Girl: Man, it's so fast, it's blinding!

What music was it?

Just simply what we were doing onstage. Basically that. Just rock & roll. Plus we wanted to have one extended cut on it. But in reality, the way we played was not really too much the way that record was. Usually we played tunes that lasted a long time because we like to play a lot. And when you're playing for people who are dancing and getting high, you can dance easy to a half-hour tune and you can even wonder why it ended so soon. So for us the whole time thing was weird 'cause we went down there and turned out songs real fast – less than three minutes, which is real short.

It was weird, and we realized it. The first record was like a regular company record done in three nights, mixed in one day; it was done on three-track, I believe – it wasn't even four-track, Studio A in L.A., an imposing place. And we really didn't much care about it while we were doing it. So we weren't surprised when it didn't quite sound like we wanted it to.

It's hard for me to go back to the past in terms of the music, because for me it's a continuum and to stop it at one of those points it's got . . . to me, it always looks underdeveloped and not quite working. Which in fact it was.

Then on the second record, we went the whole other way. We decided we'd spend time on our record. We're going to work on it, we're going to make sure it sounds good, we're really going to get into recording and go on some trips with it. So our second record turned out to be a monumental project. We started out by recording for a couple of weeks, experimentally, in L.A., where we accomplished absolutely nothing. Then we went to New York to try some studios there, and we got our producer so excited that he quit. We got him uptight because we were being so weird, and he was only human after all and didn't really have to go through all that, so he decided not to go through it and we decided, "Well, we can do it ourselves." So we just worked and worked and worked – mostly Phil and I – for months, maybe as long as six months, at least six months. It was an eight-track recording, and we worked a lot in San Francisco. We assembled live tapes, and we went through the most complex operations that you can go through in a recording studio.

Did Phil use his background, or did you just learn it from scratch?

Phil used what he knew, and I was learning from scratch. I had had some experience after working with the Jefferson Airplane, pretty nominal, but at least I had some idea. And we had an engineer, Dan Healy, who is, like, a real good fast-on-his-feet, able-to-come-up-with-crazy-things engineer. And we worked and we assembled an enormous amount of stuff, and since it was all multitrack, it all just piled up.

With *Anthem of the Sun,* after an enormously complex period of time, we actually assembled the material that was on the master tape. Then we went through the mixing thing, which really became a performance, so *Anthem of the Sun* is really the performance of an eight-track tape; Phil and I performed it, and it would be, like, four hands, and sometimes Healy would have a hand in. We'd be there hovering around the boards in these various places at Criteria Studios, Miami, and in New York. We selected from various performances we did the performance which seemed the most spaced, and we did that all the way through. So that's a spaced record if there is one.

There's parts of it that sound dated, but parts of it are far-out, even too far-out. I feel that that's one of those things . . . see, it's hard for me to be able to listen to any of that stuff objectively 'cause I tend to hear a thing like *Anthem of the Sun* matching it up against what it was that we thought we were gonna do, intellectually speaking. So I have to think of it in terms of something we were trying to do but didn't succeed in doing. I listen to what's wrong with it. I tend to listen to it in the inverse way. But on the other hand, if I have the right kind of head and I'm not on an ego-involvement trip with it . . .

Did the next record mark any kind of change?

No. The next record was really a continuation of the *Anthem of the Sun* trip – called *Aoxomoxoa* – a continuation in the style of having a complex record. When we started, *Aoxomoxoa* was an eight-track record, and then all of a sudden there was a sixteen-track recorder in the studio, so we abandoned our entire eight-track version and went to sixteen-track to start all over again. Now, at the time we were sipping STP during our session, which made it a little weird – in fact, very weird.

GARCIA

We spent too much money and too much time on that record; we were trying to accomplish too much, and I was being really stupid about a lot of it, because it was material, some new tunes that I had written that I hadn't really bothered to teach anyone in the band, and I was trying to record them from the ground up, and everybody was coming in and doing overdubs. It was weird; we went about it in a very fragmentary way. We didn't go about it as a group at all.

Some of the music is pretty strange.

Now, I like that record, personally, just for its weirdness, really. There are certain feelings and a certain kind of looseness that I kinda dig; but it's been our most unsuccessful record. It was when Hunter and I were both being more or less obscure, and there are lots of levels on the verbal plane in terms of the lyrics being very far-out. Too far-out, really, for most people.

That was one of my pet records 'cause it was the first stuff that I thought *was* starting to sound like how I wanted to hear songs sound. And the studio stuff was successful. I'm really happy with the remix . . . I hope you get a chance to hear 'em. All the new mixes that are coming out will say on them, "Remixed."

The next one is 'Live Dead.'

It's good. It has "Dark Star" on it, a real good version of it. We'd only recorded a few gigs to get that album. We were after a certain sequence to the music. In the sense of it being a serious, long composition, musically, and then a recording of it, it's our music at one of its really good moments.

Live Dead was actually recorded about the same time we were working on *Aoxomoxoa*. If you take *Live Dead* and *Aoxomoxoa* together, you have a picture of what we were doing at that time. We were playing *Live Dead*, and we were recording *Aoxomoxoa*. When *Live Dead* came out, it was about a year out of date.

After *Aoxomoxoa* we hadn't made a studio record for almost a year since *Live Dead* came out in its place. We were anxious to go to the studio, but we didn't want to incur an enormous debt making the record like we had been. When you make a record, you pay for the studio time out of your own royalties. That costs plenty. *Live Dead* was not too expensive, since it was recorded live. It ended up paying for the time on *Aoxomoxoa*, which was eight months or some really ridiculous amount of time. A hundred grand or even more than that – it was real expensive. And we ended up at our worst, in debt to Warner Bros. for around $180,000.

So when record time came around and we were getting new material together, we thought, "Let's try to make it cheap this time." So we rehearsed for a month or so before we went in to make *Workingman's Dead*. We rehearsed and we were pretty far into the material, and then we got busted in New Orleans. After we got busted, we went home to make our record. And while we were making our record, we had a big, bad scene with our manager. Actually, making the record was the only cool thing happening – everything else was just sheer weirdness.

How had your music changed?

We were into a much more relaxed thing about that time. And we were also out of our pretentious thing. We weren't feeling so much like an experimental music group but were feeling more like a good old band.

What songs on 'Workingman's Dead' do you particularly like?

I liked *all* those tunes. I loved them all [*laughs*], to give you the absolute and unashamed truth. I felt that they were *all* good songs. They were successful in the sense you could sing 'em and get off and enjoy singing 'em. "Uncle John's Band" was a *major* effort, as a musical piece. It's one we worked on for a really long time, to get it working right. "Cumberland Blues" was also difficult in that sense. The song that I think failed on that record is "High Time." It's a beautiful song, but I was just not able to sing it worth a shit. And I really can't do justice to that kind of song now . . . I'm not that good of a singer.

But I wish someone who could really sing would do one of those songs sometime. I would love to hear some good singers do that stuff. I mean, it would just tickle me. There are some people doing "Friend of the Devil," I understand. But other than that, we haven't heard of any people doing our songs at all.

What stands out in your mind about 'American Beauty'? Each song sounds closer to the others.

There isn't too much difference. And that's . . . well, I tried to block that whole trip out. You see, my mother died while we were making that record. And Phil's father died. It was raining down hard on us while that record was going on. They're good tunes, though. Every one of 'em's a gem, I modestly admit.

What side of you does 'American Beauty' represent?

Well, let's call *Workingman's Dead* a song record, a singing record, because the emphasis is on the vocals and on the songs. And *American Beauty* is another record in that trend where the emphasis is on the vocals and the songs. And that's basically what we're doing, the music being more or less incidental – not incidental – but structural rather than the end product.

The records are not total indicators, they're just products. Out of the enormous amount of output that we create in the course of a year, they're that little piece that goes out to where everybody can get it.

The new live double set is like listening to the old Grateful Dead.

It's us, man. It's the prototype Grateful Dead. Basic unit. Each one of those tracks is the total picture, a good example of what the Grateful Dead really is, *musically*. Rather than "*this* record has sort of a country, light acoustics sound," and so on, like, for a year we were a light acoustics band, in somebody's head. The new album is enough of an overview so people can see we're like a regular shoot-'em-up saloon band. That's more what we are like. The tracks all illustrate that nicely. They're hot.

* * *

WHAT HAPPENED AT ALTAMONT? *Did you see what was coming?*

No. God, no. It was completely unexpected. And that was the hard part – that you can have good people and good energy and work on a project and really want it to happen right and still have it all weird. It's the thing of knowing less than you should have. Youthful folly.

Reich: But the things you didn't know about had nothing to do with music; they had to do with logistics and they had to do with things commercial and economic . . .

Yeah, but it was the music that generated it. I think that the music knew; it was known in the music. I realized when the Rolling Stones were playing at the crowd, and the fighting was going on and the Rolling Stones were playing "Sympathy for the Devil," then I knew that I should have known. You know, you can't put that out there without it turning up on you somewhere.

When you look back on it, do you see anything in those moments leading up to it?

No, not really. I was completely unsuspecting. There was one thing beforehand that we all should have spotted. [Emmett] Grogan wrote up on the blackboard up at the Grateful Dead office, just as the site had been changed from whatever the first one was, he wrote a little slogan up on the blackboard which said something like, "Charlie Manson Memorial Hippie Love Death Cult Festival." Something along those lines, something really funny but ominous. And there had been – the street, certain people – certain elements of the street had been saying . . . it was a very weird time on the street in San Francisco at that time, if you recall. There was a lot of divisive hassling among all the various revolutionary scenes; the Red Guard was on one trip, and Chicanos on some other trip, and people were carrying guns and stuff; there was a lot of that kind of talk.

Originally the idea was that the Stones' thing was going to be a chance for all these various community elements to participate in a sort of party for the Rolling Stones. That was the original concept, but then we couldn't have it in Golden Gate Park, so that really was the end of the plan as it was supposed to have happened. That eliminated the possibility for any community scene in San Francisco because of the transportation problem – how many Chicanos, Chinese or blacks or anything like that are going to be able to get a bus to wherever-the-fuck? That was really the end of the original plan. And then we began operating on sheer kinetic energy . . . Rolling Stones was in the air, Rolling Stones, Rolling Stones, and thus it was just being swept along. But everybody was feeling – and it was all good people – everybody was feeling good about it. Chet Helms was there doing stuff, and Emmett and Chip Monck and these solid, together, hardworking people, but somehow the sense of it escaped everybody.

* * *

*H*ow would you *describe your guitar playing?*
I don't know . . . I would describe my own guitar playing as descended from barroom rock & roll, country guitar. Just 'cause that's where all my stuff comes from. It's like that blues instrumental stuff that was happening in the late Fifties and early Sixties, like Freddie King.

When did you decide to stop doing the blues stuff, the harder rock & roll thing, and go into the stressed harmonies?

That was really the result of hanging out with [David] Crosby and those guys . . . just because they could sit down in any situation and pick up an acoustic guitar, and it's instant music; these beautiful vocal harmonies.

I think that nothing really communicates like the human voice. It is really the ultimate instrument. I used to think of myself as a guitar player, but hearing singing, and seeing it up close, has kinda made me want to sing a lot; it just makes me want to do it. I don't really know what it is . . . and it's real satisfying to sing. I've always gotten off on a good singer, and that's what I'm basin' it on.

That's part of where our music wants to go, but it's record companies and the music business structure that's making it that difficult. It should be possible for everybody to do everything, especially in music, where music can only get better when people get together in different combinations. But record companies wanna be exclusive. They're getting looser and looser, and hopefully the thing could get loose enough where everybody could do whatever they want. That would be ideal.

What guitarists have you learned the most from?

I think Freddie King is the guy that I learned the most volume of stuff from. When I started playing electric guitar the second time, with the Warlocks, it was a Freddie King album that I got almost all my ideas off of.

Reich: I have a question right off one of the evening talk shows, "Dr. Garcia, how do you stay so high?"

I smoke a lot of dope.

Reich: Do you think that's . . .

Would you like some?

Reich: Do you think that that's it?

Well, in reality I don't really stay that high, although I get high a lot, smoking a lot of pot, is what I'm trying to say. That's what it comes down to, but that doesn't necessarily mean that I'm high. A certain amount of seeming to be high has to do with my being more or less well rehearsed in the role of Jerry Garcia, 'cause it's kinda been laid on me. In reality, I'm, like, lots more worthless than any of that would make it appear.

Reich: Among the different things the kids say about you, one is "Mr. Good Vibes."

Yeah, but that always is part-true bullshit, because my old lady can tell you about how often I'm on a bummer. Really, I'm just like everybody else, and it's just that I really love those times when I'm high, so my trip has always been to make them count as much as possible.

Reich: What I'm trying to get at is that you believe in being high, and many other people not only don't believe in it but think it's dangerous and hateful.

Well, you know, one man's poison is another man's dope.

Reich: For instance, I believe in being high, but not as much as you believe in it. In other words, I have more reservations about it than you do – or less experience with it. How about that?

That's it right there. I don't have that many illusions about it, because I was never around in that world where you had to read about it. For me, it came in the form of dope. You got a joint, you didn't get a lecture; and you got a cap, you didn't get a treatise on any of that shit. You just got high. You took the thing and found out what happened to you; that's the only evidence there is. Being programmed by dope talk or any of that stuff is like somebody trying to tell you what it's like to fuck if you've never fucked anybody.

I think that the whole discussion about drugs, whether to

take them or not, is like . . . well, I don't think that there is a *side* on that. I know a lot of people who I respect superhighly that don't take anything, and, of course, I know people that get really high, and I respect them as highly, too; and I know far-out junkies. There are people doing everything, and I just don't think that *anything's* it.

Reich: How do you manage to be so optimistic?

Music is a thing that has optimism built into it. Optimism is another way of saying "space." Music has infinite space. You can go as far into music as you can fill millions of lifetimes. Music is an infinite cylinder, it's open-ended, it's space. The form of music has infinite space as a part of it, and that, in itself, means that its momentum is essentially in that open place.

Reich: You said you would only play on optimistic days, or I said I would only write on optimistic days.

That might be optimum, but my experience has been that a lot of times we've played sets that we didn't like or that I didn't like or I didn't like what I was doing, but it got on and it sounded good on tape and the audience got on. There's lots of degrees. I don't like to try to paint everything in those real, specific cartoony figures, because there's degrees all over the place. For example, if I'm super-, super-depressed, I sometimes play the highest music I play.

Reich: How do you do it?

Because music can contain all of it. It can contain your bummers, it can contain your depressions, it can contain the black despair, man, it can contain the whole spectrum. The blues is a perfect example. The blues is that very effect operating in a very sublime way. You hardly ever hear anybody say they're depressed because they've heard a lot of music. That's a pretty good example, right there. Even the worst music – the poorest, baddest, most ill-thought-of music on earth – doesn't hurt anybody.

Reich: I read a book on rock & roll recently that said the real medium of rock & roll is records and that concerts are only repeats of records. I guess the Grateful Dead represents the opposite of that idea.

Right. Our records are definitely not it or ever have been. The things we do depend so much upon the situation we're in and upon a sort of a magic thing. We aren't in such total control of our scene that we can say, "Tonight's the night, it's going to be magic tonight." We can only say we're going to try it tonight. And whether it's magic or not is something we can't predict and nobody else can predict; and even when it's over and done with, it's one of those things where nobody's really sure. It's subtle and it's elusive, but it's real.

Reich: And the magic comes not just from you but from the whole thing.

The whole thing. The unfortunate thing about the concert situation for us is the stage; and the audience has either a dance floor where they all sit down or seats where they all stand up. It's too inflexible to allow something new to emerge. It's a box that we've been operating in, and we've been operating in it as a survival mechanism, yet hoping to get off when we can. But basically it's not set up to let us get off, and it's not set up for the audience to get off either. The reason is that anarchy and chaos are things that scare everybody, or scare a lot

of the people – except for the people that get into it.

Why doesn't it scare you?

Because I've had enough experience with it to where I like it. It's where new stuff happens. I have never understood exactly why people get scared, but they do get scared for reasons, like to protect oneself, to protect one's own personal visions of oneself. They're all paranoid reasons. That's the thing you stimulate if you fight it. It's like any high-energy experience: If you fight it, it hurts; if you go with it, it's like surfing, it's like catching a big wave.

Reich: Why is it important to get high? Why is it important to stay high? What good does it do anybody – the world, the community or people themselves?

To get really high is to forget yourself. And to forget yourself is to see everything else. And to see everything else is to become an understanding molecule in evolution, a conscious tool of the universe. And I think every human being should be a conscious tool of the universe. That's why I think it's important to get high.

Reich: Getting zonked out or unconscious is a whole different thing.

I'm not talking about unconsciousness or zonked out, I'm talking about being fully conscious. Also I'm not talking about the Grateful Dead as being an end in itself. I don't think of that highness as being an end in itself. I think of the Grateful Dead as being a crossroads or a pointer sign, and what we're pointing to is that there's a lot of universe available, that there's a whole lot of experience available over here. We're kinda like a signpost and we're also pointing to danger, to difficulty, we're pointing to bummers. We're pointing to whatever there is, when we're on – when it's really happening.

You're a signpost to new space?

Yes. That's the place where we should be – that's the function we should be filling in society. And in our own little society, that's the function we do fill. But in the popular world, the media world and so forth, we're just a rock & roll band.

We play rock & roll music, and it's part of our form – our vehicle, so to speak – but it's not who we are totally. Like Moondog in New York City, who walks around, he's a signpost to otherness. He's a signpost to something that isn't concrete. It's that same thing.

Where did you get the idea about pointing to some new place?

We never formulated it; it just was what was happening. We were doing the Acid Test, which was our first exposure to formlessness. Formlessness and chaos lead to new forms. And new order. Closer to, probably, what the real order is. When you break down the old orders and the old forms and leave them broken and shattered, you suddenly find yourself a new space with new form and new order which are more like the way it is. More like the flow. And we just *found* ourselves in that place. We never decided on it, we never thought it out. None of it. This is a thing that we've observed in the scientific method. We've watched what happens.

What we're really dedicated to is not so much *telling* people, but to *doing* that thing and getting high. That's the thing; that's the payoff, and that's the whole reason for doing it, right there. ☯

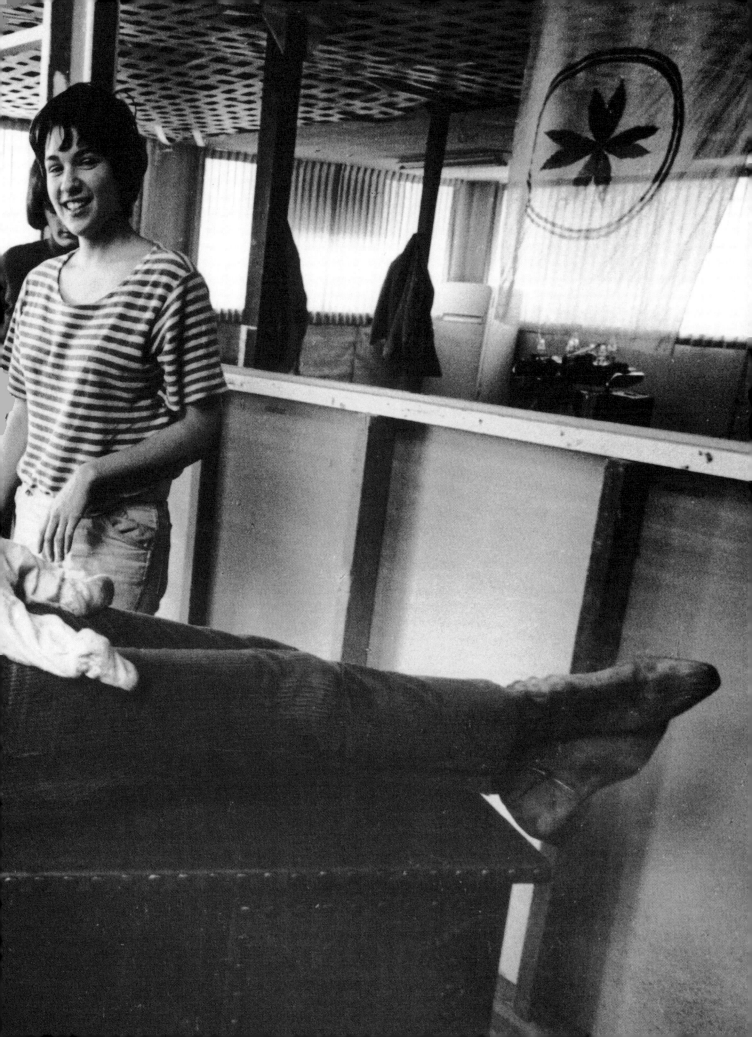

DEAD HIT EUROPE

BY * JERRY HOPKINS

THE BEAUTIFUL

IN PARIS, the Grand Hôtel is a big deal. Across the street is the historic and opulent Opera House, and running off in several directions are the city's famous tree-lined avenues. In one corner of the massive structures is the Café de la Paix, the sidewalk meeting place in all those romantic Hollywood flicks. Nearby are the shops of Saint Laurent and Dior.

The hotel itself is so big you can get lost in the hallways. Single rooms start at $35 a day, and all are equipped with balconies and small automated refrigerators that dispense liquor and beer and champagne at ridiculous prices. There are jewelry shops, restaurants, hairstylists, masseurs, art galleries, theater booking agencies, shirtmakers. Everyone on the staff speaks fluent English. It is a popular favorite of visiting Americans.

"Are you still expecting the Grateful Dead?" I asked the reservations clerk.

"The Beautiful Dead, monsieur?"

"Uh . . . not quite. The Grateful Dead."

"Oui, monsieur. Would you spell the surname, please."

"D-E-A-D."

"   ."

"It's a musical group," I said, filling in the silence. "From America."

"We are expecting a thirty-seven-piece orchestra . . ."

Only the figure was incorrect. The Grateful Dead, halfway through a two-month tour of Europe, numbered not thirty-seven but, depending upon who you talked to, up to forty-eight. There were seven musicians and singers, five managers, five office staff, ten equipment handlers (handling fifteen-thousand pounds of equipment, not counting the sixteen-track recording system), four drivers and seventeen assorted wives, old ladies, babies and friends. In its one hundred years of catering to the tourist elite, the Grand Hôtel had never seen anything like it.

The Dead arrived late Monday, not quite fresh from a two-day overland haul from Hamburg, Germany. Yet when they awoke on Tuesday, just as on the first day in each new country so far, their own Xeroxed newspaper, the *Bozos & Bolos News,* had been slipped under their hotel room doors.

The Dead began drifting into Room 4600 about noon. This was the office suite, where Rosie McGee prepared the *Bozos & Bolos News* and others manned the telephones, while Sam Cutler greased the Dead machine – changing German marks into French francs and handing out daily "road money" ($10 for the ladies, $15 for the gentlemen, for food), dispatching couriers to check an English festival site and see why the latest Dead single wasn't getting the desired promotion, worrying about lights and sound checks and transportation and luggage and laundry.

When the Dead arrived in Paris, they'd been on the road exactly a month. They'd played two nights in London (eight thousand each night) and to smaller crowds in Copenhagen and what seemed to be half the cities in West Germany. The Dead had appeared at a festival in England in 1970, had performed at a free concert in France in 1971, but never had they done the Grand Tour, long *de rigueur* for American bands anxious to improve European record sales.

Outside Room 4600 the day was warm, the sky a cloudless blue. In small groups, the Dead set out to see the sights.

"Today is a free day," the *Bozos & Bolos News* had said. "In the evening, Kinney is hosting a dinner for all of us (and a few discreet press people) at a very fine restaurant located in the Bois de Boulogne (the city park, but what a park!). It is called La Grande Cascade, and holy shit, is it ever neat! You might even feel like dressing special for it, although you don't have to. It's just that kind of place . . ."

At 7:00, Sam Cutler was telling the bus drivers he was sorry, but could they *please* do this one thing . . . yeah, he knew he'd given them the day off, but they could have the next two days off, there was just this one dinner . . .

Downstairs, in a lounge the size of half a football field (with a fountain in the middle), the Grateful Dead were assembling. Jerry Garcia dropped into an orange imitation-leather chair. "Almost every place we went today was closed," he said. "The Louvre is closed Tuesdays. We went to the Notre Dame and we saw that – really boss, but we couldn't climb the tower. We went to the Cluny. We saw that. It was sacked by the Barbarians in the year 300, and before that it was a Roman bath. Flash flash. History everywhere you look. Far-out. Stunning."

What about the rest of Europe so far?

"There's a lotta energy in Germany. Like the U.S., it's opted for the material thing. Everybody looks pretty well fed. It has the same external trappings, factories, apartments, cars, lotta roads. The thing that made it for us was the world war flash – all those movies. Germany has had its culture cut off, and it had to start again. It's not like France or England, where it's still all there."

Around the huge room, other Americans in Paris swung their heads, mouths open, staring at the tie-dye and denim and hair. Was this the Grand Hôtel?

By 8:00 the "labor dispute" had been settled and we were off by bus to La Grande Cascade, a splendid wedding cake of a room with oval walls of glass that look out onto a lawn of blossoming chestnut trees. The dinner lasted three and a half hours (as long as a Grateful Dead concert set). During the serving of liqueurs, which followed the wine and champagne, things got a little loose. That was when the Dead turned the waiters on.

"Here ya are, *mon-sore,* do yer head some good."

The waiter stood stiffly in his black tie and tails. Timidly he allowed the pipe to be raised to his lips. He sucked deeply, there was a cheer, he smiled, and the pipe was passed.

* * *

THE DEAD were to play the next two nights at the Olympia Theater, two blocks from the hotel. Jerry Garcia seemed anxious: "I got a letter from one of our fans here, and he said the police like to put plants in the audience to cause trouble, and then the police use that as an excuse to clear everybody out of the show."

"Just let 'em try it," said Phil Lesh, leering with anticipation. "We'll go up to 'em, and we'll say, 'Come along, Officer – have a drink of this Coca-Cola.'"

It had been four years to the month since students nearly brought the French government to its knees; it was true that

the police – the flics – got nervous whenever young people gathered. So when the Dead walked to the theater, there were seven busloads of police at the curb, many of them in riot helmets and armed with rifles.

Inside it was friendlier, as twenty-two hundred ticket holders (each of whom paid about $4.50) began swarming into the old theater to the recorded sounds of Jefferson Airplane, Ike and Tina Turner and the Rolling Stones.

"*Bonsoir, mes amis,*" said Phil Lesh. "Uh . . . that's about all the French I know."

The music began at 9:00, reaching the first climax two hours and fourteen songs later with "Casey Jones." It was clear this was a gathering of Grateful Dead freaks. The opening rhythms of every song were greeted with joyous shouts and applause, and between the numbers there were happy requests.

The Dead took a half-hour break at 11:00, then played for another two hours. During "Truckin'," as the mirrored ball near the ceiling revolved, reflecting light, the audience rose as one, weaving and yelping and applauding the long, jazzy drum, guitar and piano breaks. This set closed with hard rock, the familiar Bo Diddley rhythm pattern in "Not Fade Away" and the Dead's new single, "One More Saturday Night." Now Donna Godchaux, singing backup, and some of the Ladies Auxiliary were boogying on the crowded stage.

So mellow was the mood at the concert's end, the police outside had nothing to do but smoke cigarettes.

"It's called muscle fatigue," said Garcia the following day. "We couldn't have played any longer if we'd wanted to."

But Jerry Garcia wasn't quite satisfied.

"Everywhere we've been, the audiences have been Grateful Dead audiences," he said. "We've had the German equivalent of the guy who gets up on the stage and takes his clothes off. We've had the English freakout, the Danish freakout. But we haven't been playing *enough*. I'm a music junkie and I have to play every day. The gigs are too far apart. It's like we're not fucking off enough to enjoy that or we're not playing enough to enjoy that."

The second night at the Olympia was better than the first. There were only thirty or so cops on hand – down from one hundred eighty the night before – a unique sort of "review" of the Dead's music and audience, when you think about it. Again all twenty-two hundred seats were filled. Again the audience crawled forward in a friendly, inquisitive Gallic swell, applauding, cheering and chanting "one more one more one more" at the end of another four-hour-long set. And this time, Jerry Garcia admitted afterward, "We played peachy."

Next morning, it was raining as the Dead began piling luggage in the hotel lobby. They would play that night at Lille, at the other end of a high-speed motorway near the Belgian border. That'd make it three concerts in a row. Maybe Jerry Garcia and some of the others would find more satisfaction on this tour after all.

As all the tie-dye and denim and hair gathered in eddies, the other Americans in Paris began swinging their heads, mouths open. If this was the famous Grand Hôtel they'd heard about – and were going to spend at least $35 a day to enjoy – then who were all those freaks? ☾

SPLENDOR IN THE BLUEGRASS
BY JOHN GRISSIM

MARIN COUNTY'S newest bluegrass band, Old and In the Way, was playing at the Lion's Share in San Anselmo, California, and smoothly moving into "The Hit Parade of Love" when Jerry Garcia gave it away: It was their first time out. He had gone into his banjo solo before he realized he wasn't plugged in to an amplifier. He grinned and quickly took a long step up to the microphone so the folks in the back could hear. The goof was understandable, because Garcia, along with the rest of the Grateful Dead, had only the day before returned from a two-week tour of the Midwest.

Playing mandolin was Dave Grisman, an old sidekick from Garcia's Menlo Park days; guitarist Peter Rowan, who'd previously played with Bill Monroe; and all-around bassist John Kahn, plunking away on a vintage acoustic upright. The four picked and sang close harmony through more than a dozen fast-paced numbers, including Bill Monroe's "The Old Crossroads," "White House Blues" and "Panama Red," a Rowan tune.

"God, it's been eight years since I've played banjo," Garcia recalled later. "Playing music isn't hard or anything, but playing bluegrass is a kind of a sweat, though. I'd forgot how physical it is. But it sure is fun." Garcia, Grisman and Rowan live within a few blocks of one another in Marin County. "We all used to be heavily into bluegrass, so we got together a little over a month ago, started playing and then decided, Shit, why don't we play a few bars and see what happens? And John Kahn is working out beautifully on bass, because a lot of bluegrass is really stiff, and with his R&B background he gives us a great boogie-woogie bottom. We're developing a rhythmic feel that's kind of groovy.

Garcia first played banjo as a folkie in the Sixties. Above: Garcia and Dave Grisman, still playing together decades later.

"We're thinking about finding a fiddle player and then doing some of the bluegrass festivals this summer. It's a whole different world from the rock & roll scene – really mellow and nice. People bring their families and kids and grandmas and dogs and lunch. And they're all aficionados who really get off behind the licks. That'd be a lot of fun."

Finding the time for the summer festivals may be a problem, however, in view of the new immense popularity of the Dead. During its Midwestern tour the group played major halls (seventy-five hundred seats and up), selling out most concerts (including Chicago for the first time) and coming surprisingly close to it in Salt Lake City.

The Dead may sell out handily in any of a score of cities but nowhere else quite like in New York. A few years back the group played six nights in Port Chester, New York, selling out all six performances within a day. One night a bomb threat was received, presumably from irate Dead fans without tickets. Three thousand filed out while police searched the hall, and six thousand filed back in after the all-clear. That same year, the Dead headlined Fillmore East for five nights, all the tickets for which were likewise snapped up within hours.

The Dead's two concerts last week at the Nassau Coliseum on Long Island were sold out by word of mouth within two and a half hours after going on sale at Ticketron outlets. At one point six thousand tickets were sold within thirty-one minutes. Bill Graham then took out an ad in the *Village Voice* to announce the sellout and the addition of a third concert, bringing the total Dead audience to sixty thousand for the three dates.

Jerry Garcia laughed at the sellout news: "I don't know what to think about it. Basically, I try to keep my attention focused on whether I can play or not. It's like more unrealness, more Grateful Dead fever." ☯

LIVE DEAD

BY LENNY KAYE

NASSAU COLISEUM MARCH 19 1973

IT HAD TO HAPPEN: Even the Dead have gone glitter. Resplendently suave in Nudie-type sequined suits, the group appeared on the stage of this comfortably sized Long Island arena as formal gentlemen, playing before a sold-out and devoutly clamoring Monday crowd who nonetheless held true to their flannel shirt and dungaree colors. The music was consistently superb and was delivered with a professionalism and class that might even be taken for granted were it not so historically precarious, caught as it is in the double bind of massive anticipations and internal complexities, good nights mixing inevitably over the bad.

Still, instead of wrestling with the hyper-reactions of their audience – as was once the case – the Dead have resigned themselves to that unquenchable factor, even to the point of enjoying it, learning ways in which it might be manipulated and controlled. Their technique here involved pacing: stretching out the four hours of their pair of sets so that the crowd moved with – rather than against – them. The long breaks between songs served the dual purpose of relaxing the audience as well as the band.

The Dead came onstage to the usual mass eruptions, played a quick Western shuffle and closed it off before Garcia took even the glimmerings of an extended lead. They moved deliberately into "He's Gone," Jerry leaning to the microphone in the evening's only apparent reference to the recent death of Ron "Pigpen" McKernan, reeling out the final chorus: "Ooooh, nothin's gonna bring him back . . ."

The improvement and strength of the group's vocal harmonies were readily apparent; no more do their voices quaver up and down the scale trying to find the right series of notes. Joined by Donna Godchaux, the blend registered chorally near-perfect, if a shade eccentric.

The group then opened into its repertoire, which has become so large as to be in the main unrecognizable. Alternating between Bob Weir and Garcia, the band offered such things as a sharp, clicking rendition of "Mexicali Blues," matched by "Looks Like Rain," "The Race Is On," "El Paso" and finally, the first semi-oldie of the night, "Box of Rain." Instrumentally, they were in high form: Phil Lesh bottoming well, Keith Godchaux wrapping piano fills around Weir's and Garcia's tone-perfect guitars.

It was the longer songs that got them into trouble, but not by much. "China Cat Sunflower" began the launch into what has become the Dead's extended trademark, and as they took it in a roundabout way to "I Know You Rider," it seemed as if the night was sure to be tinged golden. But later, over the hump of "Around and Around" and the sing-along chorus of "Tennessee Jed," it proved to be a false start. The big song of the set, "Playing in the Band," never caught the handle they were searching for, gears touching but not quite in mesh.

The rest of the night belonged to Garcia. Returning from a short intermission and several filial descendants of "Cumberland Blues," he forcibly led the band through a combination of old and new material, capped by a beauteous ode to a woman named Stella Blue. A long jam around "Truckin'" was successful in parts, as was a followup slice from "The Other One," and with the band now beginning to group around Kreutzmann in a semicircle, concentrating on making contact, they finally got what they wanted in a long, jazz-oriented piece, the sound very free, gunning and spooking one another in a continuous upchurned spiral.

They left the stage after "Johnny B. Goode," all those hours of playing not diminishing its strength. To call them back, the audience set off a few matches in the orchestra, a few more responding along the balconies, expanding outward until the whole inside of the arena was lit by candle power. The Dead returned with "Casey Jones," responsive puffs of smoke rising from the banks of amplifiers, the band chugging along as a revolving mirror-ball refracted minispots around the audience, all ridin' that train. ☘

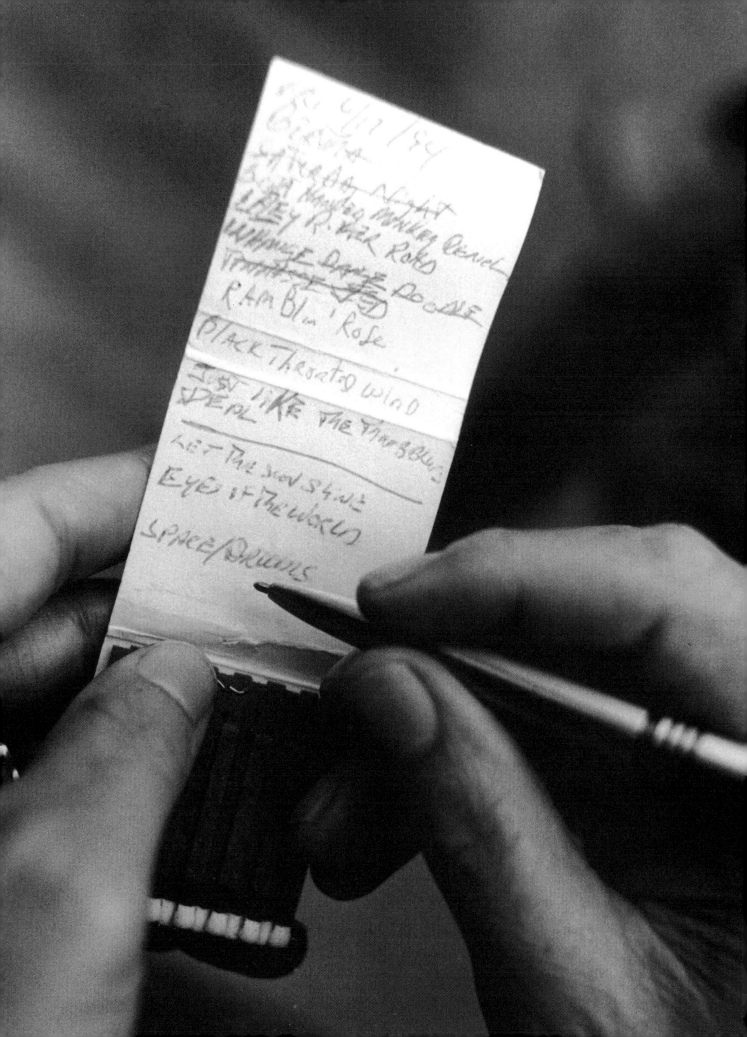

A NEW LIFE FOR THE DEAD

BY CHARLES PERRY

A MESSAGE TO GARCIA, that's what she has. "Who do I see about getting backstage?" she asks with musky urgency. "I've got a message for Garcia. It's *very important.*"

She's not sure she's hitting on the right party; her expression is guarded and nearly indecipherable in the Dead-loud murk of the Fairgrounds Arena, except for the urgency in her eyes. Groupie urgency? Space urgency? There are variations of this movie. "He's such an amaaaazing dude . . . I've driven all the way from Dallas here to Oklahoma City . . . Tell them my old man died last year and I've got to talk to Jerry."

A message to Garcia. Everybody around the Grateful Dead knows about messages to Garcia. Keith Godchaux, who has played keyboards for the Dead for two years, remembers with an ironic grimace having to go through the meeting-Garcia movie before he could show his stuff. It seems everybody who has ever gotten high behind a Dead album has to talk to Garcia.

Jerry Garcia stands for the Dead for a lot of people. He's the lead guitarist and singer, most of the song credits are his, he's extraordinarily articulate and, most of all, everyone senses his special spiritual authority in the band, his permissive guru-figure status. But at the same time he never puts himself in front of the band. Even in the matter of composing credits, he is so far from claiming the spotlight that the group has just adopted a "Plan C," under which royalties are not distributed exclusively to the composer and lyricist – the parties of the "original creative flash," to use Jerry's term – but a percentage also goes to all members of the band to acknowledge their part in the finished version of the song.

For that matter, the Dead depend on their road crew of sixteen – they won't use any P.A. system but their own – and, in varying ways, on larger and larger circles of people, ultimately including the whole Dead family of perhaps one hundred fifty persons. That's friends, old ladies, coworkers, resident artisans, side trips – everything from Grateful Dead Records Corporation to Sparky and the Ass Bites From Hell.

* * *

THE OFFICES OF Grateful Dead Records, Inc., are in a classically funky Victorian house in San Rafael, California. Classically funky by definition – a reminiscence of the Haight transplanted here in Marin County – because it used to be the Dead House before their office operations outgrew it. An audacious idea is afoot down the hall from the painting of Mickey Mouse and Pluto: a rock & roll artist-owned record company. Not a record label, such as Apple or Grunt, under the corporate wing of an established record company, but a company that presses and distributes its own discs and takes the consequences.

"I got the idea for the company on the eighteenth of March, 1972," said company president Ron Rakow, characteristically beaming mellow relaxation and at the same time twisting around in his chair from a slight overplus of animal energy. "I was driving on Highway 1 between Bolinas and Olema, and I saw a picture of the whole system, how it would work. So I went on the road to research it. I started at the Securities and Exchange Commission, Xeroxing the big record companies' financial statements. That gave me enough information to

start asking questions. I ended up writing a ninety-three-page report with several hundred pages of bibliography, which got called the 'So What Papers.' That title is said to have been born of a psychedelic meditation on the metaphysical ramifications of the phrase 'so what.'

"I presented the papers to the band on July 4, 1972. I was surprised they didn't okay it right away, so I went on the road as part of the equipment crew to work off my frustration. It was finally approved on April 19, but of course in changed form." The original plan called for a radical distribution system, completely bypassing record stores: Good Humor trucks, for instance, mail ordering and distribution through head shops. But the conservative faction of the Dead, anchored by business manager David Parker, prevailed to the extent that Good Humor–type trucks will not deliver the *first* record, anyway. The first record on the label, *Wake of the Flood,* is already in record stores, distributed in the U.S. by distributors chosen by Grateful Dead Records and in Europe through Atlantic Records' distribution.

"The sale of the foreign rights to Atlantic brought $300,000, which financed the operation," said Rakow, "and we also have a financial umbrella in the First National Bank of Boston, which has approved and underwritten the distributors we're using. That's the big load off our backs. Here, this is our cash-flow chart." He held out an accordion-folded sheet of accounting paper, dense with categories, entries and subtotals. "Feasibility and function are clearly laid out. I've estimated income conservatively and expenses liberally," Rakow added cheerfully. "We have to satisfy the paranoid viewpoint." A unique thing about this record company is that a percentage of the records delivered to any distributor, based on local market sales of the most recent Dead album, are *final* sales; that is, paid for by the distributor whether they get sold or not.

Garcia took such interest in the proposed record company that he spent five hours going through the flowchart with Rakow even before the So What Papers were presented, and an explanation of the chart based on their afternoon in Ron's barn went to each of the band members at their request. "That chart is essentially unchanged from June 1972," said Rakow, "and I'd like to point out that the financing came two days before the chart called for it, and the studio work on the album was ended on the exact day.

"It's a no-risk deal. If the company folds, the band is free to sign with any company they want, except that Atlantic has foreign rights to four records in two years' time. If the band were to break up, what would happen is that Garcia would be obliged to make one record for Atlantic for both foreign and domestic distribution.

"We've sent engineers, people who've worked in recording studios, from this office to each of the three pressing plants we're using, just to maintain quality control," said Rakow, fondling the borderline of his curly sideburns and his five o'clock shadow. "There are four people out there, checking – in each shift – to see that the mother is pressing true, that the vinyl is mixed right. Just their presence has made a difference in standards, because the plant workers are not used to having people from record companies take an interest. The original reason we did this was to get top quality, but it turns out that's impossible. The petroleum shortage is resulting in lower-quality vinyl – we've noticed a difference this week as against last week – and the best we can do is minimize defective pressing.

"But we're doing as much as anyone can. We even pulled out of one pressing plant on October 3 – and the record was due in the stores on the fifteenth – because it wasn't meeting our standards. Whew. It was like redirecting the Normandy Invasion."

Joe Smith of Warner Bros. has disinterested best wishes for the fledgling company, but as president of the Dead's former label he has, as might be expected, a jaundiced view of the operation. "Originally," he commented, "they felt there was a problem in our distribution system – we weren't using mail order or head shops. We weren't getting to their people. Initially, as I understand, they looked into this system of distribution and found it would be suicide, and so they ended up going through independent distribution, which reaches the exact same places Warner Bros. distribution does. So there's nothing unique about the operation except that it's artist owned. When they have to start paying for advertising themselves, they may wonder why they did it. If I were starting a label today, I wouldn't try to go it alone as an independent company. You can't duplicate the facilities of a full-line record company in sales, promotion, marketing and so on."

And as for the quality-control program: "You can't do it. There's no way. I think they're kidding themselves if they're trying to get out thousands of records at the same time. They were always overconcerned about complaints about surface noise and clicks – when there were a hundred complaints in hundreds of thousands of records, that was a big thing."

"Did you see that crow on our label?" asked Rakow. "So many people have had reservations about this company of ours, we decided to put the crow on our album and the labels. That crow's for eating. Either we or a lot of other people are going to have eat that crow."

* * *

RON RAKOW was first associated with the Dead as "the rocker's dream of the guy who's going to put up the bucks." He had a background in economics as a Wall Street arbitrageur – one who buys and sells simultaneously in two different markets to take advantage of a price difference; it's part of the worldwide pricing system. He lent the Dead money for equipment in 1965 and within months got swept up in the scene, dropped out of his company, Guaranteed Factors, and moved in with them as a photographer. Later he was a partner with the Dead and Jefferson Airplane in running the Carousel Ballroom, a venture that went deeply into debt and ended with the hall falling into the hands of Bill Graham, who renamed it Fillmore West. Now Rakow is Grateful Dead Records. No doubt about it, he's part of the Dead *karass,* to use the term from Kurt Vonnegut's *Cat's Cradle:* an involuntary association of people working outside the structure of any human institution to accomplish ends of which they are unaware. The Dead scene works largely by karass.

Take Jon McIntire, for instance, thirty-two-year-old manager of the Dead and the New Riders of the Purple Sage. When he met the Dead, McIntire had been pursuing a complicated academic career, never quite obtaining a degree at a series of institutions but lecturing in philosophy courses such as Symbolic Logic. He had also been acting, from the National Theater to gigs in Iceland, and singing in a Chicago nightclub. The Dead, he recalls, "rearranged my internal organs." He got into the trip, becoming successively manager of the Carousel's restaurant, superintendent of concessions and finally hall manager; then, after the Carousel's demise, part of the Dead office. Under the management of Lenny Hart, father of drummer Mickey Hart, there were many temporary defections from the office, leaving McIntire comanager. When Lenny left, he found himself manager.

Or take Rock Scully, current road manager. The same age as McIntire, he had an even more baroque college career after a childhood in Seattle, Chicago and Europe. He studied psychology under Kurt Adler at the University of Vienna, and graduated in history and literature from Earlham College in Indiana; a refusal to take a loyalty oath led him away from a post as administrative assistant to California State Senator Fred Farr and back to college – this time to the proto–Haight-Ashbury ferment of San Francisco State College in 1964. While putting on benefits for SNCC (Student Nonviolent Coordinating Committee) on the State campus, he also turned on a friend named Luria Castell to rock & roll, and her Family Dog organization eventually presented the first San Francisco rock concerts. From there on it was simple: Owsley Stanley, the Dead's early benefactor, invited Scully to manage the band. So Scully set up the short-lived management firm of Frontage Road, Ltd., with partner Danny Rifkin (who soon left for Guatemala but returned to become a member of the equipment crew). Scully also compiled *The California Book of the Dead* and served as the Dead's publisher, then as the liaison with Warner Bros. Since the band's termination with Warners, he has become road manager.

"In this scene," as McIntire puts it, "when you need something, you just hang on until somebody comes to fill the space." A classic example is the story he tells of how he heard that Keith Godchaux had joined the band: "I saw Garcia and asked him what it was all about, and he shook his head, very amazed, and said, 'Well, this guy came along and said he was our piano player, and he was.' " (Little wonder that Alan Trist, head of the Dead's publishing firm, Ice Nine, was fascinated by the scene – he'd been a social anthropologist.)

Joined to the karass like its shadow is the concept of Hypnocracy. You'll get a confusing variety of answers if you inquire the meaning of the word. In fact, it's considered bad form to ask. "It's for me to know and you to find out," said Garcia. "I used to know," said Frankie Weir [Bob Weir's wife], adding that it depended on whether you asked a Bolo or a Bozo. Frankie's partner Rosie McGee, an eight-year member of the family, stumbled and fell to one knee when asked; this was widely admired in the Dead family as an explanation of Hypnocracy.

Neither a Bolo nor a Bozo, Scully had a historical explanation. "It started when we were on the European tour last year. It was just a way of generalizing your trip. One busload of us got to being called the Bolos and the other bus was the Bozos, and while this kind of meant that everybody has two sides, an individual and yet able to submerge into this group thing, that's how it started.

"We were something like an invasion, because there were so many of us we could just take over a hotel or a restaurant. That's the meaning of the big American shoe coming through the rainbow on the cover of *Europe '72.* Most of the people had never been to Europe before, and it was also the longest Dead tour ever, so a group consciousness developed that tended to exclude the surroundings. I had spent ten years in Europe and was extremely conscious of how we seemed to them – I mean, we were ordering off the menu all the time, running Europe a little crazy. We were the All-American Kid in Europe, in a sense a little spastic about relating to people. That's how I see the Ice Cream Kid" – the "doofo" on the cover of *Europe '72,* spastically hitting himself on the forehead with his ice cream cone.

Many would disagree with Scully's cosmopolitan explanation, and even he admits there is something to the idea of Hypnocracy as symbolizing the group's "undiscovered common goals." Indeed, Bob Hunter, the chief theoretician of Hypnocracy and the lyricist who collaborates with Garcia, has offered this explanation:

"When asked the meaning of life, St. Dilbert replied, 'Ask rather the meaning of Hypnocracy.' When asked the meaning of Hypnocracy, St. Dilbert replied, 'Is not Hypnocracy no other than the quest to discover the meaning of Hypnocracy? Say, have you heard the one about the yellow dog yet?'"

Speaking of the one about the yellow dog, Hunter has acknowledged that quippie jokes are hypnocratic. The jokes told about the equipment crew are an idiosyncratic mixture of Polack and Shaggy Dog. Sample: "Why did the quippie run the truck into the wall?" "Because it was rented."

Perhaps – one must be tentative when speculating about deep matters – it has something to do with the Acid Test legacy of psychedelic faith, the sense that the unexpected and inexplicable are truth on the hoof, and when it comes down to it, all you can do is run along. And philosophic meditation on the doofo may be inevitable when you're in a scene that runs on the karass principle rather than on some narrow-minded program of eliminating fuckups.

* * *

TAKE FLY BY NIGHT TRAVEL as a karass example. The president ("Melon in Charge") is Frankie Weir; the specialist in booking bands is Rosie McGee, who came from Alembic, the Dead-associated hi-fi workshop.

"The idea had been in the air to have a travel agency for about four years," said Frankie, sitting behind a business desk with a nose-ring stud glittering in her right nostril. "So we bought an agency in February – it would have taken three times as much capital to start one from scratch – and opened up here. I don't expect it to make money for five years. It's really mostly a convenience for the bands."

Located in the same building that now houses the Dead offices, three blocks from Grateful Dead Records, Fly by Night shares the same hideous sort of office carpeting and stuccoed ceilings as the rest of the new building. As in the others there is an attempt to make it more livable with tie-dyes by family artisan Courtney Pollack and visionary fairy-

tale illustrations by Maxfield Parrish. Unlike in most travel offices, there is not a single travel poster.

"One reason we got it is that Garcia, for instance, won't come into an agency," said Frankie, who knows from rock & rollers. She danced her way from San Luis Obispo, California, to *American Bandstand* and was even a Rockette for a while before becoming George Harrison's secretary at Apple. "Another reason is that we want to be sure that the bands aren't getting booked into unfriendly or unsuitable places. We're keeping a file on hotels, limousine services, restaurants that stay open late – a clearinghouse of information on places all over the country. We're going to make this information available to anybody." Comments run from "low-key and close to everything" to "hates longhairs" and "The Mayfair is a fleabag and a whorehouse and don't ever send us there again."

Fly by Night has handled about fifteen acts, including the Dead and its spinoffs – the New Riders of the Purple Sage, Garcia's bluegrass group Old and In the Way, and so on – and a number of Bill Graham's groups. On average McGee is handling three tours at once. But like any travel agency with ambitions to commercial viability, Fly by Night is not counting exclusively on rock & roll, even though it accounts for 75 percent of the business. It also handles "commercial accounts," the traveling businessmen who are the regular diet of most agencies. The rock & roll connection has caused Fly by Night some grief in this regard: It seems an early assistant, in setting up the bookkeeping, was busted June 30 for LSD possession and – bad luck – hot airline tickets. On investigation it was found that the hot tickets didn't come from Fly by Night and that the fellow was no longer with the agency. Then, about the time that scandal was quieting down, the bustee's roommate was busted for acid. The "acid" turned out to be $300 worth of vitamin tablets, but, bad luck again, he happened to be Ron Rakow.

One hopes everybody will keep in mind what St. Dilbert has said: "How can you tell a St. from a Snr. without a program?"

* * *

THE DEAD FAN CLUB dates from the double album *Grateful Dead* (a.k.a. Skull and Roses), which contained a note that read, "Dead Freaks Unite – Who are you? Where are you? How are you?" and a promise to "keep you informed." About three hundred fifty people responded.

"The album was sort of offering people something," said Eileen Law in the Deadhead office, an office once again like all the others in the building but decorated with plants, old dance posters and letters from Dead fans. "So we were sort of compelled to respond."

The office is shared by some other Dead operations: One door leads to a bookkeepers' office, another to the "boys' room," the office of the Dead's equipment crew. Law met the Dead because she was a fan: "If you went to all the concerts, you just inevitably met the band. And if you fit in, you became part of it." So she understands the people who write in. "People are always asking for energy," she said, "and they always want to know the dates of concerts." The office regularly sends to Deadhead members tour itineraries and irregularly something called the *Dead Heads Newsletter.*

"We're trying to do a newsletter about two times a year," said Mary Ann Mayer, a former Dead light-show operator. The newsletter contains drawings, poems and occasional statements from the band. Sometimes it will answer frequently asked questions, such as how the band spends its money (in 1972 the $1,424,543 was split up this way: 27 percent salaries, 27 percent road expenses and agency, 18 percent equipment purchase and maintenance, 17 percent office expenses – including 2 percent for the Deadhead office, 8 percent tax and 3 percent operating profit); how the speakers are set up onstage; and such perhaps unthought-of questions as "What is Hypnocracy?" The newsletter, in fact, is the chief way even members of the Dead family have of keeping up on Hunter's latest redefinition/obfuscation of Hypnocracy.

There are Deadheads in every part of the world – even in unexpected places like Poland, Kuwait and Malaysia – and the rate of new memberships has reached fifty a day. The Dead make occasional special use of their fans. For example, a mailing announcing that Grateful Dead Records was about to swing into operation brought about three thousand responses, mostly asking how to be of help. The volunteers are going to be put to work checking to see that the record gets delivered to stores and played on radio stations.

Membership is free and as of September 25 had climbed from the original 350 names to 25,731. It might seem to be getting out of hand, but Law hopes it gets bigger: "It's getting more fun."

* * *

THE BACK OFFICE shows a very resolute attempt to overcome the sterility of its quarters, with tie-dyes covering the fluorescent lights and rough stained wood planks lining the walls. From time to time you might see a cadaverous bearded fellow whisk into an office decorated with a tapestry of the Skull and Roses album cover; that's Scully. The cultivated-looking gentleman with longish blond hair will be McIntire, who, despite his scholarly manner, can pick up a telephone and storm at promoters with the best of them.

Next door is the office of David Parker, business manager, who also happens to be an eleven-year friend of Garcia's. At one time he played washboard and kazoo in Mother McCree's Uptown Jug Champions. Next to his office is the New Riders office. Around a corner in the Grateful Dead office is the cubbyhole presided over by Alan Trist. This is Ice Nine, which publishes all Dead songs and at one time, confesses Trist, was "a sink to keep people on the payroll." Ice Nine has published three songbooks.

Across the hall are the offices of the Dead's agency, Out of Town Tours, where the struggle with stucco seems to have been won a little more to everybody's satisfaction. "We like it better in this building than the Dead do," said Sam Cutler in his languorous English accent.

Cutler represents as much as anyone the karass principle in operation. He met the Dead while tour-managing for the Rolling Stones in 1969; indeed, he is the one usually charged with having the inspiration of inviting the Hell's Angels to police the ill-fated Altamont concert. But he had soon become part of the karass; he took over as road manager for the Dead when Scully went into retreat in Woodstock after Altamont, then decided during the European tour to start an agency for the band. Now he is mutating from being the Dead's agent to being an independent agent, specializing in Marin County bands, "to maintain a close flow with both musicians and clubs."

* * *

OF COURSE, any band needs a practice studio. Sometimes the Dead use the New Riders' studio, located in the San Rafael industrial neighborhood. The studio is rented, natch, from an old friend of the Dead's, Don Wrixman. He rents another part of the building to some woodcraftsmen, and yet another is the Dead's sound and lighting equipment warehouse. The original Dead warehouse, which the equipment has long since outgrown, is now a workshop for repairing electronic equipment and building speaker cabinets.

As for a practice hall for the Dead themselves, they might build one someday on a piece of land they own known as "Deadpatch." When Weir's home studio is complete, the band could fit there, though Weir built it – with some of the heaviest insulation ever put into a building – so he could practice by himself. "I'm one of those people who can't stand to be overheard when they're working something out," he says.

And then there's Hart's studio out in the woods near Novato. Hart, it will be remembered, was with the band during the period when it had two drummers – including, alas, the brief period in '69 and '70 when his father managed the band and embezzled perhaps $150,000 from them, of which they got $63,000 back. A few months after Lenny Hart was brought to justice, Mickey's musical directions led him away from the Dead, but he's remained in the karass. These days his studio, or "experimental situation," as he calls it, serves for practice and also for recording. Both Bob Hunter and Barry Melton of Country Joe and the Fish have recorded and mixed albums in the studio, and Hart did his own album *Rolling Thunder* there.

As would be expected, Dead spinoff bands such as Old and In the Way have messed around in Hart's studio as well. A new spinoff group is soon to be launched from this mysterious hideout: an electronic-music outfit consisting of Phil Lesh, an MIT music student named Ned Lagin and Hart himself. "It's biofeedback music," said Hart, "neurosensory-system music. Highly evolved music. We've been sitting around late into the night out here in the forest working on it, and we're gonna bring it out pretty soon. We've been building special equipment to play it. What are we gonna call ourselves? Ha! The other night we were thinking of 'Warp Ten.' We don't know yet – anyway, it's Warp Ten to me."

The only other hint we're going to get for a while is from Scully: "I hear one time they just put their instruments down facing each other with the speakers on and walked around among them – and the instruments were, like, *talking* to each other, man, holding a conversation."

One other side trip needs to be mentioned: the Neal Cassady Memorial Foundation. Rakow had mentioned it as "one of the measures we're taking to ensure that the Dead are never financially secure." Garcia gives the details: "When I recorded *Garcia,* I found for a while I was rich, so I started giving the money away. And I found after a while that it cost me $1,500 to give away $1,000. So we're getting an institution registered to promote research in the arts, sciences and education, so I can give away my money easier. So far it hasn't done anything.

"Well, yeah, it ought to keep us insecure."

* * *

WHEN THE BAND goes on the road, life is quite different. Instead of kicking around in the woods and hanging out with family, the cast of characters is reduced to the basic touring party of twenty-three. This is six musicians, a road manager and the sixteen-member crew: two drivers for the forty-foot semi carrying the sound equipment, a lighting crew of three plus a lighting designer, nine sound quippies and the T-shirt lady. Other old ladies may come along, particularly when the band's playing an interesting place – New York is popular – but they pay their own way. The social scene widens when the Dead run into a fraternal band such as the New Riders, the Allman Brothers or Doug Sahm, or when the nonpayrolled band of friends known as the Pleasure Crew pops up.

So much for the comers and goers. Now for the crew – the quippies, objects of many a hypnocratic joke, the T-shirted gang glimpsed hulking about the stage during a show, the villains of many a wild-assed kid trying to leap on the stage or climb the speaker towers. Let Steve Parish, sentimental giant and acknowledged "loudmouth" of the group, speak his piece: "We've shown a rough exterior to a lot of people, but that's because you get jumpy on the road after a couple of gigs, getting up at eight in the morning and working till show time, then spending another four hours tearing everything down, so we don't get to quit till four in the morning.

"But we're not gorillas. We're all really sensitive guys."

Part of the gorilla reputation derives from the quippies' former habit of destroying hotel rooms. "Well, yeah," says Parish, grinning and wiping his black mustache, "it used to be a big thing to flip out. We were experts at flippin' out. And we did a lot of machoing out, too – a brotherhood swaggerin' kind of thing." Scully points out also that, contrary to the reputation of roadies the world over, this crew is usually too busy to have a shot at picking up groupies, which makes for a certain tension. "Only, after a couple of weeks out," he adds, "one night – you can never predict it – suddenly everybody'll score."

The Dead's sound system is immense. The equipment weighs about twenty-three tons, all of it needed if the Dead are to have the sound they want: a sound that will fill an arena clear to the back at any level of volume, from a whisper to a fortissimo you can feel in your kidneys, but completely clear and distortion-free. But as it happens, at the moment the Dead are thinking of getting away from the use of this titanic accumulation of amps and speakers.

"The direction of the last year was dictated by overspending in 1972," says Sam Cutler back in the Out of Town offices. "There's the matter of growing demand, too, but the Dead are supporting, directly or indirectly, forty or fifty people. Whether you want to call this the family or not is a matter of definition – when the Dead plays Winterland the guest list runs to three hundred fifty people. Anyway, the overhead

is $100,000 a month, and that's forced us into the larger halls. There don't seem to be any halls in the country between about six thousand capacity and ten thousand, so the band has been forced to provide sound equipment for those gigantic ice rinks.

"The band prefers to play in the smaller clubs; they make it possible for people to be in a much better space because they don't require police to be there and aren't as subject to absurd early curfews. But if the band plays, for instance, a three-thousand-seat hall, and tickets are $5 apiece, they will make $7,500 for the night. At that rate they'd have to play fifteen gigs a month, and the Dead don't want to work that hard. They want to work long enough to satisfy the music withdrawal symptoms. And they're road-fragile – they're not built for it. They don't have the gypsylike mentality of some other bands.

"But they don't like playing the large halls, and they haven't been happy with their performances in the last year. So next year we're compromising: We'll have maybe two tours of large halls, concentrating on the ones that have acoustically redeeming features and no hall management or police hassles. And then four or five small-room tours. There are some other ideas in the air, too . . . weird ones.

"It means we'll have to prune the tree a little to make for better blossoms. How exactly will we do that? That's the million-dollar question."

At the Hilton Inn in Oklahoma City, Garcia adds his angle: "The record company may alleviate economic forces that have put us in this place. Right now, somehow, we've ended up successes. But this ain't exactly what we had in mind, twelve-thousand-seat halls and big bucks. We're trying to redefine. We've played every conceivable venue, and it hasn't been it. What can we do that's more fun, more interesting?"

* * *

FOR THE TOURS of small halls, the sound equipment will be cut back from twenty-three tons to seven, and modularized so that a crew of two or three men could set it up. As for what happens to the crew then, the Dead karass will provide. The Dead are setting the quippies up in a company called Quality Control Sound Products to build speaker cabinets with the rock & roll tour in mind, cabinets that won't fall apart like commercial pressboard models. They've already sold some to the Allman Brothers. There are also plans for a quippie consulting service and a J.B. Lansing speaker franchise.

The quippies are a company, then, as well as a crew, like so many of the Dead family back in Marin. If that weren't enough, they're also – are you ready? – a band. The Dead have been coaching them on instruments, and the New Riders' rehearsal hall sometimes pulses with the rock & roll sound of Sparky and the ABs – Sparky and the Ass Bites From Hell.

"So if everything were to collapse and even the band broke up," says Garcia with a benevolent grin, "I'd have to do a record for Atlantic. I'm the consolation prize.

"But our scene is always healthiest when it's really struggling. Basically our situation is on the borderline of collapse all the time anyway." ☾

IN 1974 I WAS THE MUSIC CRITIC for the *Philadelphia Bulletin*. Being a regular writer for a major-city daily newspaper at the age of twenty-four was rewarding and gave a certain satisfaction to a young rock fan's life. Getting paid to see and interview bands like the Grateful Dead was at times so much fun, it almost seemed illegal. But, someone had to do it, so . . . . Anyway, that summer

OH

WITH JERRY GARCIA

of '74, the Grateful Dead were booked for two nights at Philadelphia's Civic Center. My job was to do a preview story in the *Sunday Bulletin* on the band. Their publicist approved an interview with Bob Weir (Jerry Garcia, I was informed, "wasn't talking to the press") and provided me with tickets to see a show in Providence, Rhode Island, a couple of weeks before Philadelphia, and off I went.

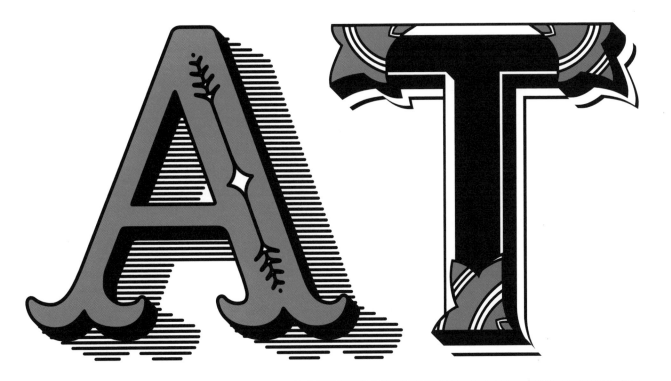

AT
BY STEVE WEITZMAN

THE SHOW THAT NIGHT at the Providence Civic Center was a five-hour extravaganza, leaving everyone – band and audience alike – drained and exhausted but in a state of euphoria. A few minutes after the last encore, I noticed Jerry Garcia, wearing a dark green T-shirt, Wranglers and Acme boots, leaning against a wall backstage, winding down. I went over to say hello and asked him about a new (at the time) song from *Mars Hotel* with which they had closed the show.

Spotting the tape recorder I was carrying, he said, "I'm not doing interviews this year," in the same tone of voice he might use to order an after-dinner wine. "I hate all my records," he added. "The Grateful Dead don't make good records."

Was he satisfied with the performance they had just given? "If I was ever satisfied," he added totally seriously, "I'd quit playing."

Two years later in a New York hotel room, on April Fools' Day, 1976, Garcia agreed to an in-depth interview. Following two years of low Grateful Dead activity (which were filled with rumors of retirement), Garcia was in town with a solo band featuring John Kahn, Ron Tutt and Keith and Donna Godchaux. Being into gadgets, he inspected with interest a new tape recorder I had just bought, and we began.

* * *

I SPOKE WITH YOU briefly backstage at the Providence Civic Center two years ago. You told me, "I'm not doing interviews this year," and then you said, "I hate all my records. The Grateful Dead don't make good records."

[*Laughs.*] Yeah, that's true.

That's true that you said that or that's true that they don't?

Well, both of them are true. But it's a matter of objectivity. It depends on which side of the coin you're on. For example, if I buy somebody's record – a Rolling Stones record or something – what I hear obviously is the finished record, the finished music and the whole thing

Garcia, with the Dead and his other bands, paid homage to such heroes as country-music pioneer Jimmie Rodgers (left) and (right) bluesman Reverend Gary Davis.

that's already happened. In other words, with a Grateful Dead record, part of what I'm dealing with is the dissonance between the original version, the original flash as a composer. When a song comes into my head, it comes with a complete sound to it, a complete arrangement, a complete format and a complete *thing* more often than not, which represents my relationship to a personal vision. So, for me, comparing the record to the vision, I always feel that it fails.

That doesn't discourage you to the point of not wanting to record?

It *could*. But it doesn't, because there's enough to making records or making music that there are enough other ways to get off. So I'm not that hung up on the relationship to the vision except that it produces sort of a feeling

of disappointment. You want it to work a certain way, and sometimes it doesn't work as well as you want it to. Like, I had a whole long thing I was working on as far as *Blues for Allah* was concerned that was a technical trip, and it required a certain amount of developing hardware to go along with the idea, which is often the case with things I get involved with. Often I want to do something that you can only do by developing or interfacing a number of existing possibilities.

With *Blues for Allah* there was a thing I wanted to do that had to do with an envelope shaper and stuff like that, that didn't come together the way I wanted it to. And so, when I listen to it, I think, "Well, shit, it isn't quite where I wanted it to be." But in the long run, after, like, however many records – nineteen records or something like that – you feel that at least your percentages are getting closer and you're able to score on other levels. Like, on our earlier records, if I listen to them now, they are embarrassing for reasons like they're out of tune.

And your recent records are never out of tune.

[*Laughs.*] Now they're much more together on those levels than they used to be. We're much more able to pull off the technical aspect without having to sacrifice feeling. In terms of *Blues for Allah,* the latest Grateful Dead record I can talk about in this frame, I think that's the first record we've made in years where we really had fun. We laughed a lot and got good and crazy. We had an opportunity to get weirder than we normally get. First of all, because we didn't have the pressure of having to go out and tour and travel and thus break the flow.

A couple of years ago you weren't doing interviews. Now you are. Why the switch?

I like to do 'em when I feel like I have something new to say. Every couple of years my viewpoint changes, you know what I mean? So I have something to say. I have some substance. Also, at the end of a year of rapping – if I have only one rap [*laughs*], one good thing to say and I spend a year saying it – pretty soon I'm burned out, and I can't stand to listen to it anymore. But the fact that I haven't been out traveling a lot and I'm not road-weary also has something to do with it.

In our brief conversation two years ago, you said – in response to whether you were satisfied with the show – "If I was ever satisfied, I'd quit playing."

Yeah, I think I might, in the sense that part of it is the thing of trying, taking chances.

So why now, at this point in time, do you have something to say? Your solo album?

The solo album is one thing. I think the movie is the thing [*The Grateful Dead Movie*].

Tell me about the movie.

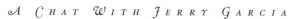

When we decided we weren't going to perform anymore, our farewell show, so to speak, was five days at Winterland. It was after we got back from our second trip to Europe – October '74. About a month before the Winterland dates, I got the idea that it would be neat to be able to film it, just because I didn't know if we were going to perform again. Or if we were going to perform in that kind of a situation again. And that five nights in a place would at least give us the possibility, numerically anyway, that we would have one or two really good nights. In about two or three weeks the whole production thing came together to make the movie.

At first we thought, let's just make a record of the idea, and I want it to look good. I wanted it to be really well filmed, but I didn't really know a lot about film when the idea got under way. But when it was time for the show to start, we had about nine camera crews and a lot of good backup people, good lighting people, and the whole thing was already on its way to happening. It was chaotic but well organized in spite of the relatively short preproduction time we had. After the five days were over – and during that time I involved myself mostly with the music; I didn't really get into the film part – we had a couple of hundred thousand feet of film in the can. So then it was, What's going to happen with this? Originally, we were thinking in terms of, What about a canned concert? Would something like that work? Could we send out a filmed version of ourselves? Then, after getting involved and interested in the movie as a project, I started looking at the footage and the concert

stuff, and I felt there was a *movie* there. A movie in a movie sense rather than a movie in a canned-concert sense. Then there was the thing of putting all that together, and that's what I've been working on the last year and a half, ever since the filming was over, really.

I've noticed your concerts don't change as much from show to show as your albums do.

That's true. That's because albums get to be a certain time and space, and the concert thing is a flow.

And you know what to expect from a Grateful Dead concert.

In a way, but we're trying to bust that, too. That's one of the reasons we dropped out.

You have so many members of the Grateful Dead on your solo album, 'Reflections,' it could almost be a Grateful Dead album.

A lot of energy from that record is really a continuation of the *Blues for Allah* groove that we got into. We sort of continued the same energy because we were having a lot of fun doing it.

One of my favorite things you've been involved with in the last few years is the 'Old & In the Way' bluegrass album you did with Vassar Clements, David Grisman and Peter Rowan.

That was a good band. It was satisfying and fun to be in.

Was the reason you only put out the 'Old & In the Way' album and didn't do a whole lot of touring with that band because of the fact there's only a certain amount of acceptance bluegrass can get?

That, and also we ran into a really weird problem in terms of dynamics, which was that bluegrass music is like chamber music; it's very quiet, and if the audience got at all enthusiastic during the tune and started clapping or something, it would drown out the band, and we couldn't hear each other.

What an album. I didn't know you were such a hot banjo player.

[*Laughs.*] Oh, I was real hot when I was a kid. Now my reasons for playing banjo and my reasons for liking bluegrass music are completely different from when I started, 'cause then I was really hot.

I think that 'Old & In the Way' album may be the best bluegrass album ever recorded.

Wow. Thank you. I'm happy with it too, but the truth is, we had much better performances than were on that record.

That's hard to imagine.

Oh, yeah. We had performances that were heart-stopping. And perfect, you know, but there weren't as many that were recorded that well.

That banjo solo you did on "Wild Horses" and Vassar's violin solo in "Midnight Moonlight" . . . Jesus.

Well, that was really a thrilling band. And I think that was the nicest that Vassar's played, too. When he was playing with Old & In the Way, he played the maximum of mind-blowing but beautifully tasty stuff, and the music had enough interesting kinds of new changes and new things happening – Pete's good songs, for example – so that Vassar had a chance to blow with a lot of range. More than he does normally. That was neat.

The Grateful Dead have been a strange band for my taste, in that, if I like a band a lot – and some of your stuff I've liked an awful lot – I normally like just about everything the band does. But with the Dead, some of the stuff you've done has just gone right by me, while other stuff just blows me away. And it's the same way with your concerts. Say you're in the middle of a jam; I'll be half asleep for a few minutes, and all of a sudden, you'll do something for five or ten seconds on guitar that will make my hair stand on end.

See, I have that kind of reaction to the Grateful Dead myself. The Grateful Dead is not anybody's idea of how a band or music should be. It's a combination of really divergent viewpoints. Everyone in the band is quite different from everyone else. And what happens musically is different from what any one person would do. For me the band that I have right now I'm real happy with. I haven't been as happy with any little performing group since Old & In the Way, in terms of feeling "this is really harmonious, this is what I want to hear." This band that I have now is very consonant. The Grateful Dead has always had that thing of dissonance. It's not always consonant. Sometimes it's dissonant.

Sometimes it's real ugly-sounding and just drives you crazy.

Do you spend a lot of time in San Francisco?

Yeah, I spend most of my time working. I'm very taken with our scene. It's very interesting.

Your records are getting softer. In fact, there's only one uptempo song, "Might As Well," on your new solo album.

That's true. That's probably the worst thing about it, the lack of balance of material.

When I listened to it, I thought maybe you didn't like to rock & roll as much anymore.

No, uh . . . it's not that. All these things have to do with luck. And timing. For example, the way that solo album was recorded, really a lot of material was performed with the intention of using it on the record, but of the takes that I felt were acceptable, they tended to be more of those softer tunes. So I decided to go with those, because I felt the feeling of the tracks was better, not because of wanting it to be that way.

Your guitar playing has remained fairly constant in the last few years. The only real deviation was on this album's track "Comes a Time." You used a mild fuzz.

I just used a small amplifier.

There was some nice sustain on your playing. It sounded terrific.

Yeah. I do those things more on other people's sessions than I do on my own. I tend to be real off-handed about my guitar playing on my own records. In fact, on Grateful Dead records, too.

What other records are you referring to?

Well, when I just go and do sessions with somebody more or less anonymous.

You don't do sessions that often, do you?

Not anymore.

Who are the last few people you've done sessions for?

I did a whole spasm of local ones, like all those Merl Saunders [*Live at Keystone, Fire Up*] records. Tom Fogerty's records. And the Airplane session. Stuff like that. I used to do more than I do now.

Kingfish and your band are both on similar – and sometimes identical – tours at the moment and sometimes even cross paths, but you never share a bill. Are the two bands' identities so different that it would hinder playing together?

Well, it's just that neither one of us wants to try to cash in on the Grateful Dead notoriety. And, also, the people that are in our respective bands have identities of their own to support. So rather than get everybody under the big Grateful Dead umbrella, it's better if everybody can have their own little shot. Because, for example, it would be possible for Kingfish to go out and work without Weir. They're a band without him as well as a band with him. There are those kinds of considerations, because when we start working on Grateful Dead stuff, which we'll start doing pretty soon, those bands will have their own survival problems. Not so much my band because Ron [Tutt] works with Elvis. John [Kahn] does studio stuff, and he's always got stuff going on.

Are both you and Kingfish ending up your tours at about the same time?

Yeah. The Grateful Dead has to start rehearsing.

Are you going to do a big summer tour like everybody else?

We're going to approach it differently. We're going to try to do small places. We're going to do theaters. We're not going to do any barns.

Why, at this point, have the Grateful Dead decided to get back together?

We're horny to play. We all miss Grateful Dead music. We want to be the Grateful Dead some more.

What kind of material will you be doing?

Probably some old stuff but more new stuff, and I think probably the biggest change will be that we have Mickey back in the band.

When you look back on your records – you still probably maintain that you hate all your records . . .

I don't listen to 'em. I *can't* [*laughs*].

Are there any that you hate less than the others?

Well, I always like the one we're working on, or the one we've just finished. That's the one I feel closest to. But after that, I have to disqualify myself. I can't judge them against anything but an emotional situation that I'm in, in relation to the Grateful Dead. Either they recall to me what was going on at the time we recorded or something else. It's more personal than anything else.

When you work on songs, can you tell which ones may become classics with your audience, like "Sugar Magnolia" or "Truckin'"?

Uh . . . not really. I can't. 'Cause often, the ones that get me don't get anybody but me [*laughs*].

Which ones haven't gotten many other people?

Well, I don't know, but there are some songs that I really loved . . . like, I really loved "Row Jimmy." That was one of my favorite songs of ones that I've written. I *loved* it. Nobody else really liked it very much – we always did it – but nobody liked it very much, at least in the same way I did.

"U.S. Blues" got real popular in the summer of '74 and became a big number for your live shows . . .

Well, that kind of figured to be. Some of 'em, you can say, "Well, this'll at least be hot. If nothing else."

I like "Scarlet Begonias" a lot.

Yeah, that's another song, too. That's a song I like. "Ship of Fools" is a song I like an awful lot. But my relationship to them changes. Sometimes I really like a song after I've written it and I don't like it at all a year later. And some of them, I'm sort of indifferent to, but we perform it and find they have a real long life. For me to sing a song, I really have to feel some relationship to it. I can't just bullshit about it. Otherwise, it's just empty and it's no fun. There has to be something about it I can relate to. Not even in a literal sense or a sense of content, but more a sense of sympathy with the singer of the song. It's a hard relationship to describe, but some songs have a real long life and you can sing them honestly for a long period of time, and others last just awhile and you don't feel like you can sing them anymore.

When you write with Robert Hunter, you write the music and then he writes the lyrics?

More often than not. But also it's a little freer than that, too. I edit his work an awful lot and, for example, a tune like "U.S. Blues" really will start off with three hundred possible verses. Then it's a matter of carving them down to ones that are singable. Other songs are like stories. A lot of times I edit out the *sense* of Hunter's songs.

So you're the reason he seems so deranged.

Yeah [*laughs*]. I'm an influence in that. And when I edit his stuff, he really treats it with skepticism, but we have a thing of trust between us now so that he usually laughs when I hack out the sense of the song. Dump it. We have a real easy relationship.

By the way, you have one of the strangest record company bios I have ever read. It was credited to Hunter.

I actually think that bio was written by Willy Legate.

Who is he?

Willy Legate is this guy who's an old, old friend of me and Hunter's and Phil's and our whole scene, and he's a lot of things. And one of those things he is, is sort of a Bible scholar. And he's a madman. We were exposed to him really a lot during a formative period of our intellectual life. And he's still around in our scene.

He's the guy who wrote, "There's nothing like a Grateful Dead concert," and he wrote the little blurb inside the *Europe '72* album about the Bolos and the Bozos. We also call on him to do various things. One time we asked the Deadheads to send us their thoughts, just to get some feedback from them. And they sent us lots and lots of letters, and we gave 'em all to Willy. And he ended up with, like, a two-page condensation of all the letters, with every viewpoint, that was just tremendously amazing to read. It was just so packed with information.

Willy is someone who has a lot of different kinds of gifts. He also even wrote some lyrics to some of our early songs before we started recording, but we've subsequently stopped doing the tunes. But he's another creative head in our scene that operates way back from the public.

What kinds of things do you care a lot about these days?

[*Pauses.*] I think the thing I'm most into is the survival of the Grateful Dead. I think that's my main trip now.

Was there ever a point when you didn't care a lot about that?

Yeah, always.

So this is pretty new?

Yeah, pretty new.

How long has this been going on?

I would say about a year.

Why is that?

Well, I feel like I've had both trips, in a sense that I've been in the Grateful Dead for ten or twelve years, and I've also been out of it, in the sense of going out in the world and traveling and doing things just under my own hook. And, really, I'm not that taken with my own ideas. I don't really have that much to say, and I'm more interested in being involved in something that's larger than me. And I really can't talk to anybody else either [*laughs*]. So, sometime in the last year, I decided, yeah, that's it, that's definitely the farthest-out thing I've ever been involved in, and it's the thing that makes me feel best. And it seems to have the most ability to sort of neutrally put something good into the mainstream. It's also fascinating in the sense of the progression. The year-to-year changes are fascinating.

I would say that's the thing I'm most concerned about now. Everything else has gotten to be so weird. And I've never been that attracted to the flow politically.

Never?

No. It just isn't interesting to me.

Do you vote?

No. Vote for *what?* Even looking for decently believable input from that world is a scene. So I haven't developed that much interest in the motions of the rest of the world. I'm mainly interested in improving the relationship between the band and the audience and being onstage and playing.

How about causes, like the legalization of marijuana, that kind of stuff?

It's all passing stuff. I don't know. I don't have anything to say about moral things. Or legal things. I think there's a lot of confusion on those levels. Basically, my framework politically or anything like that is, I'm into a completely free, wide-open, total anarchy space. That's what I want [*laughs*]. Obviously, I'm not going to be able to sell that to anybody [*more laughter*]. Nobody's going to dig that.

You can't even give that away . . .

Exactly. So I don't even bother. If I have a flag to wave, it's a nonflag. But as a life problem, the Grateful Dead *is* an anarchy. That's what it is. It doesn't have any . . . stuff. It

More of Garcia's favorites: (left) the Carter Family (Sara, A.P. and Maybelle) and (above) Delta bluesman Skip James.

doesn't have any goals. It doesn't have any plans. It doesn't have any leaders. Or real organization. And it works. It even works in the straight world. It doesn't work *too good.* It doesn't work like General Motors does, but it works okay. And it's more fun.

I'm curious to see what effect your newfound affection for the Grateful Dead is going to have on your music.

It'll be interesting. See, I've always been real ambivalent about it. It's like one of those things that I've always wanted to work out, but I never wanted to try and make it do that. And, in fact, everyone in the Grateful Dead has always had that basic attitude. So we'll see what happens. ☯

CHARLES M. YOUNG BY

THE
AWAKENING OF
THE DEAD

BOB WEIR and Phil Lesh don't even look up as the roar of barely muffled Harley-Davidsons thunders into their Palladium dressing room from the New York City street two stories below.

"I'm telling you, I couldn't hear myself play," says Weir during the forty-minute intermission. "I'm just guessing what it sounds like to the audience."

"So I'll turn down my bass," replies Lesh. "But I can hardly hear myself onstage as it is. I'll have to stand right next to the speakers . . ."

A huge Hell's Angel – about six foot seven and 280 pounds – throws open the door to a chorus of "Hi, Vinny!" from the Grateful Dead. Followed by a couple of his compatriots, he strides around the room shaking hands like a great woolly mammoth graduate of the Hubert Humphrey School of Charm. "Whuss happnin'? I mean, ya know what I mean? Uh? Uh? Whuss happnin'?" His hair and beard are two feet long; he is dressed in a sheepskin hat and sleeveless leather jacket that is open to reveal a tattoo-covered torso.

Jerry Garcia asks Vinny how he has been.

"Just a couple of assault charges," says Vinny. "Nothin' serious; $500 in bail, *phffffftttt*. Ya know what I mean?" He pulls out a large knife. "I only use it for operational purposes."

One of the roadies' children, a three-year-old boy with long curly blond hair, toddles over and holds up a deflated rubber toy. "Giraffe?" he says. "Giraffe?"

"The kid don't speak nothin' but Lithuanian? Uh? Uh?" Vinny says as the child walks off again. "I guess he don't like skinny guys."

A roadie announces five minutes to show time and says to me, "Vinny is the only man on earth I'd trust with my kid."

Seeking some opening for conversation, I ask Vinny what a grime-obscured tattoo on his biceps says. He recites an obscene poem, then thinks better of it and grabs my notebook. "That's personal," he explains, crumpling the top sheet and throwing it on the floor. "I wanna hear 'Truckin'.' You ain't done 'Truckin'' yet, have you?" he says to the band as they head downstairs. Another twenty Angels and maybe twice that number of Dead friends freely wander in the wings.

"In all the time we've known them," says Weir, "I've never really talked that much with the Angels. I never know what to say to them."

* * *

WE'RE STILL as confused as we ever were," Garcia assures me in his hotel room on the second day of a five-night stand. "But it's a new world now, and we can't be wasteful anymore. We're using as little energy as possible and keeping everything simple. The old Dead trip was getting to be a burden, so we sacked it and went on to new projects. We're having fun again."

So the Grateful Dead Cadillac of Anarchy – incorporating every hood-ornament idea of the counterculture and every electronic gadget – has been traded in for a Grateful Dead Volkswagen of Ecology. So their $450,000 sound system – once one of the seven wonders of rock & roll – has been cannibalized, and they are using (God forbid) a borrowed (from Bill Graham) sound system. So their road crew of twenty-five quippies has been slashed to nine. So they aren't a record company anymore. So there isn't enough beer in their dressing room for a self-respecting Hell's Angel to get high on. So even though they still take ten-minute tuneups between songs, their performances are more purposeful and less self-indulgent than in the past. So they readily spit on tradition and got an outside producer (Keith Olsen) for their new album, *Terrapin Station.*

"Why not?" laughs Garcia. "We've tried everything else. It actually sounds like a record. People won't believe it's us."

"It's the Dead without all those wrong notes," adds Weir, sitting across the room. "And it's not completely overdone, either. Our past albums were like Dagwood sandwiches because you had to listen to them thirty or forty times on very sophisticated equipment to hear everything we'd dub in. We have seven very strong opinions about what should be done with a song, and it got too cumbersome in the studio. If you made a suggestion to put something in, then you'd have to let everybody else put in their suggestions, too. We needed one authority to make the decisions. Also, Keith is very short, so no one will hit him."

After ten albums on Warners, four on their own label and one on MGM, the Grateful Dead seem finally to have made a good, accessible album, this time for Arista. On past Dead efforts – even such songs as "Not Fade Away," whose appeal is 80 percent rhythm – the drums were not recorded with enough power to push the tune along. Olsen (their first outside producer since their first album) has remedied the problem with fairly involved orchestration between Bill Kreutzmann and Mickey Hart and by bringing the sound level up to about the point where Led Zeppelin mixes John Bonham. This has freed Garcia, still one of rock's most accomplished guitarists, to play melody lines instead of filling space. Some early listeners have gone so far as to call the effect "DiscoDead" – and the music is, in fact, quite danceable. Vocals are improved, with almost Beatles-like harmonies. And keyboardist Keith Godchaux's wife, Donna Godchaux, is emerging as a distinctively breathy and sexy vocal stylist.

The Deadheads' fanaticism remains as fierce as ever. The Palladium shows sold out in a few hours, and scalpers have been getting up to $75 per ticket. Groups of up to two hundred have been standing in front of and behind the theater for hours for a glimpse of Garcia. The formal Deadhead organization has fallen into disarray (its last mailing was about a year ago), but about twenty-five requests for concert schedules still arrive every day at the San Francisco head-quarters. The audiences, which one might have expected to consist of aging hippies, instead are composed of young hippies. Their hair is longer than that of the band members, who now appear to be seeing stylists regularly. Some of the kids have even been wearing tie-dye T-shirts.

"We're definitely getting a younger crowd," says Garcia. "I think it's because of the hassle of buying tickets."

Sometimes, I suggest, it looks as if the Dead could play "Louie, Louie" for two hours, and their audiences would still eat it off a stick.

"We've done it!" chuckles Garcia. "Things that were tremendously dull, and the audience didn't mind. They *expect* us to go pearl diving and occasionally come up with clams. They know what's going on. They're not as critical as we are, of course, because we're at every performance."

Deadheads will finally get a chance to see the band all they want in June, when the movie *The Grateful Dead* is released. The film centers on the Winter-land concerts of October 1974 but is "not a documentary or concert film," according to Weir. "It's impossible to describe."

"It's entertaining, though. I was surprised," says Garcia. "We used nine crews and ended up with one hundred fifty hours of film. It got to be a dance between them and us onstage. Some of the footage is startling. Then we went through two years of incredible doubt, crisis after crisis, as the movie was endlessly eating bucks. Every time I thought about something, my mind would come back to the film and I'd get depressed. It's boiled down to two hours and ten minutes now, but it sure took a lot of energy."

In pursuit of technical perfection, the Dead took the film to Burbank Studios, the most advanced facility for film sound-tracks but still relatively primitive by recording industry standards. They wanted it synced to within one frame, and went ahead with the mixing even though the gadgets needed to get their tape onto the film hadn't been invented yet. Working closely with the engineers, the Dead finally succeeded, causing considerable excitement in the movie community.

I quote a line to Garcia from a ROLLING STONE interview in 1972, when he said he didn't have a particular personal philosophy; all he had was the ability to perceive cycles. Where, I wonder, are the Dead on their cycle now?

"I have no idea what I meant by that," he says. "I can say anything when I'm asked a question. Bob and I once set up a formula to deal with interviewers: Depending on how the question was phrased, not the content, we would answer yes or no. It's not uncommon for me to say things that aren't true. Honesty right now has nothing to do with ultimate truth. That's why I try to leave a lot of possibilities for different interpretations in my lyrics. People can fill in their

own ideas and make new connections. There's a greater level of participation."

I ask Garcia if the small-scale tour and the reliance on outside professionals for the new record and movie were a concession that traditional Grateful Dead anarchy doesn't work.

"We still have the fundamental formlessness of the music," he says. "What makes it interesting is its ability to come to form at any minute. A producer is not a matter of form. He's there to see where our ideas are going and make sure they get there."

Garcia walks into the adjoining suite and rummages around. He returns with a four-page paper called "With Future Events Having an Increasingly Less Predictable Nature." It says things such as, "Undeniability in concept and translation/transmission will be greatly more important. Language will have to be treated more precisely, creatively, and seriously. Manners will increase in effective use as precise shortcuts for defining day-to-day relationships."

"That's what it's all about: future events having an increasingly less predictable nature," says Garcia. "That was written by our old manager, Jon McIntire, a tremendous cat. He's fallen in with some futurists at Stanford. He's interested in formalizing the attitude of the Grateful Dead community philosophically. The trick is to be as adaptable and changeable as possible. What they're studying in physics now – the smallest observable phenomena in nature, charmed quarks and whatever – nobody knows what it is. It could change our entire structure of reality. Literally anything is possible."

"We could even be watching our own minds in those sub-atomic particles," says Weir. "There's this theory that the nuclear reaction of the sun is only on the surface. Inside could be consciousness. *The universe could be a mind.*"

Time for sound check. We head downstairs through a lobby full of Deadheads and into a limousine. Hart, dressed in a silver Porsche jacket, leans back over the front seat and tells how he was walking around the Village in the morning and was approached by an old bum. "He followed me for a whole block, giving me this sob story about how bad off he was," Hart says. "The guy really had his rap down, so I gave him ten bucks. He about had a heart attack. Begging here is a lot more professional than in San Francisco. It's a matter of survival in New York."

The biker-Dead alliance dates back to mid-Sixties San Francisco; at left and on the following pages, Hell's Angels rev their motors in front of the Winterland, 1967.

Backstage, an Angel is talking to Lesh about how a friend of his got into a fight and the opponent pulled off the guy's wooden arm and clubbed him with it. After a respectful silence, I ask Lesh if anarchy can work without big bucks.

"You answered your own question, man," he replies. "You can't have it without a whole lot of money." ℭ

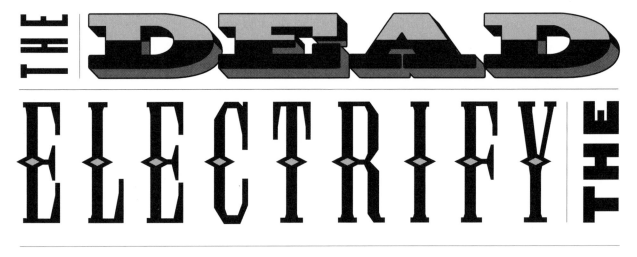

THE GRATEFUL DEAD'S ten-year dream climaxed on September 16, when the band played its third and final concert under a full moon at the foot of the Great Pyramid. Despite some problems – musically and otherwise – neither the Dead nor Cairo is likely to forget the historic first rock shows at the Pyramid.

Though the Egyptian concerts were more or less a personal whim on the part of the band, they became the basis for a serious pilgrimage for hard-core Deadheads. A chartered jet from California touched down in New York to pick up East Coast Deadheads and then continued to Cairo. The scene on board the plane resembled Haight-Ashbury, circa 1967. Ken Kesey was there, along with his brother Chuck, their families, assorted Pranksters, Owsley, Mountain Girl – all familiar faces from psychedelia – and younger Deadheads.

Amazingly, the 110 Deadheads sailed through customs at the Cairo airport without a single bag being searched.

The Dead had already shipped in twenty-five tons of equipment for sound, lighting, filming and recording the concerts for a live album and movie. The venture cost the band $500,000, and proceeds from the concerts (tickets cost from $1.50 to $7.50) were donated to the Egyptian Department of Antiquities and to the Faith and Hope Society, a home for the handicapped.

The entourage occupied the first day in the 110-degree desert heat by exploring the pyramids. Basketball star Bill Walton, who accompanied the Dead, was filmed by Ken Kesey climbing inside the Great Pyramid. The hotel's bars, restaurants and gardens became filled with American and British hippies, and Dead music poured out of cassette machines everywhere. Jerry Garcia hovered around the hotel in a good mood. "This should be strange enough," he said on his way over to the Great Pyramid to oversee the miking of the five-thousand-year-old tomb of Pharaoh Cheops, which was used as an echo chamber for the Dead's shows.

The band's first performance, September 14 at the Sound and Light Amphitheater, was less than spectacular musically. Before about two thousand persons – Deadheads, young Americans and Britons living in Egypt, Western travelers passing through and a mixed crowd of Egyptians – the Dead came onstage after an opening set by Hamza El-Din, a Nubian oud player. Garcia tuned up for fifteen minutes, and then the band eased into "Eyes of the World." That suddenly segued into Buddy Holly's "Not Fade Away." Bob Weir did a set of ill-received country songs, and the show came to a close with "Around and Around." There was no encore.

Before the second concert, a Merry Prankster named George climbed up the Great Pyramid to plant a Dead banner at the top. Again, Weir performed country songs, like "Mama Tried." The Merry Pranksters undertook a long jam of electronic noise, and the show ended with "Terrapin Station" and "Sugar Magnolia."

The Dead's third night was their best. Playing during a lunar eclipse, the band opened the first set with "Bertha" and closed with "Deal." But the audience didn't really come alive until after the intermission, when the Dead's new reggae song, "Shakedown Street," woke everyone up. Then, in what Bob Weir called an act of "questionable taste," Kesey and his Pranksters set off rockets and started taunting the Egyptians in the crowd with chants of *"Bakshish, bakshish,"* a phrase used by Egyptian beggars, which, loosely translated, means, "Tip me, rich Yankee." The night ended with the Dead's only encore of the three concerts, "One More Saturday Night."

"I think I kind of left my little reality at that point," Weir said about playing during the eclipse. "It was so surreal that I wouldn't even try to describe what went through my mind."

Bill Graham treated the whole crew to dinner at the nearby Sahara City nightspot to celebrate Kesey's birthday and then produced a surprise: The promoter had rented fifty camels and horses for the entourage's return to the hotel.

Graham, back in the States, was ecstatic: "You know, I've never danced in public before. I was never relaxed in front of a crowd. But the third night was one of the great experiences of my life – dancing to 'Sugar Magnolia' in front of the Sphinx and the Great Pyramid. In my old age, if I remember major events in my life, this will be one of them."

Weir was equally happy with the excursion: "Everybody feels somehow different from the experience. I don't know how to explain it. But I'd love to do it on a regular basis." ℰ

PYRAMIDS | BY LARRY KELLEY

BY KEN KESEY

REVISITING THE PYRAMIDS

" '*Bukra fil mish-mish*' is kinda the Egyptian version of the Mexicans' '*mañana*.' It translates as 'Tomorrow, in the time of the apricots.' But dig: There isn't any apricot season on the Nile . . ."

PLEASANT HILL, OREGON
October 17, 1995

DOWNWIND by a couple decades, peeking back through cracked mind mirrors because ROLLING STONE recently published a chunk of "The Search for the Secret Pyramid" and Jann had asked me to try to come up with the most memorable scene from that historic assignment. A grand gallery of Egyptian etchings comes flapping to mind:

– like that first night in Cairo, when the Ramadan fast ended and seven million uproarious believers broke out in a teeming rash of discordant harmony, heralding the rise of global Moslem might . . .

– or that afternoon our motormad taxi driver T'ud ("*Thud!*" I screeched from the backseat. "This gear-grinding tire-burning pedal-to-the-metal maniac's name is *Thud?*") drove me from Gîza out to Sakara, where a tunnel beneath the sand led us past hundreds of stone boxes big as Buicks, all of them coffins for the bulls that were elaborately sacrificed every year for hundreds of years thousands of years ago, each coffin carved from a solid block of rare black granite, and every one of them empty, enigmatic and depressing . . .

– or that chilly dawn my shadowy little Not-guide, Marag, guided me down through the dark throb of his ancestral village to score me some hash.

Great memories, but I'm afraid I had to disappoint Jann. The Egyptian memory that stands out most happens on another trip, four years later, when I finally convince friends and family to return with me to that fabulous land of the Pharaohs . . . by chance the same time hard-shell Baptist Jimmy Carter was getting hard-nosed Hebrew Menachem Begin to sit down and schmooze with Moslem moderate Anwar Sadat in the name of Peace . . .

– in the Time of the Apricots, when the Grateful Dead played the Great Pyramid.

Sadat's old lady helped put the gig together, explaining to Egypt's less than enthusiastic Arab allies that she understood their concern about infidel Rok'n Rollies playing the World's Most Ancient Temple, but in this particular case she did not consider it blasphemous as the promoters agreed that all prophets from the concert would go toward the construction of a soccer field for the use of the underprivileged children of Cairo.

Right. Prophets. But the Arab elders went for it. How could they have known what rough beast was lurching its way toward them across the desert by the truckful? How could they have imagined the prophet-gobbling appetite of a Rok'n Rol army on a full-scale campaign? Even the

gig's promoters never dreamed how un-prophetable the gig was gonna be. Only seven hundred tickets sold, mostly to hard-core Deadheads, government operatives and spoiled Saudis who motored over by the limo load. Local sales were zip. What need for the villagers to purchase tickets to these Gîza gigs? The Bedouin in the surrounding dunes enjoy better seating and get better sound than the spoiled Saudis in the expensive front row. Seven hundred measly tickets.

"Ah, well," the promoters sigh as they strap on their most philosophical Woodstock Grin. "Some things you gotta write off as the Will of Allah."

Bill Graham isn't one of these promoters. He was too sharp a businessman to back a dollar loser. But he shows up anyway, right on cue, for the sound check. This is the scene I mean . . .

It has been a hard, crazy afternoon. The Dead road crew is about the only thing that's properly wired. The equipment is unfamiliar (it's borrowed from the Who and shipped into Alexandria to save $), and the Egyptian electricity is uncooperative. The stage is a cruel anvil of hot stone situated right off the right paw of the crouching Sphinx. The sun is pounding like a brass hammer. It's a bitch.

The band is prowling around the black towers of amps and speakers, trying to find a little shade – "Let's fucking get this over with before this fuckin' guitar melts!" Hamza el Din, the opening act, is trying to tune his crook-necked instrument in front of a goose-necked mike. The instrument is an eight-stringed oud. Hamza's a Nubian, black as Mystery Itself. His backup group is twenty-five other Nubians, clustered uncomfortably around him on the hot stage. They're Hamza's school chums from his village, to the south. He thought it might make a nice diplomatic gesture if the Dead flew them in to help with the little Nubian homeboy chant that Hamza was planning to open the show with. Mickey Hart of course loves the idea:

"Twenty-five Nubians doing an African nursery rhyme? Groovy, fly 'em in."

None of them has ever been away from home before in their lives; now Yankee sound guys are trying to tell them where to stand and what mikes to use. The poor nervous Nubians did not speak American, they did not speak English – even *Egyptian* they did not speak! Nobody is communicating with anybody. "Yibble *yabble*," the Nubians chant. "This mike!" the sound guys yell. "*Eee-e-ek!*" the tortured equipment screams. A stone bitch of a sound check.

It is into this hot and hectic tableau that Bill Graham comes stalking, right out of the Sphinx's gritty armpit. I caught the crux of the moment on a cheap cassette.

"Uncle Bill!" Bob Weir calls. "You just couldn't keep away, could you?"

GRAHAM, hands on hips, shaking his head at the stir-fry of strange ingredients sizzling before him: "Never thought it would happen, not in a million years."

ME: "Quite the mixed bag, huh, Bill?"

GRAHAM, awed but not overwhelmed: "Never woulda believed it. Seemed insurmountable. What a mishmash."

ME, oracular and ominous: "Nobody has any idea what a mixture like this might produce."

RAMROD: "Witch-doctor shit. Ting tang, wallawalla bing bang."

NUBIANS, chanting along with the tune Hamza is finally coaxing from his oud: "Yibble, *yabble* gobble dobba dobba doom boom . . ."

MICKEY, stirring in another rhythm on a little hand drum: "It's a twelve-tone scale worked into twelve different rhythm sequences, repeated twelve times, got it?"

GRAHAM: "Mickey's in hog heaven."

NUBIANS: "Hotcha motcha gotcha gotcha *zoom* zam . . ."

PHIL, hunched turkey-necked over his bass: "Thomma *boom* zoom sorta got it –"

NUBIANS: "Hotcha motcha gotcha gotcha getcha *zoom* zam –"

JERRY, stepping at last into the dangerous desert sunshine, tentative, like a gray old lion in tinted sadglasses: "Zwangle, squeedle dweedle dorngle gottit *now* zwornk!"

GRAHAM: "Tasty . . ."

And suddenly, at that moment, under that acetylene sun, it all fluxes together – like silver solder fluxing together with gold, a twist of bright wire, stringing all these different rhythms and races, these alien scales and ancient civilizations, into a kind of necklace of sound, say, might mail to, say, Queen Hatshepsut if he had her address. Indeed, a tasty trinket.

GRAHAM, hot and getting hotter: "Damn, I hope somebody with a good tape machine has the sense to record this."

* * *

NOBODY DID, as far as I know, except me and my sixty-buck Sanyo. But even on the crappy cassette, you can hear how the hectic scene started changing for the better from the moment Bill Graham showed up – as though the bastard were some kind of bad-vibe blotter. The hotter he got, the cooler the scene became until, at some secret signal, the whole stage full of chanters and drummers and rockers shifted out of Nubian homeboy raga into Buddy Holly rock as smooth as the transmission on one of those Saudi limos, from "Hotcha motcha gotcha gotcha gee" to "I'm gonna tell you how it's gonna be" without nicking a cog.

Now, lo these many years later, listening to the tape, it all seems to flux together again . . . and, by golly, you know, maybe it was all part of that ROLLING STONE assignment after all, the same way the concert at the Sphinx was part of Uncle Bill's business whether he promoted the damn thing or not.

That night at the gig, a conjunction of profound events went down: As the Grateful Dead were playing "Dark Star" through the Who's equipment between the paws of the Sphinx at the foot of the Great Pyramid in the Season of the Apricots, the *Sahara moon* underwent a total and completely unforeseen eclipse (check it out, September 17, 1978) at the very hour that *Keith Moon* was blacking out and dying from an overdose at his flat in London!

What does it all mean? Probably nothing. But it was a trip, a for-sure trip, and I was glad to be on board. ☯

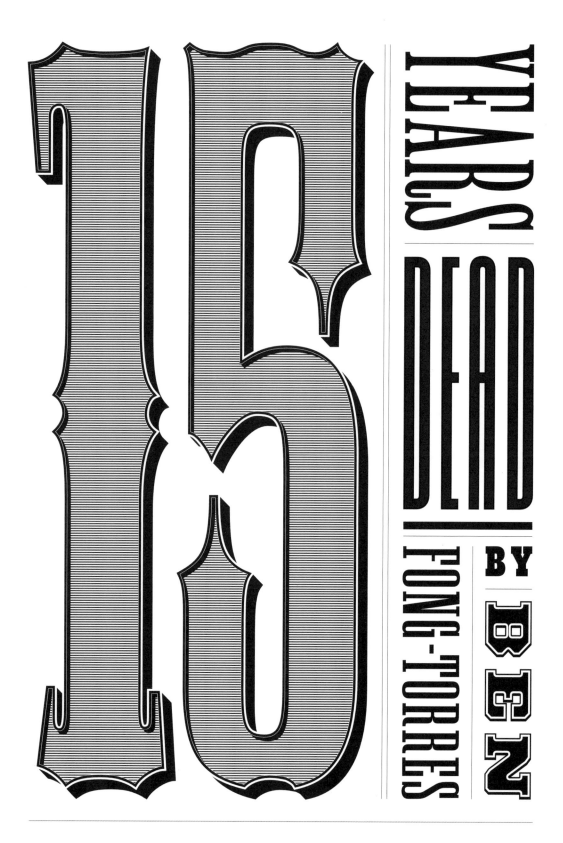

15 YEARS DEAD

BY BEN FONG-TORRES

THEY DIDN'T SING "Happy Birthday" to the Grateful Dead, who turned fifteen on June 7 in Boulder, Colorado. Not that they didn't try. Pockets of Deadheads in the crowd of fifteen thousand at Folsom Field, on the campus of the University of Colorado, attempted to work up the simple song. It wasn't that they were met with stony silence or anything. The problem was that it was impossible to be heard over this . . . *rumble* of noise that started as soon as Warren Zevon finished his set. The mix of whooping and whistling, of screeching and screaming, filled the air during the Dead's ten-minute tuning-up. It rose in volume with the beginning of each new song and settled into mere pandemonium between numbers. But Boulder, where Deadheads had gathered by the thousands the day before, was calm compared to New York.

Three weeks earlier, the Dead had played Long Island's Nassau Coliseum. For three straight nights – well, for three *consecutive* nights, anyway – crowds of seventeen thousand Deadheads packed the joint and gave out a nonstop screech reminiscent of a Beatles crowd. The only quiet moments were for the sweet, slow songs that Jerry Garcia sang. Those were like campfire sing-alongs, everybody joining in on "Sugaree" and "Candyman," arms and cassette microphones swaying side to side in the air. The rest of the time, it was get up on the chair, Jack, and scream the night away – through two sets (three hours, plus the legendary "break"), through a fiery drum duet by Mickey Hart and Bill Kreutzmann, and through songs ranging from "Johnny B. Goode" and "El Paso" to the newest stuff, like "Alabama Getaway," which was received as an instant classic.

"New York," one of the Dead family had said before the first concert, "is extra intense." For the Dead, the East Coast has been intense for years. This time about fifty-one thousand tickets were sold with no advertising, save some radio station announcements. On their end of the deal, the Dead turned an arena into a cozy room, keeping the people wired with a mix of Sixties vibes and Eighties technology. Throughout the auditorium, one noticed the reach and clarity of the rented sound system.

Microphones, on stands, sprouting out of the packed floor area, invariably connected to expensive portable tape decks, such as the Nakamichi 500 being operated by a young man with a scarf on his head and a knapsack on his back. Near the middle of the hall, another mike was attached to a crutch, held aloft and angled toward the stage speakers.

The dancing, true to the Western-based music of the Dead, was free-form hoedown. "The Woodstock Sun Grope," as one writer aptly put it, is alive.

The people doing the dancing, passing the joints and making the tapes were by no means all time-warped hippies. Probably half the crowd was under eighteen, and there were even some first-daters making out in the balcony while the newest Dead member, Brent Mydland, performed "Easy to Love You." His is a plains-of-California voice, high like Neil Young's and romantic like Jesse Colin Young's. His keyboards – electric piano and organ – give the Dead the extra coloring they'd been missing in the last years of Keith and Donna Godchaux's membership in the band.

Fifteen years after arriving on the San Francisco scene, and after having gone through acid, financial burns, Haight-Ashbury, busts, death and creative highs and lows as extreme as drugs could take them, the Grateful Dead are still drawing bigger and younger crowds. As a band, they sound fresher than ever. And they may be on the verge of their first hit single.

Of course, their albums have always jumped onto the charts – but that's because of the automatic 250,000 or so snapped up by Deadheads. The Dead have even placed a few singles on the charts – "Truckin'" and "Uncle John's Band" reached the bottom half of the Top 100 ten years ago, and more recently, "Good Lovin'" (from *Shakedown Street*) threatened. But through the years, the Dead, saddled with an image as washed-up hippies, have been anathema to most radio programmers.

That is, until *Go to Heaven* and its first single, "Alabama Getaway." Showcased on *Saturday Night Live* in April, "Alabama" almost immediately became the most-played album track on album-oriented rock radio stations.

* * *

ON THE EVE of the first concert in Boulder, Garcia sat on a bed in his Holiday Inn room. The beds were covered with blue velour spreads Garcia had brought in himself. In the tradition of touring rock artists, the TV set was on with the sound off. At 10:00 p.m., Garcia for once wasn't wearing shades, but his glasses were tinted a smoky gray. He wore – what else? – a plain black T-shirt and beige tennies. The subject was hit records, and Garcia was chortling.

"That's incredible," he said about the airplay "Alabama" was getting. Of course, he's often thought about having a hit. "Oh, sure," he agreed. "We were sure our very first record was going to be a hit." He laughed heartily.

Fifteen years ago Garcia had no idea how long the band might last. "I wasn't thinking about time," he said. "I was hoping it would do something like what it's done. It went way past all my expectations."

Despite the years and the tolls the Dead have paid, Garcia sees few fundamental changes. "The only big difference," he said, "is that our functioning ability has gotten to a point where it's competent. On our worst nights we're competent. It used to be on our worst nights we were just *bad*." He chuckled. The Dead, after all, were famous for dropping acid before shows and, subsequently, for many musically wasted nights. "Now I'll walk away from the bad ones not nearly as wounded as I used to feel. And not only that, it's more *the whole band* will feel that we haven't had a good night rather than one of us. Used to be that thing where everybody might have a good night but me. That tells me that somewhere along the line our whole aesthetic has gotten more focused. We share more of a common vision."

Going on thirty-eight, Jerry Garcia obviously doesn't feel his age. "I try not to lose touch with my more youthful self," he said. "I still basically don't think of myself much differently than I did when I was about seventeen. I may have a case of extremely protracted adolescence. I still get treated like a kid in certain circumstances." Garcia is, in fact, often in a protective bubble, watched over by band associate Rock Scully, with whom Garcia shares a Marin County house.

"It's just . . . I mean, anybody who's a little off the wall is not a member of that invisible adult class that moves gracefully through every aspect of life – everything from walking into banks, insurance, tax, all that straight shit. I certainly see it, but I don't feel that I'm part of the adult world. Nobody I know's like that. The only other side of that world is the kids. Like walking through an airport, which is as close as I get to the public – apart from walking through the streets – you're thrown in with lots of more or less normal people; if there's a family traveling, it's usually the kid I can relate to, if I have to."

In Boulder, Garcia didn't hide from people. He often sat in the small lobby of the Holiday Inn, talking with friends. But for every stranger who ventured up to him, there were knots of others, decked out in Dead T-shirts, who grabbed an eyeful, then walked away, affecting nonchalance.

When Garcia does talk with teenagers, he said, it's "one-on-one." There are exceptions, of course, but he thinks he's no longer a spiritual guru to the counterculture, the gifted rapper known as Captain Trips. "Most people who've gotten at all past a very superficial involvement have read the interviews and stuff and heard me talk my way out of that space," said Garcia, laughing. "So if that space surrounds me somehow, or I'm identified with it, they know it's not something I subscribe to personally. And most people don't come on to me as if that were the case. If they experience anything, it's the normal celebrity fear. I get that myself. I was always afraid to meet the people who awed me." Those, he said, were mostly bluegrass musicians. "I would never have the nerve to introduce myself. I was much too shy for that. But I'd go see them." To Garcia, then, the younger Deadheads "are really the same kind of people we were when we were their age. The thing they like about Grateful Dead music has something to do with what we like about it. It's not a case of mistaken identity. They know who we are."

* * *

WHAT WE STAND FOR, and what we represent to a lot of people, is misfit power," said guitarist Bob Weir. At age thirty-two, Weir retains his preppie good looks. He was idly tuning his Ibanez guitar in the clubhouse of the university's football team, along with Phil Lesh, Brent Mydland and John Barlow, Weir's old friend and cowriter. Barlow, a rancher in Wyoming who was filling in for Danny Rifkin as road manager on this segment of the tour, piped up: "We're positive miscreants. Weir and I always vied for biggest asshole in our prep school." The two, only a couple of nights before, had attended a reunion at Fountain Valley School, just outside nearby Colorado Springs.

"I don't wanna talk about that," Weir snapped, but Barlow spoke up again. "We saw a lot of people our age who definitely had a little soul death," he said. This triggered Weir. "Yeah," he said with a sigh, "twenty, thirty years older than me – and chronologically maybe a couple of years younger."

Weir, who has a nervous, halting style of speaking, suddenly sounded determined. "I refuse to get hammered by age into being an old fart," he said. On the couch, working on a steak and a glass of wine, Phil Lesh jerked his head back

and widened his eyes. "I'm not clutching to my youth," Weir said, "but there is a spirit here of, 'We gotta keep things fresh.' I see friends of mine who haven't managed to keep things fresh in their lives, and I find that lamentable. I think we relate more readily to people who haven't had the life kicked out of them. Kids – and older people – who are gonna stay young forever." People such as Michelle, a thirty-six-year-old law school graduate and friend of the Dead family who'd flown in from Northern California to catch the Nassau shows. "I can't talk about it," she said backstage after the first concert. "To describe the indescribable – ta-ta! Basic problem." But she did talk, in a husky, awed voice, about the Dead as "quantum chemists" and about their ability to, if I heard right, "stretch the Taos."

Tom Davis, a writer and performer for *Saturday Night Live,* declared himself a Deadhead of ten years' standing. Sitting at our table, he concurred with Michelle. "There are a limited number of bands that are capable of 'stretching the Taos,'" he said. Then, in an officious tone, he added: "An American band, too, I'm proud to say. Even while our country is hanging its head, at least we have people like the Grateful Dead!"

A lawyer friend of Michelle's who also made the trip told about a superior court judge in Sonoma County (in the wine country north of San Francisco) who's a Deadhead. "He plays tapes on a deck in his chambers, and he's got a Dead sticker on his blotter." Michelle added: "My husband, Chris, has argued final arguments – to *juries!* – behind three nights of the Dead. His trip is so charged that he wins."

Such stories abound among Deadheads. In San Francisco's Bay Area Music Archives, Paul Grushkin, twenty-eight-year-old keeper of the books and records, spoke warmly about his twelve-year romance with the Dead. "The Dead are a very personal thing," he said. "I think half the fun of being at a Dead concert is watching the changes you go through. Watching yourself metamorphose . . . maybe in time with the music."

Grushkin recalled a high point, a Winterland show in 1972: "I didn't think I was that stoned – maybe something like hash, or peyote . . . Anyway, that *click,* whatever it is that Deadheads say about going into hyperspace, where suddenly everything is quite . . . different . . . unnatural, not your normal course of events . . . And I couldn't decide through the next three or four hours whether it was me feeling that way, or if it was because of the band, or the audience, or the drugs."

In Boulder, Garcia, trying once again to explain his band's appeal, said: "They might like us in the same spirit that people like drugs. I think we're like a drug, in that sense. People turn each other on to us. And there's that personal contact involved with every Deadhead. There are very few Deadheads who are Deadheads in complete isolation."

"They've helped me to know myself a little better," said Grushkin. "Dead concerts are a marvelous time for introspection and reflection. It's the perfect music for that. At concerts, I see people who just suddenly get the spirit, like you do at a gospel concert. You understand – not for everybody else, but for yourself. And what happens is, you are immediately, totally distant from your wife or loved one, from everyone. There are moments when it is really splendid or scary, and it's for you alone. It goes back to the [Robert] Hunter song, 'That path is for your steps alone.' I think it's 'Ripple.' "

The Dead concert experience has been crystallized in two one-liners. A bumper sticker of unknown origin declares THERE IS NOTHING LIKE A GRATEFUL DEAD CONCERT. Even better is a remark by Bill Graham, so good he even had it painted on the side of Winterland on the occasion of its closing (with a Dead concert, of course): "The Grateful Dead are not only the best at what they do; they are the only ones who do what they do."

It follows, then, that Deadheads are a unique breed. Some have even been known to steal and fence their way across the country – or, in 1978, to Egypt – to see (and tape-record) the Dead. I told Kreutzmann that many Deadheads have little more than their tape decks, backpacks and thumbs. He straightened up. "I think they're damn lucky!" he shouted. "They're luckier than hell that they don't have to be tied down to a regular old nine-to-five shit job, and get off on traveling with a pack and an Uher. I think that's sweet as hell!"

David Gans, a Dead tape collector, knows a Bay Area "tapehead" who owns upward of one thousand hours of the Dead in concert. "He's obsessed," said Gans. "He's a twenty-nine-year-old *virgin,* for Chrissakes! I said to him, 'What about women? Marriage? A little sleazy sex now and then?' He said, 'Well, I've gotten by *this* long without it.' " Gans shook his head. "You remember that April Fools' Day concert [at the Capitol Theater in Passaic, New Jersey] where they came out playing each other's instruments on 'Promised Land'? That was here, in Oakland, by the third."

Gans, twenty-six, used to be a full-tilt Deadhead, but he's begun to pare down his tape collection. "There's always a new generation of Deadheads," he said. "People grow up and out of it." Gans, a musician (whose band does a number of Dead songs) and freelance writer, struggled with having to be defensive about it. "There's a certain level of embarrassment attached to being a Deadhead," he said. "It is so frowned on by the nons. There's jazz heads who go, 'Don't talk to Gans. He's a Deadhead. He doesn't understand McCoy Tyner.' And the truth is, the thing the Dead do is jazz, only in a rock idiom. It's musical conversation, much as the best jazz is."

Paul Grushkin has no problem being a Deadhead right in the open. "I enjoy spending a weekend getting prepared for a concert, and all of my Deadhead associates do the same thing," he said. "I don't think it's quite like preparing for the Eagles or the Cars. With the Dead, there's an excitement that begins Thursday or Friday and builds. You're really bouncing off the walls, as if you're psychically getting ready to give it your all, and whatever it is, you're gonna be right on top of the mother. In fact, it's been about six months" – Grushkin's eyebrows danced – "and boy, I'm ready for another one. Goddamn!"

* * *

IN NEW YORK, Bob Weir, speaking for the band, had begged off interviews until Colorado. The Dead, he'd said, were going through some delicate changes and "learning about each other," and they couldn't have an outsider watching, listening and asking questions. Weir had sounded weary, as if he were talking about a marriage on the rocks.

Three weeks later, in Boulder, I asked about those changes. It turned out they were musical, and still incomplete. "It's not quite as manifested as I'd expected," he said, "but the old format has just about been played out. We have July and part of August and October off. In that time, I expect a fair amount of new material will be written, and there've been a lot of discussions about rethinking our mode of presentation."

"The old format," Lesh explained, "is two segments. The first is always songs, and the second is longer stuff, medleys, jams." The idea now, he said, is to "get it tighter." "Make it more succinct," said Weir. "There's got to be a way to get more music in."

Does this notion symbolize other changes within the band?

"Well," said Weir, who has a habit of giving that word a Western, Gabby Hayes twist, "I think we're a bit more flexible and musically mobile than we have been for years. We got into sort of a static situation with Keith and Donna, where we were pretty much locked into this old format. Then for the past year or so with Brent, it's been like getting to learn what to expect, and getting him to learn our operation." "Expect the unexpected," Mydland interrupted. Weir continued: "We're just now starting to loosen up to the point where we were, say, back in 1970, '72, where we can start drifting from key to key, from rhythm to rhythm, and in the jams, some interesting stuff has come up. Once again, we're tending to go to new places every night."

After seven years with the Dead, pianist Keith Godchaux and vocalist Donna Godchaux were invited to leave the band. "Essentially," said Lesh, "it was 'Don't you guys feel you could profit from being on your own, doing what it is you do best, 'cause you're not doing it with us?' " The reason given was "limitations." The Dead wanted more and different keyboard sounds; Keith stuck to his grand piano.

Brent Mydland, twenty-seven, who in June 1980 celebrated fifteen months with the Dead, had played behind Batdorf and Rodney, and then with his own band, Silver, before touring with the Bob Weir Band. When the Dead met to discuss the Godchaux situation, it was Garcia, whose own band had toured with Weir's band, who suggested Mydland.

"One of the first few albums I ever bought," said Mydland, "was the first Dead album." Weir and Lesh looked surprised. "I didn't know that," said Lesh.

"I saw them live at the Fillmore West," Mydland continued. "And one thing that stood out was 'Good Morning Little Schoolgirl.' " That song featured the vocals and keyboards of the menacing-looking Ron "Pigpen" McKernan.

Pigpen died in 1973, his liver shot through with alcohol. In a group known as the house band for the Acid Tests of Ken Kesey and his Merry Pranksters, and a band who – even into the mid-Seventies – was said to enjoy spiking anything potable, Pigpen never took drugs, except once, when he was dosed.

Now, Garcia says that the drug image was overblown. "It's always been part true and part false. It's never been anything but something you do in addition to playing music. The fundamental thing we're doing is being a band, not selling or promoting drugs. The fact that we all take drugs isn't even true. Not all of us do take drugs, and none of us takes drugs regularly. I think drugs are just a reality of American life, in one form or another. I mean, hell, they're there."

Still, there's no arguing that they were more there for the Dead than for most people, especially in the early days. Hart was talking about how the band used to drop acid before virtually every show, and that prompted Kreutzmann to mention a major change in the Dead.

"In attitudes, how you feel before you go on," he said. "We don't get all wired and crazy." An example: "We really burned hard yesterday [in Boulder]. It's like you have a bank account of psychic energy, and we used a lot yesterday. So I woke up this morning feeling a little behind and tired, and instead of going out and using stimulants to feel up, I just wait till the music comes around and let it build like that."

And the rest of the band will pick up on it? Hart replied: "The band will let it be. This band is sensitive to everything: the weather, attitudes . . ."

* * *

GOOD VIBES!" Jerry Garcia chortled gleefully. "Too much! How perfect!" I'd just told him about a visit I'd recently made to 710 Ashbury, and about C.J. Filice, the fifteen-year-old boy who lives there with his parents and sister. In his room, on one wall, are posters of Cheryl Tiegs, Farrah Fawcett and a topless woman skier. On another wall – the big one, fronting the bed – are the Grateful Dead, in posters, photos and album-cover handbills. The kid's a Deadhead, and Garcia was delighted to hear it. "That makes me feel real good," he said, chuckling again.

The Eighties have come to the Haight-Ashbury. The street is dotted with chic boutiques and restaurants, art deco stores and a gay-owned disco. But the Sixties haven't left yet. Hippies-turned-winos litter storefronts; the Haight Ashbury Free Medical Clinic is still around and needed. And at a street fair just a month or so ago, you could pick up every artifact you missed out on in its heyday.

Up Ashbury, at 710, Michael and Francine Filice live in the two-story Victorian house they bought in 1973. It was a dump when they got it, in need of exterior paint, plaster, new plumbing and a fumigation. All they knew about the house was that a commune of between twenty and thirty people – and three dogs – had just moved out, leaving behind fallen ceilings and large painted rainbows in every room. Today, the house is lovely. The Filices spent five years restoring Victorian touches and even added to the house's original stained-glass windows and trim. The kitchen, where a good amount of dope was successfully hidden during one of the notorious busts, was just featured in *Better Homes and Gardens.*

The Filices take their house's place in rock history in stride. Having bought the first Dead album themselves when they lived in Manhattan (on the Upper East Side), they are at ease with the occasional visitors. "They just sit out front and look," said Michael, a wine importer. "They are in awe. It's like a saint had lived here."

Their son, C.J., was not a Dead fan – "I thought it was kinda hick music" – until a high school friend, Gino, got him to a concert last year. Now the Dead are his favorite group, and the only other bands he likes are the Allman Brothers, Led Zeppelin and the Stones.

In the kitchen, C.J., Gino and another schoolmate, Dave, talked about the Dead. All three are clean-cut and laugh off the presence of drugs at Dead concerts. "Even though the people there are kinda weird," said Gino, "it's a calmer crowd than the punks." Asked why he likes the Dead, Gino said, "Some of the songs really get you, I guess," and laughed, embarrassed. At school, said Dave, "Out of a thousand, the majority don't like 'em. The punks have this line, 'The Dead are dead.' " But Dave is a loyalist. "I want them to play 'Ripple' at my funeral," he said, beaming. "And if they can't make it, we'll play a tape, or we'll have Beluga Oil." Beluga Oil? "That's a band. They play a lot of Dead."

I asked the boys what they know about hippies. "Revolt," C.J. said. Dave added: "To be free. They were running everything, concerts in the middle of the streets. People were doing what they wanted where they wanted." From that knowledge, do they have a positive or a negative impression of hippies?

"Positive," said C.J. "I thought it was pretty good," says Dave. "It started the Dead. Had to be pretty good!"

* * *

AFTER FIFTEEN YEARS, what's ahead for the Dead? A tighter show? Maybe. Work in other media? Definitely. Mickey Hart got a taste of film work when he scored part of *Apocalypse Now,* and he wants to do more. Jerry Garcia, who edited most of *The Grateful Dead* movie and has done musical and sound effects on such films as Phil Kaufman's *Invasion of the Body Snatchers* and Roger Corman's *Big Bad Mama,* hopes to direct a movie version of Kurt Vonnegut's *Sirens of Titan,* to which he has secured the film rights.

"Moviemaking," he said, "is something I've always wanted to do. Not all the ideas I've had are music. Making a movie is really solving problems – visual and dramatic problems – of various sorts, and I've convinced myself I can do it, and do a good job of it."

Meantime, Garcia is providing the voice, via his guitar, for a robot child in a movie, *Heartbeeps* (starring Andy Kaufman and Bernadette Peters). He has something up his sleeve with Deadheads Tom Davis and Al Franken, and he and Dead lyricist Robert Hunter are considering making a movie out of various Grateful Dead songs. "There's a latent story there that we've been fooling with all these years. There's a story that kind of runs through."

In short, lots of new beginnings. I asked Garcia if he feels lucky to have survived and to be doing just what he wanted.

"I feel very lucky indeed," he said, laughing again. "I feel we've scored real well on that one. But I also feel that, in terms of being a practical model, we haven't done anything exceptional. That is to say, anybody who can imagine themselves doing something better than what they're doing should just go ahead and do it, and have no fear of failure or success but just go for it. That's all we've done. And apart from that, it's not as though we're especially gifted. We may have been lucky – even that, I don't know about – but we have been exceptionally determined."

I was reminded of a remark by a Deadhead. The Dead, he said, were unique for their willingness to take chances.

Garcia nodded emphatically. "And we'll continue to take them. That's our shot. That's who we are. And we're also an illustration that you can go through life that way and it'll work. It might be bumpy, but it's never boring." ℭ

THE
DEAD
HEAD
PHENOMENON

BY CHARLES PERRY

Winter 1980, College Papers

« 147 »

THE MAGAZINE that really should write about Deadheads is *National Geographic,*" declares Steve, a Deadhead from California. "Get some of those intrepid photogs in their helicopters out here to cover Mars Hotel. They'd get a good shot at some exotic folkways." Mars Hotel – the nickname this Illinois farm has been given for the duration – is awash with Deadheads. By one of those mind-blowing coincidences that make Deadhead folklore, the guy who lives at the farm offered his place to the fans just as Southern Illinois University cops were telling them they couldn't camp out in the amphitheater parking lot the night before the Grateful Dead concert.

More than fifty Grateful Dead fans have crashed for the night in the hayloft of the vast barn. By the light of day, scores of them can be seen drifting in and out of the farmhouse and cornfield, or milling around the stone well. Most are in tribal costume: for the women, loose and flowing gypsy dresses; for the men, jeans, headbands, T-shirts with innumerable designs based on covers of Grateful Dead albums. Cars, painted with skulls and roses as well as lyrics from Dead songs, are, like the people, in constant motion. About every ten minutes, a car takes off through the cornfield for a keg of beer to quell the stifling, humid August heat, or shows up with hitchhikers jamming the cab and riding the fenders.

The folklore, as in all tribal societies, is strictly oral. Rumors are passed – of fantastic dope, of peaceful, woodsy places to live. Reports are exchanged of particularly hot Dead shows of the recent past, of police hassles and great hitchhiking adventures. In all, it looks like a village gathering, except that these people who greet each other as old friends so familiarly are from all over the country. Sitting around this table under a tree are people from as far away as California, North Carolina, Colorado and Connecticut.

At the concert in Edwardsville, Illinois, that evening, some of the twenty thousand people crowding the grassy amphi-theater shout out the names of songs they want to hear. But the hard cores in the audience don't demand songs – they suggest them or simply say, "Play whatever you want!" Ecstatic reunions are blossoming everywhere – two young wood nymphs in tie-dye gossamer lean on a fellow's neck as if it were a Maypole, hugging and kissing him and each other. Behind a mixing board in the middle of the field, about forty Deadheads, mostly women, dance from the first note of the concert to the last. There's no recognizable step, just leaping and twirling – the sort of dancing little kids do.

During the first set, a distant electrical storm can be seen advancing. By the middle of the second, a brilliant lightning display forms a backdrop behind the band shell. The audience cheers the lightning, almost as if they were crediting the Dead for it. Soon a heavy shower drenches the area. The rain weeds out perhaps a third of the crowd – the local kids who just wanted to hear some rock – from the Deadheads, some of whom are taking off their clothes and running around in the rain, sloshing in the mud. Shades of Woodstock, which took place eleven years ago tonight.

DEADHEADS ARE NOT like other rock & roll fans. For one thing, in its thirteen years of recording, the band they follow has never had a Top Forty hit. For another, Deadheads are the most dedicated and exclusive fans in rock & roll.

To outsiders, the Grateful Dead are unlikely objects of devotion. Jerry Garcia, the lead singer and guitarist, is a bushy, avuncular figure with no particular stage act and not the slightest inclination toward flashy costuming. His beard is even turning gray. His solos have a rambling, why-not-this-note quality, and the lyrics are obscure in a rambling, why-not-this-meaning way.

Same with the Deadheads. Outsiders usually consider them hippie holdovers, nostalgic for the 1967 Summer of Love, when the Dead played legendary free concerts in the Haight-Ashbury to aimless, druggy aesthetes in tattered gypsy rags.

But to an insider, Garcia is *magic.* The Dead's music is positive, electric, high energy. The obscure lyrics, by Bob Hunter ("Just a box of rain, wind and water / Believe it if you need it, if you don't, just pass it on"), are on the order of prophecy, and their very obscurity shows a kindly respect for the listener's spiritual growth. Deadheads usually see themselves as searching souls on a journey that's a little hard to explain, except that it's definitely with the Dead.

The Dead's audience has been like that from the start. In 1965 the Grateful Dead were the house band of the Acid Tests, where everybody was encouraged to act exactly as weird as they felt. One of the principles of the Acid Tests was that there was no *show* that you came and watched – everyone in attendance was part of the performance. From the beginning, the Dead and their audience had a communal identity, a huge formless organism with sensed but unstated aims.

Trying to understand such an organism may be a doomed venture from the start, but Deadheads are sincere in their efforts to try to explain the reasons for their devotion. The afternoon before the show, Steve from California is lounging around among the vans in the amphitheater parking lot, occasionally selling some of his Grateful Dead decals. He's one of the hard core who follow the Dead around the country and support themselves by small-scale vending of Dead paraphernalia. He is wearing jeans and a blue bandanna headband; there's a distracted look in his eyes.

He still remembers the first Dead concert he attended, in 1973. "Everybody was *into* this energy of just living," he recalls. "It was just great. I was only thirteen then. Nowadays I can really appreciate what's goin' on. It's religious. Every show's like goin' to church."

He describes himself as a part-time carpenter and mechanic: "I couldn't hold down a full-time job and do this. The Dead tour eight months out of the year.

"I figure I've been in thirty states this year, following the Dead around. Being a Deadhead is a lot of fun, and it helps a lot of people meet other people like themselves. Deadheads know how to live and be honest, friendly, loving people. Not lettin' life get you down. I've been pretty low lots of times, but the Grateful Dead – the energy just brings you up."

Marilyn is a young woman in her late twenties from a small town near San Francisco. She has a flower delicately painted on her cheek, peace-symbol earrings, and four Dead buttons on her green gingham dress. These days she is reluctantly living with her seventy-year-old parents because state budget cutbacks in California have eliminated her job teaching preschool children.

What she'd like to do is earn a living making embroidery or stained glass, or run a horse ranch in Wyoming, or, best of all, work with the Dead: "I don't want to get caught up in a trip of money. So many people start making money, and they think they need more and more material things. It's a vicious circle; they get so caught up earning money, they can't really enjoy life or relax or do something like tour with the Dead. See the country, you know, and appreciate nature.

"It's like an unwritten law among Deadheads that everybody respects one another's rights. You can leave your stuff around without getting ripped off; everybody shares whatever they have, food or wine or drugs or whatever. As much as the music and the Dead themselves, I come for that feeling of closeness among the people. It's just like my lifeblood."

Back at Mars Hotel, the table under the shade tree is still crowded. Scott, a high school student from Des Moines, Iowa, waits patiently for the noise level to abate so he can speak in his quiet, serious manner.

He describes Deadheads as a mystery, "a culture that has been maintained over the years by the Grateful Dead. Other bands try to keep up with developments, and I respect that, but the Dead remain a very sacred culture that means a lot to a lot of people. As a friend of mine said, 'The Dead take care of us.' "

"I left New Jersey with forty-five cents in my pocket," a bushy-headed boy across the table chimes in. "Forty-five cents, and here I am. Something always comes along."

"I haven't missed a show yet," says another Deadhead. "Once I was really broke, and this chick gave me a ticket. *Gave* it to me."

Six guys have driven out together from college in Boulder, Colorado. Two have mustaches, one has a beard, the rest are clean shaven. To all appearances they are solid citizens, and in a certain way they are: They haven't reached the point where they will do absolutely *anything* to get to *every* Dead show. They drove out in two cars, rather than hitching, and when they catch the Chicago show, they'll stay in a hotel. For this show, they're staying in nearby St. Louis with the parents of one of them. He says, chuckling at his parents' naiveté, "They think it's great – all my 'college friends.' "

One of them is going for an M.B.A. in finance. He became a Dead fanatic three years ago. "You take a hit of acid and listen to the Dead," he says, "and you sort of just relate to them from then on. The first time I took acid at a Dead concert was when I really got into them. Now I can do it without acid."

Another one of this clean-cut crew is a hotel-and-restaurant-management major. He explains his reasons for liking the Dead with an air of having pondered the question long and hard: "They pretty much go with the moment." He has four- or five-hundred hours of taped concerts. One of his taping buddies has a twenty-five-page catalogue of Dead tapes identified and cross-referenced by date, place, audience, sound board, tape generation and performance rating.

His friend is praising this Dead concert with hoarse enthusiasm: "Oh, what a performance. When they were playing, it was tied to the weather so much . . . I got rained on today like I'll never get rained on in my life, and the people who were standing around me were my family."

* * *

D EADHEADS OFTEN describe themselves as a family. The Grateful Dead themselves are at the center of a huge extended family in Marin County, most of whom started as members of the audience.

The process of joining the Grateful Dead family has always been an instinctual one. For example, the late Keith Godchaux became the Dead's keyboard man in 1972, and later Garcia is said to have marveled, "This guy came along and said he was our piano player, and he was." Rock Scully has been manager, tour manager, Jerry Garcia's guardian and a number of other things (he's now their publicist) since the day in 1965 when he saw the Dead play in the psychedelic anarchy of an Acid Test. Owsley Stanley, the legendary LSD chemist, started his association with the group as their patron and has since worked for them off and on in various low-profile capacities.

Deadheads give the impression of being remote members of this same amorphous family, where everybody has a place, though it may not have yet been found. There is actually an organized (or semiorganized) club the Grateful Dead sponsor. It is a dues-free club that sends out occasional mailings and operates two telephone lines – one in San Rafael, California, and one in Passaic, New Jersey – to give out concert dates. The club began in 1971 (actually superseding an earlier fan club) with a tiny note on the Dead's seventh album (the one entitled *Grateful Dead,* but commonly called Skull and Roses, from the cover art). It read, "Dead Freaks unite. Who are you? Where are you? How are you?" followed by a post office box number. By 1973 there were thirty thousand members.

> *"We didn't invent our original audience. In a way this whole process has kind of invented us. I don't know why, and I can't say what motivates them. Back in the Seventies we had the same phenomenon of all these young kids. But now those are the people who are in medical school and law school – they are college people and professionals. They still come to shows. So now there are Deadheads everywhere. They've kind of infiltrated all of American society – everybody knows one."*
> *~Jerry Garcia, 1989*

Now there are about ninety thousand members, and a woman named Eileen Law looks after them. She works out of a Victorian house north of San Francisco, answering queries, sorting out letters of interest to various band members, filing proffered tapes of Dead concerts and acting as curator for the world's largest collection of Dead-inspired art. For anyone who suspected that Deadheads were mostly a bunch of leftovers from the Haight-Ashbury days, Eileen reports receiving an average of fifty letters a day, mostly from new members who are in high school or college. The greatest concentration of Deadheads is now on the East Coast, in places like New York and New Jersey.

A very important subtribe of the Deadheads is known as the "tapers." Tapers tape Dead concerts, and Deadheads swap tapes avidly – particularly if they've been to the taped concert and want to relive every microsecond of the show. There are a lot of tapers, as shown by a Brooklyn-based magazine called *Dead Relix* (now simply *Relix* and no longer exclusively devoted to Dead tapes), which has a circulation of twenty thousand. A more recent magazine, called *In Concert Quarterly,* also reviews the quality of taped performances (mostly of the Dead) available on the tape-swapping circuit.

Unlike most rock groups, the Dead tolerate tapers with equanimity. Concert floors bristle with microphones, and on occasion the Dead's soundman has let tapers plug into the band's sound board for current. Tapers repay the favor by sending to the Deadhead office copies of their tapes, which sometimes give useful information on the quality of the Dead's sound system.

Some Deadheads say they're into the Dead for religion, some for community, some for a party, some for the music or the lyrics.

But some people say that the reason Grateful Dead followers are so loyal is simply because they're all acidheads, and the Dead's music is addressed to people who are stoned on acid. Though there are plenty of Deadheads who don't drop acid, it probably *is* true that more Deadheads are into acid than are any other followers of rock groups. Steve from California speculates that there are some fifty thousand doses present at this concert, although, because it is the first concert of the tour, most of the acid is being saved for later.

* * *

THE APPEAL OF THE DEAD is not just that their music sounds good to someone stoned on acid, though, but that they bring together people attracted by many of the things associated with psychedelics: love of mystery and the unexpected, a search for community, quiet ideals, arts and crafts, even a way of dancing. Before the Haight-Ashbury, in an excess of optimism, invited the media publicity that ended up destroying it in 1967, San Francisco hippies were living in much the same way that Deadheads do today.

Says one New York Deadhead, dressed in a Day-Glo bathrobe, "Now it's harder, you gotta be dedicated. If you want to see the Dead shows, you gotta go through a lotta bullshit." There's no Haight-Ashbury: You have to follow the Grateful Dead around, probably dead broke yourself, and find your way into a much more clandestine psychedelic community. Deadheads nowadays appear to think of themselves less as the vanguard of a spiritual revolution, like the Haight hippies, than as a group of people whose devotion to the Dead sets them apart as a sort of nomadic tribe.

Jerry Garcia has credited the famous Deadhead loyalty to the fact that the Dead have "gamely stuck to the initial possibilities of bigger and better things for consciousness." By this he means the initial psychological and existentialist investigations of the Acid Test sort: supernatural harmony among people (with the possibility of telepathy not excluded), finding a deep and heroic meaning in everyday life, continual creativity and spontaneity.

The Dead stand virtually alone in sticking to the psychedelic adventure. Where old Beatles records may remind people of those days, the Dead still *tour.* Their concerts are regular gatherings that reinforce this psychedelic community's sense of itself and provide living examples of people who've spent a long time getting weird and seem to be surviving. This may be why hard-core Deadheads unanimously report that their conversions began not with a record but with a live Dead concert.

All is one, Deadheads tend to say, which makes it hard to say anything else. The closest the Grateful Dead have come to explaining what their trip is all about was a series of essays by Robert Hunter that appeared in the Deadhead newsletter in 1973 and 1974. They propounded a philosophy called Hypnocracy (the Greek word would appear to mean "government by sleep") and frequently quoted a smart-mouth sage known as St. Dilbert.

Deadheads camp out for three days waiting for tickets to go on sale for an upcoming Grateful Dead show at New York City's Radio City Music Hall, 1980.

For example: "When asked the meaning of life, St. Dilbert replied, 'Ask rather the meaning of Hypnocracy.' When asked the meaning of Hypnocracy, St. Dilbert replied, 'Is not Hypnocracy no other than the quest to discover the meaning of Hypnocracy? Say, have you heard the one about the yellow dog yet?'" This could be a Zen koan, a psychedelic metaphor for the mysterious burgeoning of existence from nonexistence, or simply a reference to how hard it is to "come to a logical conclusion" when you're stoned on LSD.

And while this may sound like unlikely intellectual baggage for a bunch of rock fans, the Deadhead office gets plenty of mail that suggests Deadheads understand it perfectly. Recently, a letter arrived that quoted from Lewis Carroll:

"What is a Caucus-race?" said Alice . . .
"Why," said the Dodo, "the best way to explain it is to do it . . ."
First it marked out a race-course, in a sort of circle ("the exact shape doesn't matter," it said), and then all the party were placed along the course, here and there. There was no "One, two, three and away!" but they began running when they liked, and left off running when they liked, so that it was not easy to know when the race was over.
And when the race was over, the Dodo announced that everyone had won and must have the prizes.

Another Deadhead, who calls himself Catfish John, sums it up this way:

"The secret is the magic. That's the whole secret. If you ever find the place where the people are dancing, and there's room, you see, like . . . God, it's too incredible. If you go where the dancers play, you'll see where total strangers are holding each other; there are big hand chains, thirty to fifty people all in a big circle, just dancing."

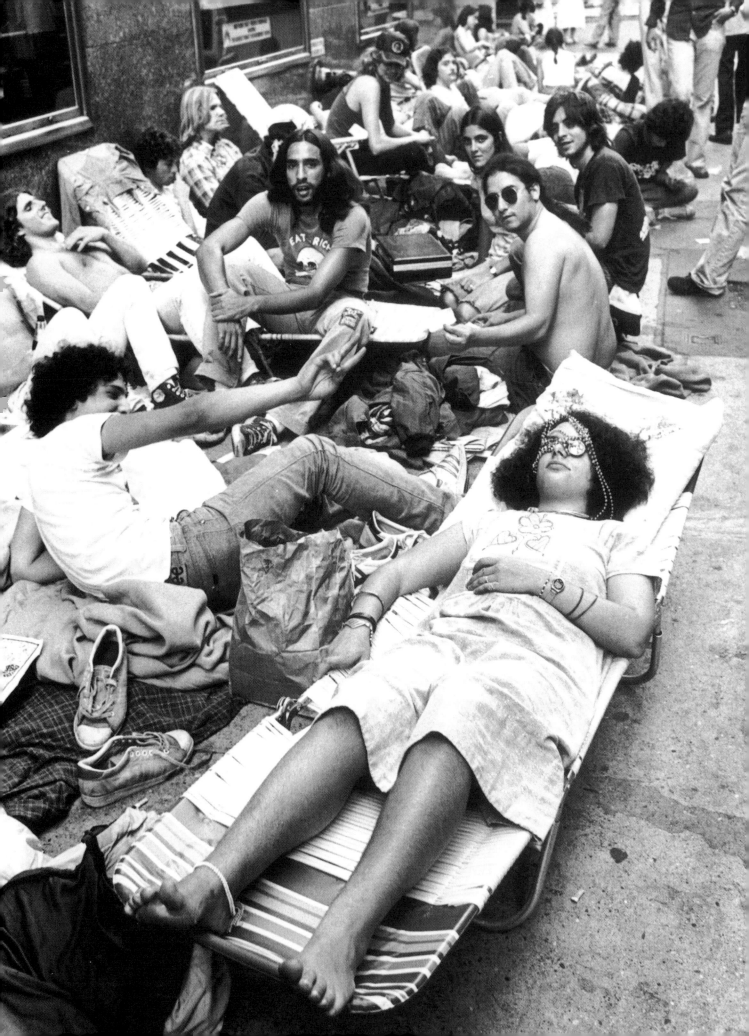

TALKING WITH

BY

DAVID GANS

&

BLAIR JACKSON

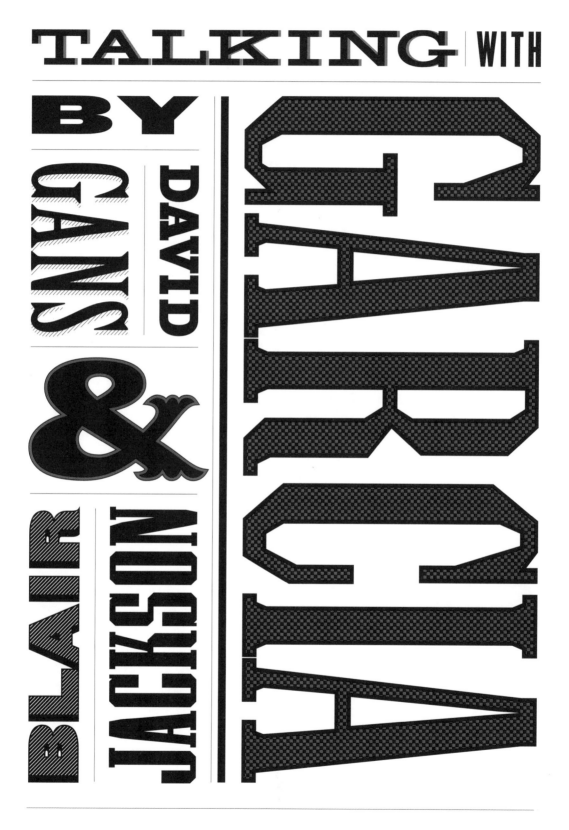

GARCIA

AFTER SEVENTEEN YEARS together, the Grateful Dead are one of America's longest-running musical arguments. Determinedly eclectic from the start, the Dead brought together influences ranging from bluegrass to avant-garde classical music to rhythm & blues, and the soup they've stirred up has bubbled, simmered down and boiled over many times. The flavor and texture have changed as various band members' influences have risen and fallen, but the core of the band – guitarists Jerry Garcia and Bob Weir, drummer Bill Kreutzmann and bassist Phil Lesh – has remained constant and committed to progress through numerous changes of peripheral personnel.

Because they eschew the normal stage and studio behavior of rock music – making admittedly weak records and playing four-hour, heavily improvisational concerts that include enough ballads to supply every other band on the face of the earth – the Dead have become something of an industry joke, symbolizing the "hippie band" way of doing business. But the Grateful Dead are true to their own vision; it would be ludicrous to imagine them changing their approach in search of a hit single.

Jerry Garcia has always been the most visible member of the putatively leaderless band, if only because he is the most genial and outgoing one. Though he rejects the mantle of guruhood with which many Deadheads have burdened him, it is obvious from his conversation that the man reads a great deal and gives much thought to the nature of existence. In the best sense of the "hippie" tradition, Garcia seems cognizant of mankind's tenuous hold on the continuum of life on this planet, and of the distinct possibility that we all may be little more than self-conscious specks in the grand scheme of the universe.

* * *

THERE'S AN EMOTIONAL TONE about the Grateful Dead that's unique. I've often likened it more to theater than to music, because I get the same mental relationship to the stage with you guys that I get at a really hot theatrical performance.

It's the same kind of chemistry.

There's much more trust happening at a Dead concert than is ever required at a James Taylor show.

That's right. The whole thing is this mutual agreement that allows the whole thing to happen. I'm conscious of that. It's definitely that for me. Being in the Grateful Dead is taxing in a way that nothing else is. When it's hard, it's the hardest thing there is, and when it's easy, it's magic. If things are happening in some kind of special way, then it's the easiest thing in the world – it's reflexive, almost. You don't think about anything, you don't plan anything, and it's no sweat.

There's not much effort involved. And for reasons we don't know, sometimes it's all there, and other times no amount of effort can make it be there.

If I tell somebody from the audience, "Tonight was really hard work, and it seemed impossible to get anything together," I always get these reports back that it was great. I'm not able to tell whether or not what happens to us emotionally or physically has any kind of relevance to the way everybody else experiences it. One of the things that's amazing about it is that everybody experiences it on their own terms. But

from the point of view of being a player, it's this thing that you can't make happen, but when it's happening, you can't stop it from happening. That's the closest I can get to really explaining it. I've tried to analyze it on every level that I can gather together, and all the intellectual exercise in the world don't do a thing – don't help a bit, don't explain it one way or another to any degree of satisfaction.

The Grateful Dead has some kind of intuitive thing – I don't know what it is or how it works, but we recognize it phenomenologically. I know it because it's reported to me hugely from the audience, and it's something that we know because we've compared notes among ourselves in the band. We talk about it, but all those things are by way of agreeing that we'll continue to keep trying to do this thing, whatever it is, and that our best attitude is to consider it a stewardship, in which we are the custodians of this thing.

One time I came home from a concert and wrote, "The Grateful Dead is immortal, but these men who play in the band are not."

That's exactly right, and that's the way we feel. It takes the responsibility out of our hands, which is comfortable. It's scary if you feel like you're responsible for it – that's a lot of energy to be responsible for. I've had to pay those dues in the psychedelic world.

Do you know how much power is ascribed to you – to the band as a whole, and to you as the focus?

Yeah, I know, and luckily I've already been able to disqualify myself from it. I know it's not me. They make the association, but that isn't the case. Well, it doesn't really matter what they believe: I know from personal, subjective testing that that is not the case.

Everybody has their own version, and that's good. That's one of the things about music that makes it a special thing. It can be experienced that way – it's so close to being perfect fascism.

What do you mean by that?

Well, it's so close to being perfectly manipulative. It borders on that, and people who use formula things on the audience are basically manipulating them in the same sense that fascism manipulates people.

You mean show-biz tricks?

Sure. That's just what they are, show-biz tricks.

There's a certain amount of that involved, though, in what you do.

Oh yeah, a certain amount of it, but our trip is to learn the tricks and then not use them. For us, we've discovered them – "Oh, far-out, when we do this, look what happens to the audience." "Yeah, let's not do that."

Do you always discard them?

Yeah, pretty much. We want for the Grateful Dead to be something that isn't the result of tricks, and we don't trust ourselves with it. We certainly don't trust anybody else with it.

It's always struck me that in your second sets, where theoretically things are very open-ended and loose, there always seems to be a time where you're in the middle of "Stella Blue," and all of a sudden it's "Sugar Magnolia," which is the most manipulative thing you can do. It says to everyone, "This is the end of the show," no matter what mood you're in. "Get into your party mood, 'cause this is it." You can't get much more manipulative.

We end up closing the door just like we open it up. In that sense, we create the framework. It has its ups and downs.

So you are conscious of it as a "show."

The contour of it, yes. And sometimes it *is* manufactured.

I've always thought it would be interesting if you ended on a down note; if suddenly the end was "Stella Blue."

We've done it. We used to end with real dire things in the old days: We used to end with "Death Don't Have No Mercy" and things like that. I like to end it gently sometimes. I really feel like I'd like for it to taper down.

Have "Black Peter" wind down and then walk offstage. But it doesn't, because here comes Weir with clang-clang, "Around and Around."

Well, there's always those possibilities. Weir pushes the show-biz stuff.

It's a good dynamic, I guess.

Yeah, it keeps people from taking it too seriously.

You don't take Weir very seriously, but in my conversations with him I've gotten the feeling that he lacks respect for you guys' attitude.

That's the thing. Weir is capable of being a tremendous cop at times. It's something he knows about himself. In the Grateful Dead, if you don't have a sense of humor, you're screwed.

When you're working in a band, you have to try to let everybody have his own voice the way he best sees it. There are always going to be things that create friction. It's part of what's interesting between he and I. He's always going to make decisions musically that I'm not going to agree with fully, but I'll go along with them anyway.

But on the other hand, there are ideas that Weir has that I would never have had, that in fact maybe only *he* has. That's his unique value: He's an extraordinarily original player in a world full of people who sound like each other. I don't know anybody else who plays the guitar the way he does, with the kind of approach that he has to it. That in itself is, I think, really a score, considering how derivative almost all electric guitar playing is.

There are so many different musics at work in the Grateful Dead, and you all seem to have learned them from their sources: Bill Monroe, Reverend Gary Davis, Hank Williams, Sonny Boy Williamson, et cetera. Younger musicians haven't been exposed to the pure goods the way you were.

The way I hear myself is that I hear my influences, to some extent, in myself . . . I've been influenced by people where I haven't been influenced by the notes they played, but by the attitude, the gesture – the other part of it. The substance rather than the form.

Give us an example.

Oh, like [John] Coltrane. I've been influenced a lot by Coltrane, but I never copped his licks or sat down and listened to records and tried to play his stuff. I've been impressed with that thing of flow, and of making statements that to my ears sound like paragraphs: He'll play along stylistically with a certain kind of tone, in a certain kind of syntax, for X amount of time, then he'll, like, change the subject, then play along with this other personality coming out, which really impresses me. It's like other personalities stepping out, or else his personality is changing, or his attitude's

changing. But it changes in a holistic way, where the tone of his axe and *everything* changes. It's a complete vertical change, then it'll narrow down to a point, then it'll open up again.

Perceptually, an idea that's been very important to me in playing has been the whole "odyssey" idea – journeys, voyages, you know? And adventures along the way. Golden Gate Park is an example of something that works that way. Walking through the park takes you through a lot of different worlds. All of a sudden you're in one of those places where everything is that weird prehistoric-looking shit, huge ferns – and it changes seamlessly from one thing to another. They really are different, their whole texture and everything. It's the work of an artist.

But in that case, it's probably a conscious construction, whereas with Coltrane it would be more instinctual.

Right, but maybe not. Coltrane was a smart guy. He knew what he was doing – he spent a lot of time studying music.

Do you always know what you're doing?

In what sense?

In a long solo passage where you play those paragraphs, and you'll maybe change something in your signal processing and start a new thing. Or sometimes it won't even be a gross change like that, but you'll change modes or scales.

Sometimes I do, and sometimes I don't. It used to be more rambling than it is now. Somewhere in the Seventies it became my goal to be more in charge, to know what I'm doing. So now if you stopped me somewhere, I'd be able to tell you what it is I'm trying to do. I've got that kind of a handle on it. When things are going really well, I know automatically; certain lengths start to be apparent. I automatically know how long eight bars is, sixteen bars, and where the one is gonna be. I can turn it around all different kinds of ways. I like to be able to know where it is, but I also like to be able to forget about it entirely.

So it becomes an ongoing, subconscious kind of thing that's there when you need it.

That's right. In the Grateful Dead, there's a certain philosophy about that. Rhythmically, you always know our policy is that the *one* is where you think it is. It's kind of a Zen concept, but it really works well for us. It makes it possible to get into a phrase where I can change into little phrase spurts, spitting out little groups of notes that are attached fives – five in the space of four, or five in the space of two is more common for me – and then turn that into a new pulse, where those fives become like a sixteenth-note pulse. Then I'm inside of a whole irregularly rotating tempo in relation to what the rest of the band is playing, when they're playing, say, the original common time. It produces this ambiguity, but all I have to do is make a statement that says, "End of paragraph, AND, one," and they all know where it is. We all have that kind of privilege – it's partly something we've allowed each other, and partly something we've gained the confidence to be able to do just by spending *a lot* of time playing together.

When we started working on "The Eleven" back in the late Sixties, we'd spend hours and hours and hours every day just playing groups of eleven, to get used to that phrase, then we started working out things in seven, and from seven we started working out things that were, like, two bars of seven, three bars of seven, four bars of seven – patterns, phrases and licks that were those lengths – and play them over and over and over again.

In an almost academic way?

Oh, yeah, a real academic way.

The band woodshedded together –

We had to do it. You can't play confidently and fluidly in those times without really knowing what you're doing.

Yet your image is not that of a studious band.

I know, but God, you can't play the way the Grateful Dead plays without working at it. It's not something that just *happened* to us. There was a long, slow process that brought that into being. It really started when Mickey first met Alla Rakha. He was completely blown out – it was the first time he'd ever heard Eastern players. He was so impressed with the level of technical ability and the time thing. The odd times got to be a big thing, because with Mickey, technique was no problem; he was a champion drummer. As far as technique, as far as hands were concerned, he was a guy of national stature.

A budding Buddy Rich.

Well, in a way. His background was fundamentals, which is more the military trip and less band music. But for him, the idea of that kind of discipline, what Indian music seems to have – the combination of tremendous freedom and also tremendous discipline – that really impressed Mickey, so he started right away studying with Alla Rakha. That influence got the rest of us starting to fool with ideas that were in certain lengths. The challenge with us was, how do you take these lengths and make them translatable to Western body knowledge. Westerners' body knowledge is basically twos and fours, smaller increments. It's harder for Western ears to hear the large divisions, the long meters.

Dancing to "The Eleven" . . . well, dancing to the Grateful Dead doesn't look like people dancing to most other musics.

No, it doesn't, but it's rooted in gravity, you know, and human body design, like all dancing is. Dancing is a function of gravity acting on the body, and the body is basically a gravity-designed thing. It's evolution. The backbone of those things are functions of this gravity on this specific planet. Dancing has to do with, like, you jump up in the air, and gravity pulls you down at a certain rate. That's the reason why the march is always 110, and when you march there's always a certain meter, which is marching meter – it has to do with the average stride length of a human.

You've put a lot of thought into this, haven't you?

Well, I haven't thought about it in some kind of methodical, mad scientist, "now-I'm-gonna-make-music-that-makes-people-dance" sort of way, but just in terms of why do these things work? Why do some things work and some things not work? Why in some grooves do you look for some slower division of the meter? If something's going terribly fast, you look for a slower part of it, the half-time or whatever. Something to get comfortable with, where your body knowledge works for you. The thing that I see – for me, where I can rock back and forth or tap my toe – it's gravity. It's that simple, it's like the test for me. It's part of what

makes music so compelling. Music is like echoing and talking about physical laws – at least locally, physical laws in this universe, on this planet. It's part of what makes it really interesting.

Other people think about music that deeply. In Indian music, they have organized it to the point where the intervals in any one of those ragas – each interval has a definite emotional connotation. It probably has to do with some kind of real, nervous-system recognition. The nervous system has some rate, which you can describe as pitch.

Have you tried to relate this to our Western music?

Yeah, but I'm not trying to codify it. In Eastern music, it's formalized. There's a raga for each time of day, and so forth. There's ragas for particular activities, and then within each raga, each of the intervallic relationships all have some definite specific emotional sense. That's the way the music is structured – it's part of the learning process.

Have you ever read [Hazrat] Inayat Khan's books on Indian music? It's fascinating as hell, especially since it's an oral tradition. You know that drummer talk – they teach you to sing it. Every Indian musician, no matter what instrument he plays, starts by learning how to sing each of those figures. It's fantastic. That's how they do the arrangements: They *talk* them to each other. They're as tight at that as any Western musicians are at sight-reading. They have phenomenal ability to remember long, long things, phrases that last the equivalent of sixty, eighty bars. One guy can sing it to another guy one time, and the other guy's got it.

I wonder how that maps into the organization of the nervous system?

That's what's interesting about these Inayat Khan books; he does talk about that. There are about four or five books on classical Indian music, and they're all far-out. It'll blow your mind how highly organized the music is.

I also have an interesting treatise by this Dutch guy about medieval church music, from before Bach, before baroque music. It's basically a study of this kind of music called *tactus*. This music is written in an early kind of notation that doesn't give any indication of the time. It's before they had rhythmic notation, but there are note values. These are like four-part vocal things, contemporary with Gregorian, but four-part instead of unison. They were written to be performed by these little groups of monks in Gothic cathedrals.

This guy ran a complicated vertical analysis of all the intervallic relationships in these works, which are commonly very short. They look like they're about eight bars long, in four-part vocal . . . harmony, you could say – early counterpoint. This guy made an effort to study all the relationships, and also to see if he could deduce what it was that they used for the time values. There's no bar lines or anything.

There's this incredible readout of all these relationships, which the guy then applies to all the alchemical and Masonic magical numerological traditions, the significance of all these really complex things, but also, it would take a monk, like, twenty years to write one of these things, and they wondered what the heck would take 'em so long, with these things that look like simple pieces of music. It turns out that they're really super-complex, highly coded, sort of magical stuff that are designed for specific architectural spaces, designed to be sung in a specific place in a Gothic cathedral.

Taking into account reverberation times, standing waves –

It basically has all that kind of physics in it, but the way they . . . in those days they had it all in octaves, remember; and the divisions of twelve for the twelve apostles; and the trinity runs all through it because of the magical significance of all those numbers. It's a huge body of complex knowledge that's codified that way. It turns out that the way this music was sung . . . there's little wood engravings and stuff like that on the illuminations that this music was written on that show the group of usually twelve or fourteen, with their hands on each other's throats. His deduction is that they got the tempo and the time relationships from the heartbeat, from each other's pulse. So the implications are very far-out.

Would that imply that eventually their pulses became synchronized?

Right. When they sang this music, they would get tremendously high in the church. In those days, the whole thing had power to make changes, the idea of music as drugs.

* * *

THERE ARE TIMES *when I've felt like the music plays the band, or that the band and the audience are definitely linked.*

We know that's the case. It's wonderful. It means that you're no longer responsible. That's the stuff, the pure gold of the experience.

How often do you get that?

Not very often.

It seems to depend very much on Phil's frame of mind at the moment. But even so, is it inaccurate to think that his role in the band diminished in the last couple of years?

Well, he doesn't sing anymore.

But even live he doesn't seem to have the same kind of presence.

It's possible. He's a different kind of guy than he used to be – he's definitely changed a lot. You'd have to ask him. He's, like, a hard guy to know, and it's also one of those things where I can't characterize him in a way that I think is fair to him. To get insight into his personality, you'd have to talk to him about it and see where he thinks of himself as being. Phil has much tighter a sine wave to who he is. He goes through his changes much more frequently than I think of myself as doing. This is really coffee-table psychoanalysis at its cheapest, I don't mind telling you.

Phil is an incredibly complex and brilliant guy. He does things for reasons of his own that are, just like his music, not easy for me to understand. I don't know why he is the way he is or why he does what he does, or what kinds of thoughts he thinks on and off. But I do know that his period of being enthusiastic and of being estranged, which we all have about the Dead – we're all ambivalent about the Grateful Dead, it gets to be a love-hate thing after awhile – that he goes through those changes with greater frequency. Sometimes during the course of the gig, he'll go through two or three great big changes.

He's much harder on himself than anybody is on him. He punishes himself in his own mental being, his own artistic space or whatever it is. But he's a tremendously brilliant guy,

and I think he has a huge role. He's like one of the fulcrumatic personalities in the band. If Phil is happening, the band's happening.

Is that cause or effect?

It's both. It's totally interactive . . . Phil has more power individually than any of the rest of us has. He really is superimportant, and it's one of those things that – the way we are, and the way our relationships are in the band is that we can see each other clearly and we can't see ourselves. That's the position that we're in relationship-wise. It's very difficult to see how you yourself fit in, and it's easy for you to see how others have power, but it's not easy for you to communicate to them the amount of power they have. You can tell somebody, but that doesn't mean they can know. We try to report to each other to some extent what it's like and what we think is happening. We have frameworks through which to talk about it; we have our own metaphors, our own ways of discussing what's happening in the Dead that make the most sense to us, but ultimately you can't tip off anybody. The Grateful Dead has this weird quality, and everybody feels this – people in the audience feel it regularly – that "if I could just get everybody to do what I wanted them to do, or do it the way they did it that night, it would just be perfect." You know? It has this fixable quality.

And it never happens.

Right. You can't do it just by knowing the symptoms. You'd think that you would be able to make corrections in music just by saying what it is you think is deficient.

According to the rules by which other musical aggregations play, you guys are failures. But you've survived outside those definitions, and it's a privilege in that respect.

You're right. We're insanely lucky, and I appreciate it like crazy! But you don't gain an improved position just by virtue of being in the Grateful Dead, for example. We're frequently seen as being privileged somehow, but being in the Dead is in no way a privilege. It doesn't exempt you from anything particularly, and the reward is a fleeting, existential kind of reality, where really the most important thing is the gig that just happened. Everything that we've done culminates in the last note that we play. If it was a bad gig, it's like there's nothing but suicide, that the only reasonable thing to do is to end it all. But the hope that there'll be a better one is an everpresent possibility. Luckily, they change for the better often enough so that it isn't complete darkness. But the nature of the experience is such that it's balanced, really, on the most recent experience. No matter how good it's ever been, if the last gig was a bum one, God, you're stuck.

Do you feel an obligation to keep the Dead going?

In a kind of large sense, yeah, I do sort of feel an obligation to it. I don't know the nature of the obligation, though.

Is it in the sense that so many people would be let down if you didn't do what you're doing?

No, it isn't that kind of obligation.

Lost lives, people running into walls . . . there are tons of people who would not know what to do if the Grateful Dead exited the planet. I know personally a lot of guys that would be broken men – and a few women.

Well, they should start stashing something.   ☯

THE NEW DAWN OF THE GRATEFUL DEAD

BY MIKAL GILMORE

JERRY GARCIA RUNS his fingers through his gray-white beard and smiles a rueful smile. "Man," he says, "if I could do it again tomorrow, I'd make it three or four times better."

It is an uncommonly warm spring evening in Marin County, California, and Garcia – the warm-faced, full-bellied, forty-four-year-old lead guitarist of the Grateful Dead – is seated in the band's San Rafael recording studio, discussing an old performance he has just finished viewing, from a video called *So Far,* which was shot nearly two years ago. The video is an adventurous and impressive work that, in its grandest moments, attests to the much touted spirit of community that the Grateful Dead share with their audience. Yet certain passages of the hour-long production probably come as rough viewing for Garcia, who looked rather heavy and fatigued during the project's taping. At the time, he was entangled in a drug problem that, before much longer, would not only imperil the guitarist's health and freedom but also threaten the stability of the band itself.

That fact lends a certain affecting tension to the better performances on *So Far* – in particular, the group's doleful reading of "Uncle John's Band." The song – a country-style sing-along about people pulling together into a brave and loving community in frightening times – has long been among the band's signature tunes, yet in *So Far,* the Dead render it as if they were aiming to test its meanings anew. Garcia and rhythm guitarist Bob Weir face off in a dimly lit concert hall, working their way through the lyrics with an air of frayed fraternity, as if this might be their last chance to make good on the music's promise of hard-earned kinship. "When life looks like easy street, there is danger at your door," they sing to each other, and from the look that passes between them in that moment, it's impossible to tell whether they are about to pull together or come apart.

It is a raggedy but utterly remarkable performance, and it seems to leave Garcia a bit uneasy. "There were so many people who cared about me," he will say later in the evening, "and I was just fucking around."

These days, things have taken a turn for the better. By all accounts, Garcia is now a revitalized man – his friends say he's as clear-witted, affable and aspiring as he's been in over a decade. Moreover, the band itself is midway through what may prove to be the most eventful season yet in its twenty-two-year history. Just a couple of nights ago, Garcia, Weir and the other band members – bassist Phil Lesh, keyboardist Brent Mydland and drummers Bill Kreutzmann and Mickey Hart – stayed up until early morning, polishing the mix on *In the Dark,* a rousing and often moving work about aging, decline, rebirth and recommitment that is, in fact, the group's first studio album in seven years. Then, the next afternoon, the band reconvened in the same studio to begin rehearsals with Bob Dylan for what may be the most out-of-the-ordinary tour of the summer: a string of stadium-size appearances that will feature Dylan and the Dead together.

Not a bad agenda – especially for a group that, two years ago, seemed bound for dissolution. "It's like we have a new beginning," says Garcia. "It's more fun now

than it's ever been; the band is just tearing up."

Garcia pauses and fishes a cigarette out of the pocket of his plaid work shirt. "The truth is," he says, "time pays off. Longevity is real special when it comes to playing music, because pretty soon you have a relationship with the other players in the band that is beyond intimate. It's closer than any other relationship you have in life. I know these guys better than I know anybody. And they still have that capacity to surprise me musically; I have to stay on my toes to keep up with them. At the same time, if I have an inspiration, they're all ears. They'll follow me down any dark alley. Sometimes there's light at the end of the alley, and sometimes there's a black hole. The point is, you don't get adventure in music unless you're willing to take chances."

Garcia stares for a moment at his cigarette and realizes he hasn't lit it, then laughs. "We're ready for anything now," he says, lighting up. "It just took awhile, that's all. I swear, it's like the Grateful Dead are the slowest-rising rock & roll band in the world."

* * *

FOR MANY, OF COURSE, the Dead have already risen. Indeed, to an intense, far-flung audience that is known, both affectionately and derisively, as Deadheads, the Grateful Dead have long figured as a cultural icon, standing for ideals of humanity, benevolence, unity and even spirituality that most other Sixties-born bands long ago forgot and that most modern rock artists have forsworn in favor of more caustic values.

This is a singular place of esteem to occupy in today's pop world, and it has helped establish the Grateful Dead as one of the biggest-drawing performing bands of our time; in fact, according to some estimates, the Dead are the single most successful touring band in rock history. What is particularly intriguing about all this is that, on some levels, the Grateful Dead are practically invisible. Unlike Bruce Springsteen, the Rolling Stones, the Jacksons, the Beach Boys or any number of popular live acts of the last generation, the Grateful Dead have never won much radio exposure, do not dominate MTV and only rarely elicit coverage from the pop or mainstream press.

Yet none of this matters, for the Dead have forged a symbiosis with their audience that, no matter how naive some may find it, is simply unequaled and probably unshakable. In fact, the Dead and their audience practically form their own self-sufficient fellowship – an alternative pop commonwealth that boasts, among other things, its own pop press (made up of several Dead-related magazines, the best of which is the Bay Area–based quarterly *The Golden Road*), its own radio program (*The Deadhead Hour,* which originates from San Francisco's KFOG and will soon be nationally syndicated), its own computer-linked database system (in which Deadheads not only trade fans' notes and debate ethical issues but also pass along their concerns directly to various band members) and its own worldwide network of tape collectors, who with the band's blessing and cooperation record all the Dead's performances and share them with other obsessive archivists. What's more, the Dead maintain one of the largest staffs of any pop act around and invite most of their employees to participate in a pension fund and a profit-sharing program that divvies up not only the group's touring revenues but some songwriting royalties as well. And finally, as much as possible, the Dead bypass conventional ticket-sales systems (and reduce scalping) by selling 50 percent of their tickets through their own scrupulously organized mail-order system.

If all this sounds vaguely utopian or communal-minded, well, that's precisely the point: The Grateful Dead and their audience function – and thrive – almost entirely outside the conventions of the mainstream pop world. Consequently, the Dead – a band rooted in the ferment and romanticism of the Sixties – somehow epitomize the two most prominently contradictory ideals of Eighties pop: They are not just a raging cult fave but also a smashing mass success.

Yet despite this achievement, for much of the pop world, the Dead are an object of indifference and, just as often, outright ridicule. That's because the band never seemed to have let go of the ideals and styles that it first laid claim to in San Francisco's Haight-Ashbury scene in the mid-Sixties, and much of its audience can still seem obsessed with that period as well. In the fast-developing, increasingly hard-minded world of modern pop, standing still can seem the greatest sin of all, and at least one critic, Dave Marsh, has described the Grateful Dead as little more than "nostalgia mongers . . . offering facile reminiscence to an audience with no memory of its own."

It is a charge that nearly every person in or around the band is familiar with, and clearly it rankles. "It's mortifying to think of yourself as a nostalgia act when you've never quit playing," says Robert Hunter, who has been Garcia's lyricist – and a hidden member of the band – for nineteen years. "We're looking at an audience of nineteen- or twenty-year-old kids. Can you have a nostalgia for a time you didn't live in? I think some of our music is appealing to some sort of idealism in people, and hopefully it's universal enough to make those songs continue to exist over the years."

John Barlow, a cattle rancher and writer who lives in Wyoming and is the band's other lyricist, has an even stronger reply. "I find it sort of curious," he says, "that there's a pejorative attachment to the fact that there are people who refuse to let go of a certain time and place – especially when the values that that time and place represented were the best that we've seen in our lifetime. These are soulless times now, and I don't see anything wrong with people who want to fix themselves on times that were a lot more enriching. But the real point is that that doesn't represent the audience at all."

So how does the Grateful Dead's appeal differ from that of artists like Bruce Springsteen and U2, who also seem to inspire a sense of community among their followings? "I think our greatest appeal is to somebody who's a bright kid, in late high school or in college," says Barlow. "Our audience tends to be intelligent enough and individualistic enough so that they don't have an easy time fitting into the mainstream in their schools. They're different, and they need refuge – they need a place they can go where they belong. There aren't any initiations or requirements or membership tests

or anything else to become a Deadhead; you just have to like it and feel like you're part of it, and then you're a brother to them all. And that, I think, is a very comforting discovery for a lot of these kids . . . You're not going to get condemned for anything you do, unless it's overtly violent. Furthermore, other people are going to take up your slack if you do something stupid, because they care about each other. Not only do you have the freedom to experiment, you have some latitude about the consequences of failure. There aren't too many places in society where that's the case."

*   *   *

"THE PUBLIC'S TASTE runs in cycles," says Phil Lesh, "and what's trendy twenty years ago is not the same thing that's going to be trendy today. But while the public's tastes go up and down in cycles, we're just like the median line that's running right through that."

The Grateful Dead's flair for constancy should come as no surprise: Though the band may have developed in a time and place that stressed cultural revolt and stylistic innovation, the band members themselves came to their vocation from backgrounds deeply rooted in the ideal of permanence. None, in fact, emerged strictly from rock & roll: The group's original lead singer, Pigpen (Ron McKernan), was a blues devotee; Jerry Garcia studied folk and bluegrass music; Bob Weir trained in folk and country blues; Phil Lesh was a student of classical music and jazz; Bill Kreutzmann played R&B; and Mickey Hart had experience in martial music. This mix of influences infused the band's early music with a quick-witted complexity and a keen earthiness that set the group apart from some of the artier exponents of late-Sixties psychedelia.

Yet at the same time, it *was* psychedelia – which is to say that at least some of it was music rooted in the idealism of the late-Sixties drug culture. Indeed, the Grateful Dead served as the house band for the Acid Tests, held during 1965 and 1966, just before LSD was made illegal. Apparently, the tenure paid off: Perhaps more than any other band of the era, the Grateful Dead succeeded in making music that seemed to emanate from the psychedelic experience – music like 1969's *Aoxomoxoa,* which managed to prove both chilling and heartening in the same measure.

"I wouldn't want to say that this music was written on acid," says Robert Hunter, who had originally taken LSD under the auspices of U.S.-government experiments at Stanford University. "Over the years, I've denied that it had any influence that way. But as I get older, I begin to understand that I was reporting on what I saw and experienced – like the layers below layers which became real to me. I would say that *Aoxomoxoa* was a report on what it's like to be up – or down – there in those layers. I guess it is, I'll be honest about it. Looking back and judging, those were pretty weird times. I was very, very far-out."

By 1970, the innocence and idealism surrounding the Bay Area music scene – and much of the counterculture – had largely disappeared. The drug scene had turned creepy and risky; much of the peace movement had given way to revolutionary fervor; and the starry-eyed dream of the emerging Woodstock generation, bound together by the virtues of love and music, had been sundered abruptly, first by the Manson Family murders in the summer of 1969, and then a few months later, by the gloomy and violent event known as Altamont. It was partly in response to these developments that the Dead entered the studio and began recording *Workingman's Dead* and *American Beauty,* a pair of 1970 albums that, like the best work of Bob Dylan and the Band, flirted with timeless American myths for the purpose of illuminating modern American troubles. Mainly, though, they were records that explored the idea of how one could forge meaningful values in disillusioning times.

"When Jefferson Airplane came up with that idea, 'up against the wall,' I was up against them," says Hunter. "It may have been true, but look at the results: blood in the streets. It seemed the Airplane was feeling the power of their ability to send the troops into the field, and I wanted to stand back from the grenades and knives and blood in the street. Stand way back. There's a better way. There has to be education, and the education has to come from the poets and musicians, because it has to touch the heart rather than the intellect, it has to get in there deeply. That was a decision. That was a conscious decision."

Sometimes, adds Hunter, it was difficult to hold on to that conviction. "When *American Beauty* came out," he says, "there was a photograph that was due to go on the back cover which showed the band with pistols. They were getting into guns at the time, going over to Mickey's ranch, target shooting. It wasn't anything revolutionary; they were just enjoying shooting pistols. For example, we got a gold record and went and shot it up.

"I saw that photo, and that was one of the few times I ever really asserted myself with the band and said, 'No – no picture of a band with guns on the back cover.' These were incendiary and revolutionary times, and I did not want this band to be making that statement. I wanted us to counter the rousing violence of that time. I knew that we had a tool to do it, and we just didn't dare go the other way. Us and the Airplane: We could have been the final match that lit that fuse, and I went real consciously the other way."

In addition, with their countryish lilt and bluesy impulses, *Workingman's Dead* and *American Beauty* were attempts to return to the musical sources that had fueled the band's passions in the first place. "*Workingman's Dead* was our first true studio album," says Garcia, "insofar as we went in there to say, 'These are the limitations of the studio for us as performers; let's play inside those limitations.' That is, we decided to play more or less straight-ahead songs and not get hung up with effects and weirdness.

For me, the models were music that I'd liked before that was basically simply constructed but terribly effective – like the old Buck Owens records from Bakersfield. Those records were basic rock & roll: nice, raw, simple, straight-ahead music, with good vocals and substantial instrumentation, but nothing flashy. *Workingman's Dead* was our attempt to say, 'We can play this kind of music – we can play music that's heartland music. It's something we do as well as we do anything.'"

In a sense, *Workingman's Dead* and *American Beauty* stand as a certain creative peak for the Grateful Dead. Following

those works, the band shifted focus, putting more and more emphasis on the length and quantity of its live appearances and issuing a series of multirecord live sets that, over the years, would at times be excitingly visionary and at other times tedious, sloppy and ultimately negligible. Though the band would periodically convene for a studio effort, most of the Dead's material in the last seventeen years has lacked the commitment and cohesion that graced *Workingman's Dead,* and it would not be until 1987's *In the Dark* that the Grateful Dead would again produce a work that attempted to reflect the temper of the times and that would adequately display the group's musical prowess.

For many Dead fans, this long standstill was actually the band's golden period – an era in which the group forswore the artifice of studio work for the comparatively riskier process of creating a constantly mutating brand of music that was rooted in the experience of day-to-day, moment-to-moment live performance. For the Dead, though, it was a fitful, sometimes difficult stretch. In 1973 Pigpen died, leaving the band without its most animated member and its one authoritative blues voice. Meantime, the band hired keyboardist Keith Godchaux and his wife, vocalist Donna Godchaux. They were both dismissed in 1979 over musical differences, and Keith Godchaux died the next year in an automobile accident. Also during this period, the Dead launched their own independent record label – a brave but costly venture that ultimately failed. Finally, in 1977, the band signed with Arista and produced a series of misdirected LPs designed for commercial airplay. "That music is not what I call Grateful Dead," says Mickey Hart. "It was produced by twits and plumbers; it was a shame and a travesty."

Says Bob Weir, "All that pressure to make commercial records more or less drew a backlash from us. I wouldn't say we were disheartened during that time so much as we just lost interest. I guess we kind of lost sight of the fact that we were really engaged in something more than a job. Maybe we lost focus on the goal ahead – which is to get on with it, ever on with it – and just started seeing the tours in front of us.

"But the one thing we knew we could do – and found a great deal of satisfaction doing – was playing live. It wasn't so much an ideal as what was realistic for us at the moment. That's the medium that works for us. There are people that you're playing to, that you're getting immediate gratification from, and that's preferable."

By 1981, the Grateful Dead found themselves in a bind. The band still owed Arista two LPs of new material but had grown gun-shy about the studio. Eventually the Dead negotiated a compromise: The group would deliver two double LPs of live material in exchange for one studio LP, then would begin work on a final record of new songs to fulfill its contract with the label. But after two weeks in Berkeley's Fantasy Studios, the studio effort came apart. "Everything was kind of lackadaisical," says Brent Mydland, who joined the band in 1979. "We'd get in there and wait around for a couple of hours, play for ten minutes, and then go get something to eat, and get back together forty-five minutes later and play for another ten minutes . . . We had the tunes, but there was no real drive

to go in and record. The attitude was, 'Why put out an album that's just going to be a throwaway?' "

There were also other problems. By 1984, concerned Deadheads had begun writing the group's fan club office in San Rafael, inquiring about Garcia's health. Some thought he seemed a bit erratic and distracted onstage; others noticed that he appeared to be steadily gaining weight and often seemed sluggish or fatigued. And still others wrote expressing distress over a rumor that had started to spread among Dead fans: Was it true that Garcia was using hard drugs?

The concerns proved well placed. Garcia had been using cocaine and heroin for several years – in fact, had become addicted – and, according to some observers, his use had started to affect the spirit and unity of the band itself. "He got so trashed out for the last few years," says the Dead's sound engineer, Dan Healy, "that he just wasn't really playing. Having him not give a shit – that was devastating."

Watching from his home in Wyoming, John Barlow thought he was witnessing the probable end of the Grateful Dead. "I was very afraid that Garcia was going to die," he says. "In fact, I'd reached a point where I'd just figured it was a matter of time before I'd turn on my radio and there, on the hour, I was going to hear, 'Jerry Garcia, famous in the Sixties, has died.' I didn't even allow myself to think that it wasn't possible. That's a pretty morbid way to look at something. When you've got one person that is absolutely critical, and you don't think he's going to make it, then you start to disengage emotionally, and I had. For a while, I couldn't see where it was all headed. I mean, I could see the people in the audience getting off, but I couldn't see any of us getting off enough to make it worthwhile.

"And it wasn't just Garcia," Barlow says. "There were a lot of things that were wrong. I don't want to tell any tales out of school, but I think our adherents have a more than slightly idealistic notion of what goes on inside the Grateful Dead, and just how enlightened we all are.

"What happened with Garcia was not unique."

* * *

D RUG USE," says Jerry Garcia, "is kind of a cul-de-sac: It's one of those places you turn with your problems, and pretty soon all your problems have simply become that one problem. Then it's just you and drugs."

It is late at night now, and Garcia sits in the cavernous rehearsal hall of the San Rafael studio. The other band members have all gone home, and only a couple of assistants linger in a nearby room, making arrangements for the next day's rehearsal with Dylan. Garcia looks tired – it has been a long day, and tomorrow promises to be a longer one – but as he sips at a Coke and begins to talk about the rough history of the last few years, his voice sounds surprisingly youthful.

"There was something I needed, or thought I needed, from drugs," he says directly. "Drugs are like trade-offs in a way – they can be, at any rate. There was something there for me. I don't know what it was exactly. Maybe it was the thing of being able to distance myself a little from the world. But there was something there I needed for a while, and it wasn't an entirely negative experience . . . But

after awhile, it was just the drugs running me, and that's an intolerable situation.

"I was never an overdose kind of junkie. I've never enjoyed the extremes of getting high. I never used to like to sit around and smoke freebase until I was wired out of my mind, know what I mean? For me, it was the thing of just getting pleasantly comfortable and grooving at that level. But of course, that level doesn't stay the same. It requires larger and larger amounts of drugs. So after a few years of that, pretty soon you've taken a lot of fucking drugs and not experiencing much. It's a black hole. I went down that black hole, really. Luckily, my friends pulled me out. Without them, I don't think I ever would have had the strength to do it myself."

In fact, says Garcia, it was the Grateful Dead who made the first move to resolve his drug problem. "Classically," he says, "the band has had a laissez-faire attitude in terms of what anybody wants to do. If somebody wants to drink or take drugs, as long as it doesn't seriously affect everybody else or affect the music, we can sort of let it go. We've all had our excursions. Just before I got busted, everybody came over to my house and said, 'Hey, Garcia, you got to cool it; you're starting to scare us.' "

According to some sources, the request that the Grateful Dead made of Garcia on that day in January of 1985 was actually a bit more adamant. The band reportedly told Garcia that he was killing himself and that while they could not force him to choose between death and life, they could insist that he choose between drugs and the band. If he chose drugs, the band might try to continue without him, or it might simply dissolve. Either way, the members wanted Garcia to understand they loved him, but they also wanted him to choose his allegiance.

Garcia reportedly made a decision: He promised the band he would quit drugs and would seek rehabilitative treatment within a few days. As it developed, he never got the chance. On January 18, while parked in his BMW in Golden Gate Park, Garcia was spotted by a policeman who noticed the lapsed registration on the vehicle. As the policeman approached the car, he reportedly smelled a strong burning odor and noticed Garcia trying to hide something between the driver and passenger seats. The policeman asked Garcia to get out of the car, and when Garcia did, the policeman saw an open briefcase on the passenger seat, full of twenty-three packets of "brown and white substances."

Garcia was arrested on suspicion of possessing cocaine and heroin, and about a month later, a municipal court judge agreed to let the guitarist enter a Marin County drug-diversion program.

Looking back at the experience, Garcia seems almost thankful. "I'm the sort of person," he says, "that will just keep going along until something stops me. For me and drugs, the bust helped. It reminded me how vulnerable you are when you're drug dependent. It caught my attention. It was like, 'Oh, right: illegal.' And of all the things I don't want to do, spending time in jail is one of those things I least want to do. It was as if this was telling me it was time to start doing something different. It took me about a year to finally get off drugs completely after the bust, but it was something that needed to happen."

Garcia pauses to light a cigarette, then studies its burning end thoughtfully. "I can't speak for other people," he says after a few moments, "and I certainly don't have advice to give about drugs one way or another. I think it's purely a personal matter. I haven't changed in that regard . . . It was one of those things where the pain it cost my friends, the worry that I put people through, was out of proportion to whatever it was I thought I needed from drugs. For me it had become a dead end."

Following Garcia's drug treatment, the band resumed a full-time touring schedule that included several 1986 summer dates with Bob Dylan and Tom Petty and the Heartbreakers. "I felt better after cleaning up, oddly enough, until that tour," Garcia says. "And then I didn't realize it, but I was dehydrated and tired. That was all I felt, really. I didn't feel any pain. I didn't feel sick. I just felt tired. Then when we got back from that tour, I was just really tired. One day, I couldn't move anymore, so I sat down. A week later, I woke up in the hospital, and I didn't know what had happened. It was really weird."

Actually, it was worse than that: Though he had never been previously diagnosed for diabetes, when Garcia sat down at his San Rafael home on that July evening in 1986, he slipped into a diabetic coma that lasted five days and nearly claimed his life. "I must say, my experience never suggested to me that I was anywhere near death," says Garcia. "For me, it had just been this weird experience of being shut off. Later on, I found out how scary it was for everybody, and then I started to realize how serious it had all been. The doctors said I was so dehydrated, my blood was like mud.

"It was another one of those things to grab my attention. It was like my physical being saying, 'Hey, you're going to have to put in some time here if you want to keep on living.'" Garcia still seems startled by this realization. "Actually," he says, "it was a thought that had never entered my mind. I'd been lucky enough to have an exceptionally rugged constitution, but just the thing of getting older, and basically having a life of benign neglect, had caught up with me. And possibly the experience of quitting drugs may have put my body through a lot of quick changes."

At first, though, there were no guarantees that Garcia would be able to live as effectively as before. There were fears that he might suffer memory lapses and that his muscular coordination might never again be sharp enough for him to play guitar. "When I was in the hospital," he says, "all I could think was, 'God, just give me a chance to do stuff – give me a chance to go back to being productive and playing music and doing the stuff I love to do. Shit, man, I'm ready.' And one of the first things I did – once I started to be able to make coherent sentences – was to get a guitar in there to see if I could play. But when I started playing, I thought, 'Oh, man, this is going to take a long time and a lot of patience.'"

After his release from the hospital, Garcia began spending afternoons with an old friend, Bay Area jazz and rhythm & blues keyboardist Merl Saunders, trying to rebuild his musical deftness. "I said, 'God, I can't do this,'" says Garcia. "Merl was very encouraging. He would run me through these tunes that had sophisticated harmonic changes, so I had to think. It was like learning music again, in a way. Slowly, I started to gain some confidence, and pretty soon it all started coming back. It was about a three-month process, I would say, before I felt like, 'Okay, now I'm ready to go out and play.' The first few gigs were sort of shaky, but . . ." Garcia's voice turns thick, and he looks away for a moment. "Ah, shit," he says, "it was incredible. There wasn't a dry eye in the house. It was great. It was just great. I was so happy to play."

Garcia smiles and shakes his head. "I am not a believer in the invisible," he says, "but I got such an incredible outpouring. The mail I got in the hospital was so soulful. All the Deadheads – it was kind of like brotherly, sisterly, motherly, fatherly advice from people. Every conceivable kind of healing vibe was just pouring into that place. I mean, the doctors did what they could to keep me alive, but as far as knowing what was wrong with me and knowing how to fix it – it's not something medicine knows how to do. And after I'd left, the doctors were saying that my recovery was incredible. They couldn't believe it.

"I really feel that the fans put life into me . . . and that feeling reinforced a lot of things. It was like, 'Okay, I've been away for a while, folks, but I'm back.' It's that kind of thing. It's just great to be involved in something that doesn't hurt anybody. If it provides some uplift and some comfort in people's lives, it's just that much nicer. So I'm ready for anything now."

* * *

ONE DAY EARLIER this year, Robert Hunter paid a visit to Jerry Garcia at the group's San Rafael recording studio. Following Garcia's recovery, Hunter had noticed, the band had seemed revivified. In fact, the group was finishing work on a long-planned video and had started rehearsals for a new, greatly overdue studio LP – though so far most of the material being considered was older fare: songs written years before but never recorded.

Hunter, though, had something fresh in hand. "Here," he said, handing a lyric sheet to Garcia. "I've written something I want you to take a look at." Garcia took the sheet, glanced at it, put it in his shirt pocket, then went back to his work.

The next day, Garcia held up work on the video project while he sat at a piano, with Hunter's lyric sheet propped in front of him. Within a couple of hours, he had framed the music to "Black Muddy River," a haunting, country-steeped lament that seemed to be about all the losses and weariness that had dogged Garcia and the Grateful Dead but also about all the hopes that had been recently rekindled. "When it seems like this night could last forever," Garcia sings on the LP, in the most mournful voice he has ever summoned, "and there's nothing left to do but count the years . . . I will walk alone by the black muddy river / And believe in a dream of my own."

Yet, says Hunter, he never planned it as a song about the band. "'Black Muddy River' is about the perspective of age and making a decision about the necessity of living in spite of a rough time, and the ravages of anything else that's going to come at you. When I wrote it, I was writing about how I felt about being forty-five years old and what I've been through. And then when I was done with it, obviously it was for the Dead."

But because "Black Muddy River" is a song that ultimately expresses hope for the future, it also raises a certain question about where the Grateful Dead may be headed: Namely, after having endured so many years of setbacks and stasis, is the band finally about to pursue the pop dream a bit more aggressively? Certainly, with an ambitious new album completed and a high-profile tour with Bob Dylan under way, the time has never been more favorable. In addition, with artists like David Byrne and Elvis Costello currently singing the band's praises, it seems that the modern pop scene may prove more receptive to the sort of freewheeling mix of country balladry, psychedelia and polyrhythmic improvisation that the Dead have always championed.

Still, while this sort of forecast might cheer most bands, in the Dead's family it elicits decidedly mixed responses. "Over the years," says Hunter, "it seemed a blessing that we were able to work and be dynamic and stay down there out of public view. That sort of attention eats people, and it eats groups; anybody who reads ROLLING STONE knows what happens. By all indications, we're going to get the record company backing in all the things that are necessary to have a hit, and it's a little frightening. Are we going to be eaten now? Who else has ever had an underground swell as large as ours and had it meet with another wave of aboveground approval? Look out: This is critical mass.

"I'm excited by it, and I have misgivings. I would like the world to know about the Grateful Dead; it's a phenomenal band. But I don't think the Grateful Dead is going to be as free a thing as it was. That's the devil we pay."

To Garcia, the prospect seems a bit more remote. "To tell the truth," he says, "it's one of those things that I'm not ready to think about. In fact, for me, it's like a jinx. If I start dwelling on it, sure as shit, this record will fail miserably. I'm used to loving something, then having it crash. Also, I've heard all this stuff before, you know? I remember people saying that 'Uncle John's Band' was going to be a big hit.

"Yet no matter what happens, if all these things fail, fall completely to the ground and shatter into a million pieces, it's not going to fundamentally affect us or what we do. We're going to keep on playing. We still have a few good years in us."

* * *

IN THE END, whether the Grateful Dead win mainstream favor may prove intriguing but hardly vital – and not simply because the band already attracts a following of hundreds of thousands. Actually, the Grateful Dead enjoy a far more significant distinction: They are one of the few bands in all pop to bind together an audience that, without the band's continued presence, would probably not cohere, or even exist.

Indeed, when the Grateful Dead play at Laguna Seca Raceway, near Monterey, California, on a weekend in May, the legion of nearly thirty-five thousand fans that attends the performances is largely the same sort of audience that

some folks have enjoyed poking fun at for nearly two decades now: in part a crowd of middle-aged sentimentalists but mainly forever-young hippie types, wearing vivid, gorgeous tie-dyes and flowing, free hair and dancing as rest-lessly and haphazardly as only impenitent tribalists can. Yet as anomalous or naive or plain hilarious as many modern pop fans may find this scene, there's also something undeniably homey and heartening about it. This is a crowd of folks for whom blitheness is not just a bond but also an act of social dissent: a protest against both the resurgent straightness of our times and the meanness and trendiness that seem to characterize much of today's pop music. And for this audience, one of the most meaningful acts of affirmation it can make is to cheer the genial music of the Grateful Dead.

Perhaps it's this sense of shared good humor that helps make the Dead's performances seem so spirited this weekend. Or perhaps it's simply the experience of witnessing a once-considerable band as it actively reasserts its skill and force, and a bit of its vision as well. In any event, in their best moments the Grateful Dead are still as eloquent and alluring as in their go-for-broke heyday. More remarkably, they still sound like a unit without any fixed center: The melodic focus still shifts somewhere between Jerry Garcia's restive guitar lines and Phil Lesh's nervy bass runs; the rhythmic impulses pull back and forth between Bill Kreutzmann's swinglike tempos and Mickey Hart's edgier attack; and the harmonic action veers between Bob Weir's fitful rhythm-guitar chords and keyboardist Brent Mydland's passion for soulful dissonance. In short, though the lineup may be slightly different, in practice this is the same band that made "Dark Star" and "Uncle John's Band" count for so much a generation ago: a band that needs all its members working and thinking together to keep things moving and balanced.

But the Grateful Dead are never more impressive than in those moments when they make it plain that, above all, they need the audience to keep things purposeful. This idea comes across with special force toward the end of Sunday's show, when Bob Weir leads the band into a hard-pushing, rough-around-the-edges version of Buddy Holly's "Not Fade Away." After a few minutes, the guitars, bass, drums and keyboards drop out of the sound,

At right: Longtime Garcia collaborator Robert Hunter, circa 1976. "As I get older, I begin to understand that I was reporting on what I saw and experienced – like the layers below layers which became real to me. Looking back and judging, those were pretty weird times. I was very, very far-out." ~Robert Hunter

and there is only the band and the audience shouting those old and timeless lyrics: "Love is love and not fade away / Love is love and not fade away."

"Not fade away!" the crowd shouts to the band.

"Not fade away!" the band sings back.

"NOT FADE AWAY!" the crowd yowls, leaning forward as one.

It keeps going like that, two bodies staring hard at one another, shouting and beaming, bound up in the promise that, as long as one is there, the other holds a hope. ☕

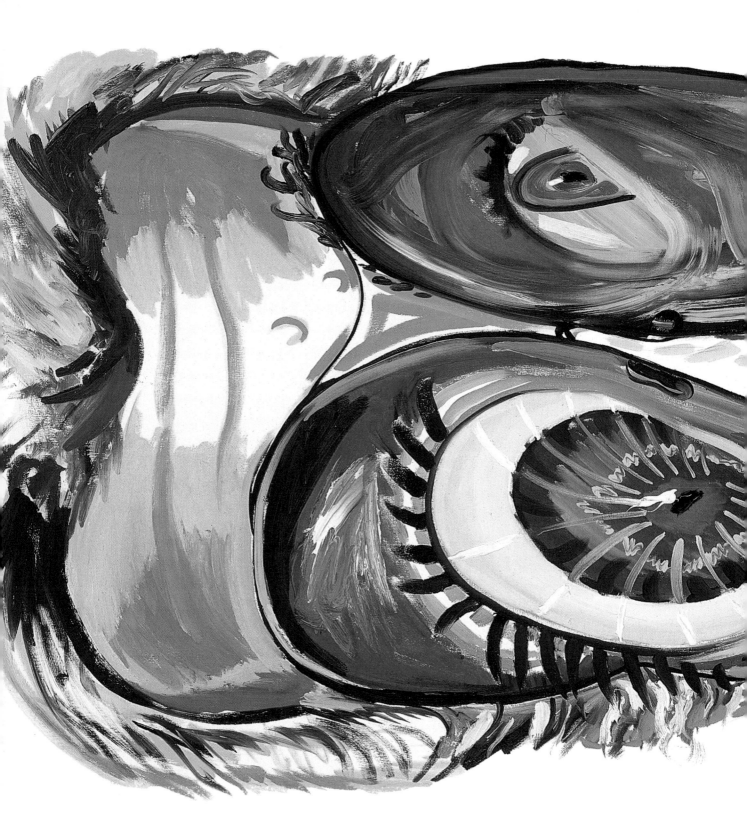

FOR ME, IN MY LIFE all kinds of drugs have a hindrance to me. So far as I'm concerned,

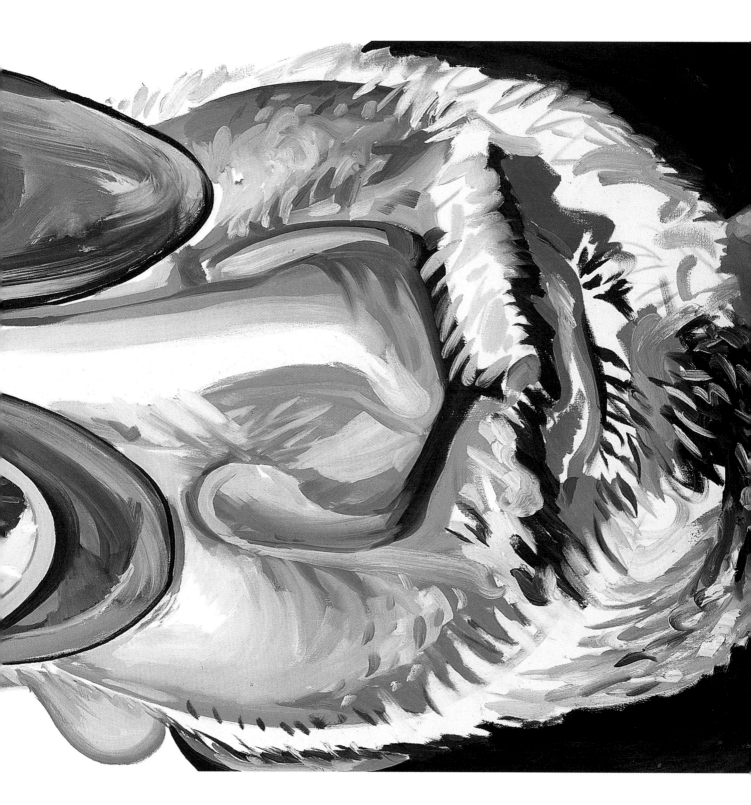

been useful to me, and they have also been
the results are not yet in." ~*Jerry Garcia, 1991*

ON A ROLL

THE ROLLING STONE INTERVIEW

WITH JERRY GARCIA

BY FRED GOODMAN

WHEN THE BUSINESS magazine *Forbes* recently published its annual list of the forty highest-paid entertainers in the world, the Grateful Dead – those outlaws of the music industry – ranked Number 29, with an estimated annual income of $12.5 million.

Money is hardly the primary measure one would select to evaluate the success of the Grateful Dead's vision. But it is indicative of the fact that after decades of touring with a consistency and success unmatched by any other band, the Grateful Dead have a relationship with their fans that is unique in the history of rock & roll. On the eve of the release of their twenty-second album, *Built to Last,* the Grateful Dead stand as an American dynasty like no other.

Performing live has always been the focus of the Grateful Dead, and until the 1987 platinum album *In the Dark* produced the single "Touch of Grey," the band had never had a Top Ten hit. But today the Grateful Dead find themselves more popular than ever, creating a new set of problems that Garcia terms "oversuccess." The cult of Deadheads has grown so large that the Grateful Dead have been forced by many arenas to ask the fans who follow them and camp out wherever the band plays to stay home unless they have tickets. This is a particularly thorny problem for a group that has always striven to avoid the conventions of the music business and considers its fans as much a part of the Dead community as the band members themselves.

The rebirth of the Grateful Dead coincides with that of their lead guitarist and reluctant figurehead, Jerry Garcia. After a diabetic coma that put him in the hospital in July 1986 and a period spent shaking a heroin and cocaine habit, Garcia – who admits to having "vacillated furiously" for most of his career about whether or not he wanted to be involved in the Grateful Dead – has regained his stride, touring and recording with his own group when the Dead are off the road. With the release of *Built to Last,* Garcia agreed to sit down at the Dead's recording studio on Front Street, in the San Francisco suburb of San Rafael, and take stock of where the Grateful Dead's decision to take their own road nearly twenty-five years ago has ultimately led.

* * *

CONGRATULATIONS *on making the 'Forbes' list. I see the Dead are Number 29 – how do you plan to jump over Van Halen and Madonna in the coming year?*

Oh, God. Success has never been part of our schedule, exactly. It's kind of been a happy surprise, but in a way it presents itself as just a new level of problems. And not that it's not gratifying – it's gratifying to have an audience. For us, it's been slow and steady enough where none of it has been a shock.

What do you think the appeal of the Grateful Dead is to listeners who weren't even born yet in 1967?

Well, in a way it gives you a curious feeling of not having changed much. There are people out there who look a whole lot like the people that we originally started playing to. So you get this kind of relativistic view of time. We have people coming to our shows who are younger than we were when we started. You wonder where these people are coming from, but they're self-invented. We didn't invent them, and we didn't invent our original audience.

In a way, this whole process has kind of invented us. I don't know why, and I can't say what it is that motivates them. Back in the Seventies we had the same phenomenon of all these young kids. But now those are the people who are in medical school and law school; they are college people and professionals. They still come to the shows. So now there are Deadheads everywhere. They've kind of infiltrated all of American society – everybody knows one: "I've got a cousin who loves you guys."

I wonder what the late Sixties means to a person who is nineteen today. The drugs were different, and you didn't have to worry if having sex with someone would kill you.

The feeling they might have missed out on some fun. Yeah, it's possible. This is a grimmer world.

Do you think that following the Grateful Dead is perceived as a way to step into that other world?

Well, really, there's no way to step out of this world. They are carrying all their baggage with them when they come to the Grateful Dead shows.

So you have no sense that the culture surrounding the Grateful Dead is isolated?

Shit. I don't think it's isolated. Of course, how would I know? I'm right in the middle of it – I have no perspective. Go ask a black person if it means anything to them. It probably doesn't. We're not at that Johnny Carson level of absolute familiarity.

But he wasn't that far ahead of you on the 'Forbes' list.

That's gratifying [*laughs*].

The fact that being in the Grateful Dead has made Jerry Garcia a wealthy man is kind of strange.

Who would have known? Yes – it's still not the point, either. I mean, the things that I'm trying to do I'm still trying to do. And having money or not having money really doesn't help it. It doesn't interact in any way. I'm not very into stuff. You know, oh, hey – a new car [a BMW 750iL]. After you've bought one or two things, that's it.

We never said that money was bad. But it just has never been our focus one way or another, pro or con. The most cogent example of how things have changed in my life is that when the Grateful Dead wasn't working I used to go and play in bars. Low profile, not many people were interested. Now this has escalated along with everything else. And the stress level has skyrocketed.

That has also caused problems at shows. One city even threatened to ban Dead shows because of the crowds you draw.

A lot of the towns we play in, we bring in more people than the population of the town. It's obviously upsetting, and when it's going on for three or four days, it's *really* upsetting.

What can be done about it?

Not a whole lot. We can pass the whole set of issues on to the fans, which we try to do. We give them handouts and say, "Here are the problems we're facing. If you have any suggestions, please let us know. Otherwise, here's what we think should happen." In other words, take this into your own hands. If you want the Grateful Dead to come back to this town, this is what they are saying we have to do. Luckily, our audience is always pretty much game enough to accept the responsibility.

What do you make of all the police busts surrounding your shows in the past year?

It's more of the same. It's probably part of the fallout of the tremendous frustration America is feeling about drugs. Just not wanting to deal with it realistically. Instead, they're going to somehow try to arrest everybody who uses drugs.

What do you think of President Bush's war on drugs?

It's a joke. Greed and the desire to take drugs are two separate things. If you want to separate the two, the thing you do is make drugs legal. It's the obvious solution. Accept the reality that people do want to change their consciousness, and make an effort to make safer, healthier drugs. When you take the greed out of it, all of the damage starts to fall away, because the criminal intent is a whole different level than the guy who takes drugs.

In terms of the situation with the police, has the band done anything to try and . . .

Oh, yeah. The police love suggestions from us.

But isn't the issue of finding places to play so great that you have to sit down and talk to the police when you want to go into a town?

Oh, definitely. The Nassau Coliseum [in Uniondale, Long Island, New York] is the primo example. Every time we played there, they busted three hundred or four hundred kids. We're not going to be bait for the police department, so we refused to play there. And they said, "Please come back. We promise we won't bust anybody. Honest to God. Come back." So we said, "Okay, we'll go back." And when we played there, they did it again. This has happened a couple of times. So they say, "Honest to God, we really aren't going to bust anybody – no shit. Please come back and play." So I just played there with my band. They busted forty or fifty kids. So the Grateful Dead ain't going to go back there. What is it about our fans that makes them so fucking offensive to everybody? They're certainly no worse than sports crowds.

What do you make of the Jefferson Airplane re-forming?

I think it's interesting, because they are all so amazingly argumentative. There was a time when they made great music together. If they find some of that chemistry – and sometimes it's the chemistry that makes you fight that makes the music good – if they can hold themselves together long enough, we might be exposed to something interesting.

Are you in touch with them?

I know that I can call up [Paul] Kantner any time. And certainly Grace [Slick] was very helpful to me when I was going through my drug trips. These people are like relatives. Also Pete Townshend. I'm really sorry I missed him on this run. He's the guy I really love.

What about some of the other musicians who were around Haight-Ashbury when the Dead got started? I understand the Dead had a friendly rivalry with Quicksilver Messenger Service. Didn't you guys used to stick each other up onstage?

Yeah. One night we raided their house – got all decked up in war paint like the Indians. We stormed in there; it was a game, that's all. Then they were going to come and stick us up when we were playing at the Fillmore Auditorium. They were going to handcuff us to the microphones and play a tune through our equipment and split. They had all of this lined up, and some cops saw them in the street in their van with plastic guns. This was during the touchy period of big shootings in the streets of San Francisco. They took them off to jail immediately.

Is there anyone you've lost touch with that you'd like to find? I never see Owsley Stanley's name anymore.

Owsley's still around. We still see him. You don't see his name because he chooses not to be in the public.

What does he do?

He's an artist. He makes jewelry and sculpture. He comes every year and visits us, comes out on the road and hangs. But he chooses to be invisible. He's a quiet and regular citizen now. But he's still Owsley, and he's still the same lunatic. I still see Kesey. We're all still good friends. The Acid Test was powerful stuff. You never erase those experiences from your life.

Considering the tenor of the times, do you think it's possible today for there to be something akin to what the Acid Test was in the Sixties?

No. Well, yes. It depends on what you think the Acid Test was. What the Acid Test really was was formlessness. It's like the study of chaos. It may be that you have to destroy forms or ignore them in order to see other levels of organization. For me, that's what the Acid Test was, that's what it was a metaphor for. If you go into a situation with nothing planned, sometimes wonderful stuff happens. LSD was certainly an important part of that for me. I also think there's an electronic hinge like computer cybernetics that's going to take us to interesting places and may work the way psychedelics do without the idea of substance.

What are you talking about?

Have you heard of this stuff called virtual reality? There's a place here where they have something you put on your head. It's got, like, a pair of goggles on it, and the goggles are two little TV screens that give you a 3-D image. There's something on top of the helmet that tells attitude – whether you are shifting out of center. And then you have this glove you put on your hand.

When you put on the goggles, you are in this room. It's a completely fictitious room. But if you turn your head around, your view of the room is 360 degrees. And you have this disembodied hand out in front of you, which is the glove. And you can pick up fictitious objects that you "see" in the room.

You can see where it's heading: You're going to be able to put on this thing and be in a completely interactive environment. There is not going to be any story, but there's going to be the way you and it react. As they add sounds and improve the image, you're going to be able to walk around in that building, fly through the air, all that stuff. And it's going to take you to those places as convincingly as any other sensory input.

These are the remnants of the Sixties. Nobody stopped thinking about those psychedelic experiences. Once you've been to some of those places, you think, "How can I get back there again but make it a little easier on myself?"

You already knew Robert Hunter, your lyricist, when he was involved in the original LSD lab research near Stanford, right?

Oh, yeah, sure. When he came back with his reports of what it was like, I thought, "God, I've *got* to have some of that."

When I was in junior high school, I saw a documentary showing a bunch of people who were taking LSD. At the time they thought it was a psychomimetic, that it produced schizophrenia. The film showed this artist who was just drawing lines, and he was obviously very moved – like at a peak ecstasy experience. I thought, "God, that looks like such fun!" That image stayed with me a long time and that notion that there is some magical substance that corresponds to the best of your dreams.

In primitive cultures that state of the shaman is a desirable state. In our society, we somehow are trying to not have that. That's a real problem. We need the visions. A lot of what we do is already metaphors for that – movies, television, all that stuff. We want to see other worlds. Music is one of the oldest versions of it. That's Mickey Hart's shot: magic in music, the magic in the drums. The primitive power of the drums. I think that stuff is all still there. The problem is we're not dealing with it consciously.

In a sense, the Grateful Dead experience is that metaphor, too. It's like, "Here's the ritual that we have been missing in our lives." We don't go to church anymore. We don't have celebrations anymore. The magic has even been taken out of the Catholic Mass. English? Sorry, it doesn't have that boom – it doesn't have that scare.

What do you make of the myths that grow around the band? There's one that says a person disappeared while you were playing. And several people claim to have seen it happen.

I love it. We get all kinds of feedback from people who get into it on all kinds of levels. We get it from quantum physics. From people who are doing brain research. From the hard spiritual to the hard science. We get people who are Deadheads who are all of those and who see a relationship. And as they elucidate the relationship between what the Dead does and what they do, we start to see ourselves as part of this complex something else. Which I think is the real substance of the Sixties. For me, the lame part of the Sixties was the political part, the social part. The real part was the spiritual part.

The Grateful Dead are unlike any other band because, aside from playing music, you are the core of a social phenomenon. Does that make it hard to just be a musician?

For me, music is as difficult as it ever was. It's really hard for me to write a song, it's hard for me to play the guitar. I have to practice a lot to do it even competently. And I feel like I'm just getting into it, just getting started. And no matter what I do, it's still that way. It hasn't made it easier, it hasn't made it more difficult. But there is that juice. When you hit a crowd of eighty thousand people and you get the *pow*, there's definitely a rush involved.

The Grateful Dead have never denied that they have nights when they're awful. But it seems as if the people who follow the band just love everything.

They're more judgmental than that. They have their favorites, but they know when we have a bad night, and they appreciate a good try. And some nights that we hate, those are the nights they love. Sometimes there are nights that are all conflict, and it's like everything you do is wrong, and when you listen to them later on, they are very interesting musically.

So in a way they've allowed themselves that latitude to enjoy a show for lots of different reasons. I think that's in their favor – no matter what the experience has been, they

don't get burned. It's not like going to a show that's a real tight show, and you miss every cue, and everything is fucked up, and you say, "Shit, that was horrible." When a Grateful Dead show is horrible, it's interesting.

Have the Dead gotten to where they want to be, musically?

It feels like we haven't really gotten to that place – you know, the perfect moment of Grateful Deadness, or whatever it is. We brush up against it occasionally. We'd know it if we saw it, but it isn't something that we can just make happen. The audience may be getting what they're after, but what we're after remains elusive and slightly out of focus. Although it's getting stronger and more clear as the years go by.

That's one of those things you can't predict when you start out: How long is this going to be interesting to me? I would never have thought I'd be interested in something for twenty-five years. That's a long time for anything. Even if we never get to that place, the process itself stays interesting, so the trip has been worth it.

The band has never been satisfied with its studio records. Are there any you've gone back to and discovered that you like?

A few. I really like *Mars Hotel*. And *Blues for Allah* is a very chancy record. Instead of writing at home, we worked on stuff together in the studio. We went every day to Weir's house for about six months and developed all the material. It was very productive, and the music had a real singular personality.

What about your new album? Did the success of 'In the Dark' have an effect on how you approached 'Built to Last'?

Not too much. When we started recording this album, we thought we'd follow the same methodology we used for *In the Dark*.

You recorded the basic tracks in a concert hall, right?

That's what we did with *In the Dark*. But on this one, about a year into it we changed our tack totally, so this record has been completely different. Instead of going after the standard bass-and-drums kind of basics, we worked from rhythm tracks – just the basic rhythm of the tune, which we'd write into a computer.

Then Bob and Phil and me and Brent would rough the tune out. So essentially, we were dealing with just one take of each tune. Mickey's got his own studio, Weir's got his own studio, and we've got Front Street here. We were able to evolve ideas – everybody at their own rate. Really nobody heard this record until we mixed it. And as the ideas were evolving, somebody would say, "I see Phil is going in this direction with this – I'll have to change my part a little bit." Then Phil would say, "Well, I see Weir has changed his part a little bit – I'll change mine." So the whole evolutionary process was accelerated.

It sounds more like you were interacting with the computer rather than with each other.

Well, we're interacting with the music more directly and not so much with each other. No one was really working in isolation.

You were once an art student. Do you find that background is intrinsic to the way you approach music?

I can't separate myself from it. I still tend to think visually, even if I don't mean to. When I listen to a mix, I see a field.

Do you think that way as a guitarist, too?

Yeah. I think of notes as objects that have perspective. They have the front part of them and the back part of them, the attack and the release. To me, it's very visual. If I had the time, I would illustrate all my solos. I could do it – I have seen them that way.

How do you feel about your work as a songwriter?

I'm not a prolific writer, I'm a default writer. In order to have original material, somebody's got to write it. It's like "Who's going to do it?" "Shit, I don't know – does it have to be me? Oh, fuck." It's been that kind of thing.

Actually, looking back, I've written some okay tunes. I'm very satisfied with them. My style, if there is one, is really very close to folk music and bluegrass. Those are my roots.

Do you still get a chance to play with other musicians outside the Dead and your own bands?

If I have the time, I love to do it. I did a thing for Warren Zevon not too long ago. It was great to work with Ornette Coleman, too.

Had you ever worked with him before?

I had met him a couple of times. He has been to a couple of Grateful Dead shows. He and his son, Denardo, asked me if I would record with them. And I said I'd love to do anything any time under any circumstances. So they called me when they were working on the album [*Virgin Beauty*]. I was flattered silly.

I hope to play live with Ornette sometime. I think I hear what it is that he does.

Critics of the Dead say . . .

What? Somebody critical of the Dead?

Sorry. The band has been called anachronistic.

We always were anachronistic, if you use it to say we're out of time. We have always been out of time. We've always been doing something that wasn't exactly the thing that was happening. We've gotten slightly more professional over the years – we don't take quite as long between tunes as we used to. We still don't do song lists. We still wing it, but we're getting very good at it.

But do you think that what the Grateful Dead do is still in tune with what's going on musically and culturally?

We are a process rather than an event. In terms of vocabulary of fashion, there's fashion in music, and we sort of keep up. But it's definitely within the context of what we're doing.

The members of the Grateful Dead really have a complex relationship. At this point it's gone beyond even blood. The Grateful Dead has been the most intimate kind of relationship I've ever experienced. There is definitely the danger of becoming insular, and we're certainly aware of that on a lot of levels. But that's kind of what we're after: a kind of community. And we have it. It's hard to stay closed. I've tried that. I spent a good long time trying a drug world that was pretty closed.

Why did that happen?

It's just wear and tear more than anything else. It's kind of like I needed a rest. I'm not very good at self-analysis. But I stopped because I care more about the Grateful Dead than I do about myself, ultimately.

In a way, the Grateful Dead has become the focus of all of our lives, even though we have families and children. The Grateful Dead – that's the center, in a way.

Have you been able to figure out why you developed such a bad drug problem?

Self-indulgence, pretty much. I mean, I liked it too much, and the more you like it, the more it likes you, and pretty soon that's just about all there is. I'm glad I'm not involved in it anymore. I really am. But I haven't come to any conclusions about drugs at all on any level. I don't think I've gained any particular insights, but I do know that I've always basically been an addictive personality. That's just who I am. So for me, it's one of those things I always have to watch out for.

Let's talk about the live album the Dead did with Dylan. There was talk that you were unhappy with it when it came out.

No. Bob wanted us to bury his voice a bit. When you're collaborating with Dylan and he says, "Hey, I think that my voice is too out front," what am I going to do? Punch him? I'll say okay against my own instincts.

By the way, I understand it was your idea to do his song "Joey," about the mobster "Crazy" Joey Gallo. Why? It might be the most laborious song Dylan ever recorded.

I love it. I don't know what it is – people from the East Coast tend to hate that song. For me, it's a folk song. You know, it's like [Woody Guthrie's song] "Pretty Boy Floyd." I don't find it judgmental; I don't think it says anything good or bad, and it's got some really touching lines in it. But I must admit, I'm in the minority here.

While we're talking about choosing material, let me ask you about the music the Dead are performing these days. Over the years, the Dead have been including more and more covers. What's that about?

There's a certain amount of laziness. Getting Bob Weir to do new tunes is like pulling teeth sometimes. He doesn't even like to do his own tunes a lot of times. We slowly stop doing a lot of his tunes, and he doesn't say anything. It's like "Hey, what ever happened to those tunes of yours?" Unless we actively do something about it, tunes escape us – they just get away. We can play five or six nights without repeating anything. So the tunes don't get played very often – that's the consequence.

You've said that the Grateful Dead took their cue from the Beats. What was your perception of Neal Cassady when you met him? Was it a conscious thing: "I'm hanging out with Dean Moriarty"?

Well, I had been a fan of Kerouac's, so a little bit, yeah. But the reality of Cassady was so much more incredible. He was *so* much more than anybody could get down on paper. As incredible as he was as a fictional character, the reality was more incredible.

There's no experience in my life yet that equals riding with Cassady in, like, a '56 Plymouth or a Cadillac through San Francisco or from San Jose to Santa Rosa. He was like the ultimate *something*: the ultimate person as art. Not only did he play into his own myth, but he also played into you specifically. He knew your trips; he knew who you were, like a person in a book. He had this uncanny ability to pick up a conversation where it stopped, even if it had been six months before. I mean *right* where it stopped. And he could

do it with, like, a half dozen people at the same time. He was just incredible; there is really nothing like Cassady.

Plus, he was the ultimate sight gag. The most incredible wit and rap. *And* the most incredible physical body. I saw him do things that were at the level of, like, Buster Keaton, in terms of physicality and timing. Only in the *real* world.

He was so much larger than life. You know, he used to have this thing where you'd take a dollar bill out and he would holler out the serial number on it. And every once in a while he'd get it right. No shit. Your mind would be so blown. There was nothing like him.

Just the privilege of seeing him talk to a cop: There were times when we got pulled over in the bus, and a cop would talk to Cassady. And Cassady had this incredible ability to mind-fuck the police. He'd instantly turn into this humble guy: "Hey, I'm just taking these college kids around. I'm a working man myself." And he'd have his wallet out, and they were asking him for a driver's license. He'd have his life story out. You know, a wallet this thick with stuff – little clippings and pictures and all kinds of shit. And pretty soon the cops would say, "Oh, fuck it!"

A lot of people couldn't handle him, and a lot of people were scared to death of him. They thought he was totally crazy. And a lot of people would dismiss him because he didn't cop center stage. He would have a little sideshow going on over here. You'd ignore it as long as possible, but you'd sort of get sucked in, and pretty soon – wham! – there you are in this world. If you went for it, it was incredible. But he'd never lay it on you. It was one of those things you sort of had to volunteer for. I had incredible experiences with him. He blew my mind hundreds and thousands of times.

Looking back, what do you think has been lost from that time?

Neal is the big thing. It would have been great to have Neal all the way up to now. I certainly miss him as badly as I miss anybody – Pigpen too. And the whole thing with the Acid Test. That was tremendously lucky; it probably cemented us more than any other experience in life so far.

Do you think the Dead's shows still have any connection to the Acid Tests?

In a way. What we're doing is not that different.

Do you think that's one of the things that the kids who come to see the Dead are trying to connect with?

They get something. It's their version of the Acid Test, so to speak. It's kind of like the war-stories metaphor: Drug stories *are* war stories, and the Grateful Dead stories are their drug stories, or war stories. It's an adventure you can still have in America, just like Neal on the road. You can't hop the freights anymore, but you can chase the Grateful Dead around. You can have all your tires blow out in some weird town in the Midwest, and you can get hell from strangers. You can have something that lasts throughout your life as adventures, the times you took chances. I think that's essential in anybody's life, and it's harder and harder to do in America. If we're providing some margin of that possibility, then that's great. That's a nice thing to do. ☙

Following pages: Timothy Leary and Neal Cassady aboard the Merry Pranksters' bus, as seen by Beat poet Allen Ginsberg's camera, 1964.

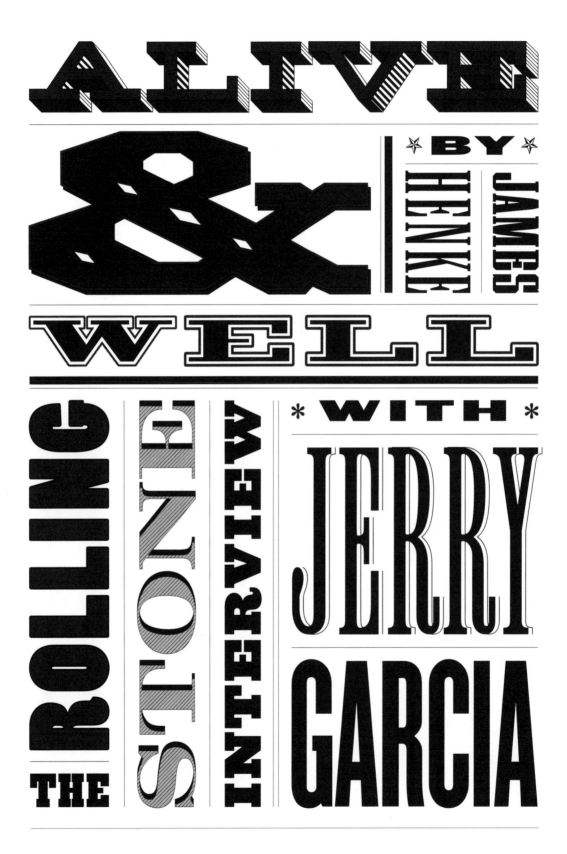

ALIVE & WELL

BY JAMES HENKE

THE ROLLING STONE INTERVIEW

WITH JERRY GARCIA

IF THERE'S SUCH a thing as a recession-proof band, the Grateful Dead must be it. While the rest of the music industry has suffered through one of its worst years ever – record sales have plummeted, and the bottom has virtually fallen out of the concert business – the Dead have trouped along, oblivious as ever to any trends, either economic or musical.

During the first half of the year, the group – now in its twenty-sixth year – grossed $20 million on the road. Over the summer, which experts have declared the worst in memory for the touring business, the Dead were the only band that chose to concentrate on – and indeed, that filled – outdoor stadiums. Their average gross per show, according to the industry newsletter *Pollstar,* was more than $1.1 million, or nearly twice that of the summer's second-biggest touring act, Guns n' Roses. And then, immediately after Labor Day, the Dead hit the road again, playing three nights at the Richfield Coliseum outside Cleveland, nine nights at New York City's Madison Square Garden and six nights at the Boston Garden. All of the shows, of course, were sellouts.

Forty-nine-year-old Jerry Garcia is as baffled as anyone by the Dead's seemingly unstoppable success – though he continues to search for explanations. "I was thinking about the Dead and their success," Garcia said on a September afternoon, as he sat in a hotel room overlooking New York's Central Park. "And I thought that maybe this idea of a transforming principle has something to do with it. Because when we get onstage, what we really want to happen is, we want to be transformed from ordinary players into extraordinary ones, like forces of a larger consciousness. And the audience wants to be transformed from whatever ordinary reality they may be into something a little wider, something that enlarges them. So maybe it's that notion of transformation, a seat-of-the-pants shamanism, that has something to do with why the Grateful Dead keep pulling them in. Maybe that's what keeps the audience coming back and what keeps it fascinating for us, too."

Even as they've continued to pull the fans in to their live shows, the Dead have been busy with other projects over the past twelve months. Last September the band released *Without a Net,* a two-CD live set culled from some of its 1989 and 1990 concerts. Then this spring the group issued *One From the Vault.* Another double CD, *One From the Vault* documents a now-legendary 1975 concert at San Francisco's Great American Music Hall, where the band first performed its *Blues for Allah* album onstage. (*One From the Vault II,* the next release in what promises to be a continuing series of CDs from the Dead archives, is due in January. It features a pair of August 1968 shows from the Fillmore West, in San Francisco, and the Shrine Auditorium, in Los Angeles.)

In April Arista Records put out *Deadicated,* an anthology of fifteen Dead songs performed by artists as diverse as Elvis Costello, Dwight Yoakam and Jane's Addiction. Proceeds from the album are being donated to the Rainforest Action Network and to Cultural Survival. Both organizations will also benefit from the publication this month of *Panther Dream,* a children's book about the rain forest written by Bob Weir and his sister, Wendy Weir, who also illustrated it.

(In addition, Mickey Hart has collaborated with Fredric Lieberman on *Planet Drum: A Celebration of Percussion and Rhythm,* which was just published by HarperCollins. An accompanying CD has also been released by Rykodisc.)

Meanwhile, Garcia has not been sitting by, idle. In July he and mandolin player extraordinaire David Grisman released a lovely CD of all acoustic music, ranging from their take on the Dead's "Friend of the Devil" to B.B. King's trademark "The Thrill Is Gone" to Irving Berlin's "Russian Lullaby." And last month Arista issued *Jerry Garcia Band,* yet another live two-CD set. Heavy on cover versions, including the Beatles' "Dear Prudence" and four Bob Dylan songs, the album features Garcia's longtime side band, which now includes John Kahn on bass, David Kemper on drums and Melvin Seals on keyboards. The band will venture out on the road in November for a series of East Coast dates, including one night at Madison Square Garden.

Garcia admits that these solo jaunts are often more entertaining than his work with the Dead, and one gets the feeling that if he felt he could easily extricate himself from the Dead and his attendant responsibilities, he might just do it. Still, when pressed, Garcia claimed the Dead take precedence. "It's still fun to do," he said. "I mean, even at its very worst, there's still something special about it. We've all put so much of our lives into it by now that it's too late to do anything drastic."

Nonetheless, Garcia believes the Dead are at a transitional point, a situation primarily brought about by the drug-related death of Brent Mydland in July 1990. Mydland, who over the years had assumed a major share of the group's songwriting duties, has been replaced by both Vince Welnick, a former member of the Tubes, and Bruce Hornsby, who has been sitting in with the band on the road but whose long-term commitment is uncertain.

During two separate interview sessions, conducted during the band's New York stand, Garcia talked at length about Mydland's death, the current state of the Dead and his attitude toward drugs. He also spent a considerable amount of time discussing his family. His openness on that topic was in part due to his renewed relationship with his eighty-three-year-old aunt – the sister of his late father, Joe Garcia – which prompted him to explore his roots more thoroughly. In addition, Garcia has been playing the role of family man recently. He was accompanied on tour by his current companion, Manasha Matheson, and their young daughter, Keelin, and – as incongruous as it may seem – much of his free time was filled with such activities as visiting zoos and taking carriage rides in Central Park.

* * *

I HEARD THERE WAS a meeting recently, and you told the other band members that you weren't having fun anymore, that you weren't enjoying playing with the Dead. Did that really happen?

Yeah. Absolutely. You see, the way we work, we don't actually have managers and stuff like that. We really manage ourselves. The band is the board of directors, and we have regular meetings with our lawyers and our accountants. And we've got it down to where it only takes about three or four hours, about every three weeks. But anyway, the last couple of times, I've been there screaming, "Hey, you guys!"

Because there are times when you go onstage and it's just plain hard to do, and you start to wonder, "Well, why the fuck are we doing this if it's so hard?"

And how do the other band members feel?

Well, I think I probably brought it out into the open, but everybody in the band is in the same place I am. We've been running on inertia for quite a long time. I mean, insofar as we have a huge overhead, and we have a lot of people that we're responsible for, who work for us and so forth, we're reluctant to do anything to disturb that. We don't want to take people's livelihoods away. But it's *us* out there, you know. And in order to keep doing it, it has to be fun. And in order for it to be fun, it has to keep changing. And that's nothing new. But it is a setback when you've been going in a certain direction and, all of a sudden – *boom!* – a key guy disappears.

You're talking about Brent Mydland?

Yeah. Brent dying was a serious setback – and not just in the sense of losing a friend and all that. But now we've got a whole new band, which we haven't exploited and we haven't adjusted to yet. The music is going to have to take some turns. And we're also going to have to construct new enthusiasm for ourselves, because we're getting a little burned out. We're a little crisp around the edges. So we have to figure out how we are going to make this fun for ourselves. That's our challenge for the moment, and to me the answer is: Let's write a whole bunch of new stuff, and let's thin out the stuff we've been doing. We need a little bit of time to fall back and collect ourselves and rehearse with the new band and come up with some new material that has this band in mind.

Do you think you might stop touring for a year or so, like you did back in 1974?

That's what we're trying to work up to now. We're actually aiming for six months off the road. I think that would be helpful. I don't know when it will happen, but the point is that we're all talking about it. So something's going to happen. We're going to get down and do some serious writing, some serious rehearsing or something. We all know that we pretty much don't want to trash the Grateful Dead. But we also know that we need to make some changes.

You mentioned writing some new material. Why do the Dead seem to have such difficulty writing songs these days?

Well, I don't write them unless I absolutely have to. I don't wake up in the morning and say: "Jeez, I feel great today. I think I'll write a song." I mean, *anything* is more interesting to me than writing a song. It's like, "I think I'd like to write a song . . . No, I guess I better go feed the cat first." You know what I mean? It's like pulling teeth. I don't enjoy it a bit.

I don't think I've ever actually written from inspiration, actually had a song just go *bing!* I only recall that happening to me twice: once was with "Terrapin" and the other was "Wharf Rat." I mean, that's twice in a lifetime of writing!

What about when you made 'Workingman's Dead' and 'American Beauty'? Those two albums are full of great songs, and they both came out in 1970.

Well, Robert Hunter and I were living together then, so that made it real easy. Sheer proximity. See, the way Hunter and I work now is that we get together for like a week or two, and it's like the classic songwriting thing. I bang away

on a piano or a guitar, and I scat phrasing to him or lyrics, and he writes down ideas. And we try stuff.

Have you ever thought of making another album in that vein?

Oh, jeez, I'd love to. But it has to do with writing the stuff, and like I said, I'm about ready now to write a whole bunch of new stuff.

Why do you think the Dead have had such problems making good studio albums?

Well, I think we *have* made a few good ones. *From the Mars Hotel* was an excellent studio album. But since about 1970, the aesthetics of making good studio albums is that you don't hear any mistakes. And when we make a record that doesn't have any mistakes on it, it sounds fucking boring.

Also, I think we have a problem emoting as vocalists in the studio. And there's a developmental problem, too. A lot of our songs don't really stand up and walk until we've been playing them for a couple of years. And if we write them and try to record them right away, we wind up with a stiff version of what the song finally turns into.

Getting back to Brent, did you see his death coming?

Yeah, as a matter of fact, we did. About six or eight months earlier, he OD'd and had to go to the hospital, and they just saved his ass. Then he went through lots of counseling and stuff. But I think there was a situation coming up where he was going to have to go to jail. He was going to have to spend like three weeks in jail, for driving under the influence or one of those things, and it's like he was willing to die just to avoid that.

Brent was not a real happy person. And he wasn't like a total drug person. He was the kind of guy that went out occasionally and binged. And that's probably what killed him. Sometimes it was alcohol, and sometimes it was other stuff. When he would do that, he was one of those classic cases of a guy whose personality would change entirely, and he would just go completely out of control.

You think, "What could I have done to save this guy?" But as you go through life, people die away from you, and you have no choice but to rise to the highest level and look at it from that point of view, because everything else is really painful. And we're old enough now where we've had a lot of people die out from under us. I mean, [artist] Rick Griffin just died.

I wanted to ask you about him.

Oh, God, what a most painful experience. I mean, he was one of those guys that you only get to see two or three times a year, but every time you do see him, you really enjoy it. That's the kind of relationship I had with Rick Griffin. I mean, I really respect him as an artist. I've been a fan of his since the Sixties. And he was a real sweet person. And now I'm not gonna be able to look into those blue eyes . . .

They had a memorial service for him, where his friends took his ashes out on surfboards – he was a surfer, you know – and they scattered his ashes in the ocean. And they had leis and flowers and all this beautiful stuff. His folks were there, and it was very lovely, and they were very satisfied. I mean, for me at this point, I'm just happy if someone dies with a minimum of pain and horror, if they don't have to experience too much fear or anything. It's always hard to deal with death, 'cause there you are confronting the unconfrontable.

the new guy; I mean, he was with us for ten years! That's longer than most bands even last. And we didn't treat him like the new guy. We never did that to him. It's something he did to himself. But it's true that the Grateful Dead is tough to . . . I mean, we've been together so long, and we've been through so much, that it is hard to be a new person around us.

But Brent had a deeply self-destructive streak. And he didn't have much supporting him in terms of an intellectual life. I mean, I owe a lot of who I am and what I've been and what I've done to the beatniks from the Fifties and to the poetry and art and music that I've come in contact with. I feel like I'm part of a continuous line of a certain thing in American culture, of a root. But Brent was from the East Bay, which is one of those places that is like *non*culture. There's nothing there. There's no substance, no background. And Brent wasn't a reader, and he hadn't really been introduced to the world of ideas on any level. So a certain part of him was like a guy in a rat cage, running as fast as he could and not getting anywhere. He didn't have any deeper resources.

My life would be miserable if I didn't have those little chunks of Dylan Thomas and T.S. Eliot. I can't even imagine life without that stuff. Those are the payoffs: the finest moments in music, the finest moments in movies.

Great moments are part of what support you as an artist and a human. They're part of what make you human. What's been great about the human race gives you a sense of how great you might get, how far you can reach. I think the rest of the guys in this band all share stuff like that. We all have those things, those pillars of greatness. And if you're lucky, you find out about them, and if you're not lucky, you don't. And in this day and age in America, a lot of people aren't lucky, and they don't find out about those things.

It was heartbreaking when Brent died, because it seemed like such a waste. Here's this incredibly talented guy – he had a great natural melodic sense, and he was a great singer. And he could have gotten better, but he just didn't see it. He couldn't see what was good about what he was doing, and he couldn't see himself fitting in. And no amount of

And I'm not a religious person; I don't have a lot of faith in the hereafter or anything . . .

Several people have told me that the Dead organization is difficult for a newcomer to deal with; that if you're an insecure person, you're not going to get much comfort.

No, forget it. If you're looking for the comfort, join a club or something. The Grateful Dead is not where you're going to find comfort. In fact, if anything, you'll catch a lot of shit. And if you don't get it from the band, you'll get it from the roadies. They're merciless. They'll just gnaw you like a dog. They'll tear your flesh off. They can be extremely painful.

I heard that Brent never really felt like he fit in.

Brent had this thing that he was never able to shake, which was that thing of being the new guy. And he wasn't effort on our part could make him more comfortable.

When it comes to drugs, I think the public perception of the Grateful Dead is that they are into pot and psychedelics – sort of fun, mind-expansion drugs. Yet Brent died of a cocaine and morphine overdose, and you also had a long struggle with heroin. It seems to run counter to the image of the band.

Yeah, well, I don't know. I've been round and round with the drug thing. People are always wanting me to take a stand on drugs, and I can't. To me, it's so relativistic, and it's also very personal. A person's relationship to drugs is like their relationship to sex. I mean, who is standing on such high ground that they can say: "You're cool. You're not."

For me, in my life, all kinds of drugs have been useful to me, and they have also definitely been a hindrance to me. So, as far as I'm concerned, the results are not in. Psychedelics showed me a whole other universe, hundreds and millions of universes. So that was an incredibly positive experience. But on the other hand, I can't take psychedelics and perform as a professional. I might go out onstage and say, "Hey, fuck this, I want to go chase butterflies!"

Does anyone in the Dead still take psychedelics?

Oh, yeah. We all touch on them here and there. Mushrooms, things like that. It's one of those things where every once in a while you want to blow out the pipes. For me, I just like to know they're available, just because I don't think there's anything else in life apart from a near-death experience that shows you how extensive the mind is.

And as far as the drugs that are dead-enders, like cocaine and heroin and so forth, if you could figure out how to do them without being strung out on them, or without having them completely dominate your personality . . . I mean, if drugs are making your decisions for you, they're no fucking good. I can say that unequivocally. If you're far enough into whatever your drug of choice is, then you are a slave to the drug, and the drug isn't doing you any good. That's not a good space to be in.

Was that the case when you were doing heroin?

Oh, yeah. Sure. I'm an addictive-personality kind of person. I'm sitting here smoking, you know what I mean? And with drugs, the danger is that they run you. Your soul isn't your own. That's the drug problem on a personal level.

How long were you doing heroin?

Oh, jeez. Well, on and off, I guess, for about eight years. Long enough, you know.

Has it been difficult for you to leave heroin behind?

Sure, it's hard. Yeah, of course it is. But my real problem now is with cigarettes. I've been able to quit other drugs, but cigarettes . . . Smoking is one of the only things that's okay. And in a few years it won't be okay. They're closing the door on smoking. So now I'm getting down where I can only do one or two things anymore. My friends won't let me take drugs anymore, and I don't want to scare people anymore. Plus, I definitely have no interest in being an addict. But I'm always hopeful that they're going to come up with good drugs, healthy drugs, drugs that make you feel good and make you smarter.

Smart drugs.

Yeah, right. Exactly.

Have you tried smart drugs?

I tried a couple of things that are supposed to be good for your memory and so forth, but so far I think that, basically, if you get smart about vitamins and amino acids and the like, you can pretty much synthesize all that stuff yourself. Most of the smart drugs I've tried have had no effect, and the ones that did have an effect, it was so small it was meaningless. I mean, if there really was a smart drug, I'd take it right now. "That's really going to make me smart? No shit? Give me that stuff!"

But I still have that desire to change my consciousness, and in the last four years, I've gotten real seriously into scuba diving.

Really?

Yeah. For me, that satisfies a lot of everything. It's physical, which is something I have a problem with. I can't do exercise. I can't jog. I can't ride a bicycle. I can't do any of that shit. And at this stage of my life, I have to do something that's kind of healthy. And scuba diving is like an invisible workout; you're not conscious of the work you're doing. You focus on what's out there, on the life and the beauty of things, and it's incredible. So that's what I do when the Grateful Dead aren't working – I'm in Hawaii, diving.

You became a father again a few years ago. How has fatherhood been this time around?

Well, at this time in my life I wasn't exactly expecting it, but this time I have a little more time to actually *be* a father. My other daughters have all been very good to me, insofar as they've never blamed me for my absentee parenting. And it was tough for them, really, because during the Sixties and Seventies, I was gone all the time. But they've all grown up to be pretty decent people, and they still like me. We still talk. But I never did get to spend a lot of time with them. So this one I'm getting to spend more time with, and that's pretty satisfying.

How old is Keelin?

She's going to be four in December. She's just at the point where animals are a burning passion for her. I took her to the zoo in Cleveland, and I had a lot of fun, feeding the animals and letting the tiger smell my hand and that stuff. And she loves the squirrels and the little birds. She got to feed a giraffe and things like that, so it was fun for her.

She also loves music. She loves to dance, and she loves to sing. She makes up songs furiously. And she has incredible concentration. She builds things. She calls them arrangements. She takes all her stuff and organizes it according to some interior logic. And she works on it for hours and hours. She's really focused. Then she brings me in to look at it, and she walks around it and points things out. And sometimes all the bunnies will be together, looking at you. Or the horses or something. And sometimes the logic defies you. But the way she focuses on it makes me think she's going to do something – that focus, it's genetic or something. That's the way I learned to play guitar, even though I'm not a particularly disciplined person. But she's got it real heavy. I don't know where she's going to go with it, or what she's going to do with it, but she's sure going to make somebody really crazy [*laughs*].

Have any of your other kids shown an interest in music?

Yeah, Heather, my oldest daughter from my first marriage, is now a concert violinist. And that's, like, with no

A walk down memory lane: (Clockwise from top left) The Warlocks on the steps of San Francisco's public library, 1965; father José "Joe" Garcia; Warlocks on Potrero Hill, 1965; Jerry and Sara Garcia at Palo Alto's Tangent Club, 1964; Garcia plays with Robert Hunter, Dave Nelson and Ken Frankle in the Heart Valley Drifters at the Monterey Folk Festival, 1964; banjoist Garcia at St. Michael's Alley coffeehouse with Dave Nelson and Ellen Kavanaugh, 1963; Garcia plays guitar with Hunter and John Winter in the Thunder Mountain Tub Thumpers at a Stanford frat party, 1962. "See, music was always a part of my life. My grandmother listened to country music, and my mother listened to opera. My father was a musician; I was in the middle of music. And nobody was saying this kind of music is good, this kind of music is bad, nobody was telling me rock & roll was out of tune." ~Jerry Garcia, 1972

input from me. Her mom, Sara Katz, tells me that she never particularly encouraged it either. I actually got together with Heather for the first time in a long, long time – I hadn't seen her in, like, eighteen or nineteen years – and I took her to see my friend David Grisman and Stéphane Grappelli, and she loved it. So I hope it's the beginning of something.

It's a funny thing when you have kids. I just relate back to my own past, and I know I still basically feel like a kid, and I feel that anyone who looks like an adult is somebody older than me – although I'm actually older than them now. It's a weird thing. My kids seem to be more mature and older than I am now, somehow. They've gotten ahead of me somehow. But they're very patient with me.

How old is your oldest daughter?

Heather is twenty-seven. I mean, I have people in the audience now who are younger than she is.

You also had two daughters with Mountain Girl, right?

Yeah, Trixie, who's just turned seventeen, and Annabelle, who's twenty-one. Annabelle has always had a good ear, but she's not very interested in music. She's like a computer-graphics person; she draws and designs stuff. And Trixie . . . Trixie is beautiful. It's like, where did *that* come from? She's really a howling knockout, a very pretty little girl.

So are you and Mountain Girl now divorced?

We're working on it. We're in the process of it, but it's been going on for some time. She's real glad to get rid of me. We had a great time, a nice life together, but we went past it. She's got a life of her own now. Actually, we haven't really lived together since the Seventies.

Your father, Joe Garcia, was also a musician, wasn't he?

Yeah, that's right. I didn't get a chance to know him very well. He died when I was five years old, but it's in the genes, I guess, that thing of being attracted to music. When I was little, we used to go to the Santa Cruz Mountains in the summer, and one of my earliest memories is of having a record, an old 78, and I remember playing it over and over on this windup Victrola. This was before they had electricity up there, and I played this record over and over and over until I think they took it from me and broke it or hid it, or something like that. I finally drove everybody completely crazy.

What instrument did your father play?

He played woodwinds; clarinet, mainly. He was a jazz musician. He had a big band – like a forty-piece orchestra – in the Thirties. The whole deal, with strings, harpist, vocalists. My father's sister says he was in a movie, some early talkie. So I've been trying to track that down, but I don't know the name of it. Maybe I'll be able to actually see my father play. I never saw him play with his band, but I remember him playing me to sleep at night. I just barely remember the sound of it. But I'm named after Jerome Kern; that's how seriously the bug bit my father.

How did he die?

He drowned. He was fishing in one of those rivers in California, like the American River. We were on vacation, and I was there on the shore. I actually watched him go under. It was horrible. I was just a little kid, and I didn't really understand what was going on, but then, of course, my life changed. It was one of those things that

afflicted my childhood. I had all my bad luck back then, when I was young and could deal with it.

Like when you lost your finger?

Yeah, that happened when I was about five, too. My brother, Tiff, and I were chopping wood. And I would pick up the pieces of wood, take my hand away, pick up another piece and *boom!* It was an accident. My brother felt perfectly awful about it.

But we were up in the mountains at the time, and my father had to drive to Santa Cruz, maybe about thirty miles, and my mother had my hand all wrapped up in a towel. And I remember it didn't hurt or anything. It was just a sort of buzzing sensation. I don't associate any pain with it. For me, the traumatic part of it was after the doctor amputated it, I had this big cast and bandages on it. And they gradually got smaller and smaller, until I was down to, like, one little bandage. And I thought for sure my finger was under there. And that was the worst part, when the bandage came off. "Oh, my God, my finger's gone." But after that, it was okay, because as a kid, if you have a few little things that make you different, it's a good score. So I got a lot of mileage out of having a missing finger when I was a kid.

What did your mother do for a living?

She was a registered nurse, but after my father died, she took over his bar. He had this little bar right next door to the Sailor's Union of the Pacific, the merchant marine's union, right at First and Harrison, in San Francisco. It was a day-time bar, a working guy's bar, so I grew up with all these guys who were sailors. They went out and sailed to the Far East and the Persian Gulf, the Philippines and all that, and they would come and hang out in the bar all day long and talk to me when I was a kid. It was great fun for me.

I mean, that's my background. I grew up in a bar. And that was back in the days when the Orient was still the Orient, and it hadn't been completely Americanized yet. They'd bring back all these weird things. Like, one guy had the world's largest private collection of photographs of square-riggers. He was an old sea captain, and he had a mint-condition 1947 Packard that he parked out front. And he had a huge wardrobe of these beautifully tailored double-breasted suits from the Thirties. And he'd tell these incredible stories. And that was one of the reasons I couldn't stay in school. School was a little too boring. And these guys also gave me a glimpse into a larger universe that seemed so attractive and fun and, you know, *crazy.*

But there were a couple of teachers who had a big impact on you, weren't there?

I had a great third-grade teacher, Miss Simon, who was just a peach. She was the first person who made me think it was okay to draw pictures. She'd say, "Oh, that's lovely," and she'd have me draw pictures and do murals and all this stuff. As soon as she saw I had some ability, she capitalized on it. She was very encouraging, and it was the first time I heard that the idea of being a creative person was a viable possibility in life. "You mean you can spend all day drawing pictures? Wow! What a great piece of news."

She enlarged the world for me, just like the sailors did. I had another good teacher, Dwight Johnson. He's the guy that turned me into a freak. He was my seventh-grade teacher, and he was a wild guy. He had an old MG TC, you know, beautiful man. And he also had a Vincent Black Shadow motorcycle, the fastest-accelerating motorcycle at the time. And he was out there. He opened lots and lots of doors. He's the guy that got me reading deeper than science fiction. He taught me that ideas are fun. And he's alive somewhere. I ran into some guys not long ago who said Dwight Johnson's alive and is teaching down in Southern California – Santa Barbara or something. He's one of those guys I'd like to say hello to 'cause he's partly responsible for me being here.

With the Dead and especially with your own band, you tend to cover a lot of Dylan tunes. What is it about his material that attracts you?

You can sing them without feeling like an idiot. Most songs are basically like love songs, and I don't feel like I'm exactly the most romantic person in the world. So I can only do so many love songs without feeling like an idiot. Dylan's songs go in lots of different directions, and I sing some of his songs because they speak to me emotionally on some level. Sometimes, I don't even know why. Like that song "Señor." There's something so creepy about that song, but it's very satisfying in a weird sort of way. Not that I know anything about it, because you listen to the lyrics, and you go, "What the hell is this?" But there's something about it emotionally that says: This is talking about a kind of desperation that everybody experiences. It's like Dylan has written songs that touch into places people have never sung about before. And to me that's tremendously powerful. And also, because he's an old folkie, he sometimes writes a beautiful melody. He doesn't always *sing* it, but it's there. So that combination of a tremendously evocative melody and a powerful lyric is something you can do without feeling like an idiot.

I have a real problem with that standing onstage anyway. I feel like an idiot most of the time. It's like getting up in front of your senior class and making a speech. Basically, when you get up in front of a lot of people, you feel like an idiot. There's no getting around that, and so a powerful song provides powerful armor.

You, Bruce Hornsby, Branford Marsalis and Rob Wasserman recently recorded the music for a series of Levi's ads directed by Spike Lee. Do you enjoy playing with those guys?

I love it, any chance I get. I mean, for those ads we just fucked around, really. They mixed the music so far back that you can just barely recognize us. You can almost make out Branford. I mean, you can't hear me or Bruce.

Do you ever feel like you have more fun playing with those guys than with the Dead?

Oh, sure. Absolutely. And that's always dangling in front of me, the thing of, well, shit, if I was on my own, God I could . . . But the thing is, the Grateful Dead is unique. It's not like anything else. I mean, there are lots of great musicians in the world, and I get to play with the ones who want to play with me, at least. And that's important to me. I mean, Bruce, Branford, Rob and I have actually talked about putting something together. I had this notion of putting together a band that had no material, that just got onstage and blew.

And maybe one of these days, we'll make that happen.

Hornsby seems to be taking a major role onstage with the Dead these days.

Well, he's certainly been pushing me. He's got great ears. And I also have a hard time losing him. I try, "Hey, Bruce, follow this." But he's there all the time. He also has a good sense of when not to play. And he's got a great rhythmic feeling.

So is he a full-time member of the band?

Well, he's acting like it. It's a wonderful gift to the band to have him in it now. It's a lucky break for us.

You mentioned "Wharf Rat" earlier. What do you think of the Midnight Oil version on the 'Deadicated' album?

I think it's terrific. That record is full of wonderful surprises.

What other tracks do you like?

I like "Ripple" by Jane's Addiction. And I really like "Friend of the Devil" by Lyle Lovett. Very tasty. And the Indigo Girls and Suzanne Vega I really like. And it was very flattering to me to have Elvis Costello, who I think is just a real dear guy and a serious music lover, do one of our songs.

What other music are you listening to these days?

All kinds of stuff. I listen to anything anyone gives me. I always go back to a few basic favorites. I can always listen to Django Reinhardt and hear something I haven't heard before. I like to listen to Art Tatum and Coltrane and Charlie Parker. Those are guys who never seem to run out of ideas. And there are all kinds of great new players. Michael Hedges is great. And my personal favorite lately is this guy Frank Gambale, who's been playing with Chick Corea for the past couple of years.

What about pop music or, say, a band like Living Colour?

Living Colour is a great band. Their whole approach is interesting, but they're short on melodies. And unless they find something with more melody, they're going to have a hard time getting to that next level. That's a tough space where they are right now; I think the most talented guy in the band is going to look to break out if the band doesn't go somewhere.

Jane's Addiction is another band I like. A great band.

You turn fifty next year. How does that feel?

God, I never thought I'd make it. I didn't think I'd get to be forty, to tell you the truth. Jeez, I feel like I'm a hundred million years old. Really, it's amazing. Mostly because it puts all things I associate with my childhood so far back. The Fifties are now like the way I used to think the Twenties were. They're, like, lost in time somewhere back there.

And I mean, here we are, we're getting into our fifties, and where are these people who keep coming to our shows coming from? What do they find so fascinating about these middle-aged bastards playing basically the same thing we've always played? I mean, what do seventeen-year-olds find fascinating about this? I can't believe it's just because they're interested in picking up on the Sixties, which they missed. Come on, hey, the Sixties were fun, but shit, it's fun being young, you know, nobody really misses out on that. So what is it about the Nineties in America? There must be a dearth of fun out there in America. Or adventure. Maybe that's it: Maybe we're just one of the last adventures in America. I don't know. ℭ

THE MUSIC NEVER STOPS

HIRSCHFELD

THE ROLLING STONE INTERVIEW WITH JERRY GARCIA

BY ANTHONY DeCURTIS

THEY MAKE an unlikely pair – one portly, in a rumpled windbreaker, black T-shirt and jeans; the other painfully fit, impeccably turned out in an elegant silk jacket – but Jerry Garcia and Sting seem to have hit it off quite nicely. Not that they had exactly memorized each other's musical catalogue before Sting agreed to open a run of dates for the Grateful Dead during their summer stadium tour.

"I listened to *American Beauty* last night for the first time in ten years," Sting tells Garcia as the two men relax one evening in the bar of the Four Seasons Ritz Carlton Hotel in Chicago. "It was quite good. I liked 'Friend of the Devil.' And 'Box of Rain.' " For his part, Garcia, after a stunning jam with Sting's group during sound check at Soldier Field two days later, asks a bystander the title of one of the songs the band had played ("Walking on the Moon") and which album it was on.

Garcia – whom Sting has genially dubbed Father Christmas – has taken to joining Sting onstage during his sets, adding his characteristically spidery guitar lines to a moody medley of "Tea in the Sahara" and "Consider Me Gone" on the first of two Chicago dates. "Sting's an A-list guy," Garcia says before one of the shows. "Everybody knows he's a wonderful musician and a truly fine person, too. It's nice that we get to meet him, hang out with him a little bit and sort of . . . *network* a little with him. We share interests, and I think there's stuff that we could do together in the hypothetical future that would be fun for him and for us – and possibly good for other things, too."

The hypothetical future: Now fifty-one, battling diabetes and other health problems, Garcia still looks unstintingly ahead. In conversation, he is a marvel, bouncing associatively from topic to topic, sharing his amiable intelligence as if it were a gift, in love with good talk. Childlike in his curiosity and enthusiasm, he has more projects going – and more different types of projects – than most musicians half his age. The Dead are planning to record a new studio album, their first since *Built to Last* in 1989, for release next spring. As the band's summer tour crosses the country, a collection of Garcia's artwork – pen-and-ink drawings, watercolors, computer-generated images – has accompanied it, with gallery displays in the various cities the Dead have visited.

An album of traditional children's songs, *Not for Kids Only,* with mandolinist David Grisman is set to appear in September on Grisman's label, Acoustic Disc. For a collaboration with the Redwood Symphony, with which his eldest daughter plays violin, Garcia is commissioning works for orchestra and guitar. Of course, the Jerry Garcia Band is a going concern, with an East Coast tour planned for November. And Garcia also hopes at some point to pull together *another* band, featuring Edie Brickell on vocals, for shows of entirely improvised music and lyrics.

"I had this idea of putting together a band that didn't have any material, nothing worked out – just the extreme version," he says. "Edie's actually prepared to do this. I've talked to her about it. She's even ready to have people in the audience say, 'I want you to use these words,' or 'I want you to make this the subject of the song.' "

Clearly, this is not a man who has run out of either energy, ideas or passion. But Garcia's collapse from exhaustion in

August 1992 – and the consequent cancellation of a number of Dead shows – raised the specter of the diabetic coma that had nearly taken his life in 1986. Now he is back and leading the Dead through some of their best shows in years. He is also trying to change his life – cutting down on cigarettes, eating better, exercising some – motivated by his desire, eventually, to do everything. "I feel that I can honestly contribute something," he says. And as you'll see, he's looking ahead well into the next century.

* * *

EVERYONE KNOWS *about the origins of the Grateful Dead. What about your own musical beginnings?*

Music was something I was *not* good at. I took lessons on the piano *forever,* for maybe eight years; my mom made me. None of it sank in. I never did learn how to sight-read for the piano – I bluffed my way through.

I was attracted to music very early on, but it never occurred to me it was something to do – in the sense that when I grow up I'm going to be a musician – although I knew that my father had been a musician.

You never had thoughts along those lines?

Not ever. Not once.

Still?

[*Laughs.*] Really, *still,* in a way. It's like I'm still sort of surprised by it. My older brother was a big influence. He was, like, four years older than me, so I listened to the music he listened to.

What kind of stuff?

He was into very early rock & roll and rhythm & blues. I remember, like, the Crows, you know, "Gee." Very early, before it actually started to become rock & roll. That tune, "Gee," was sort of the borderline. It was basically black music, the early doo-wop groups. I love that stuff. Hank Ballard and the Midnighters were a big early influence for me. My brother would learn the tunes, we would try to sing them, and he would make me learn harmony parts. In a way, I learned a lot of my ear training from my older brother.

What about bluegrass? When did you come to that?

My grandmother was a big Grand Ole Opry fan. Now, this is in San Francisco, a *long* way from Tennessee, but they used to have the Opry on the radio every Saturday night all over the United States. My grandmother listened to it religiously. I probably heard Bill Monroe hundreds of times without knowing who he was.

When I got turned on to bluegrass in about 1960, the first time I *really* heard it, it was like "*Whoa,* what *is* this music?" The banjo just . . . it just made me crazy. It was like the way rock & roll affected me when I was fifteen. When I was fifteen, I fell madly in love with rock & roll. Chuck Berry was happening big, Elvis Presley – not *so* much Elvis Presley, but I really liked Gene Vincent, you know, the *other* rock guys, the guys that played guitar good: Eddie Cochran, Buddy Holly, Bo Diddley. And at that time, the R&B stations still were playing stuff like Lightnin' Hopkins and Frankie Lee Sims, these funky blues guys. Jimmy McCracklin, the Chicago-style blues guys, the T-Bone Walker–influenced guys, that older style, pre-B.B. King stuff. Jimmy Reed – Jimmy Reed actually had *hits* back in those days. You listen to that, and it's so funky. It's a beautiful sound, but I had no idea how to go about learning it.

When I first heard electric guitar, when I was fifteen, that's what I wanted to play. I petitioned my mom to get me one, so she finally did for my birthday. Actually, she got me an *accordion,* and I went nuts – *Aggghhh, no, no, no!* I railed and raved, and she finally turned it in, and I got a pawnshop electric guitar and an amplifier. I was just beside myself with joy.

I started banging away on it without having the slightest idea of . . . *anything.* I didn't know how to tune it up, I had no idea. My stepfather tuned it in some kind of weird way, like an open chord. I thought, "Well, that's the way it's tuned. Okay." I played it that way for about a year before I finally ran into some kid at school who actually could play a little. He showed me a few basic chords, and that was it. I never took any lessons. I don't even think there was anybody teaching around the Bay Area. I mean, electric guitar was, like, from *Mars,* you know. You didn't *see* 'em, even.

During this time, too, I was going to the art institute on Saturdays and summer sessions – they had this program for high school kids. So I was picking up that head. This was also when the beatniks were happening in San Francisco, so I was, like, in that culture. I was a high school kid and a wannabe beatnik! Rock & roll at that time was *not* respectable. I mean, beatniks didn't like rock & roll.

Because they were more literary or something?

They liked . . . *jazz* [*laughs*]. You know: "Jazz, man. Dig it." Rock & roll wasn't cool, but I *loved* rock & roll. I used to have these fantasies about "I want rock & roll to be, like, *respectable* music." I wanted it to be like *art.*

You consciously thought that?

Oh, yeah, even back then. I used to try to think of ways to make that work. I wanted to do something that fit in with the art institute, that kind of self-conscious art – "art" as opposed to "popular culture." Back then, they didn't even

Garcia with fellow San Francisco musician and Woodstock veteran Carlos Santana, 1977.

talk about popular culture. I mean, rock & roll was so *not legit,* you know. It was completely out of the picture. I don't know what they thought it was, like white-trash music or kids' music.

The Beats, though, not only played a role in opposing the dominant culture of the Fifties, but they helped in the transition from the Fifties to the Sixties, as you did with Ken Kesey and the Acid Tests.

Well, it was very resonant for me. The arts school I went to was in North Beach, and in those days the old Coexistence Bagel Shop was open and the Place; notorious beatnik places where these guys – Lawrence Ferlinghetti, Kenneth Rexroth – would get up and read their poetry. As soon as *On the Road* came out, I read it and fell in love with it, the adventure, the romance of it, everything.

You've said that one of the reasons for the traveling culture sur-rounding the Grateful Dead is that it offers the possibility for the same kind of adventure that 'On the Road' represents.

I think it does. It is this time frame's version of the arche-typal American adventure. It used to be that you could run away and join the circus, say, or ride the freight trains.

One of the things that was fun about the early hippie scene was, all of a sudden all those people were around and you could meet them. I mean, Neal Cassady, meeting him was tremendously thrilling. He was a huge influence on me in ways I can't really describe.

Like an attitude or . . .

Yeah, lots of things, though, kind of *musical* things in a way – rhythm, you know, motion, timing. I mean, Neal was a master of timing. He was like a twelfth-dimensional Lenny Bruce in a way, some kind of cross between a great stand-up comedian like Lenny Bruce and somebody like Buster Keaton. He had this great combination of physical poetry and an incredible mind. He was a model for the idea that a person can become art by himself, that you don't necessarily even need a forum.

Did you ever get to meet Lenny Bruce?

Yeah, very briefly. I worked for a secretary transcribing tapes of his performances for his trials. I learned so much about Lenny Bruce's mind, because sometimes he was so methed out that he would condense, like, a paragraph into one word. This is after he stopped doing routines – he would just sit down and blow. He'd have, like, a *Newsweek* or a *Time* magazine, and he'd thumb through them, and whenever something caught his eye, he would just start riffing. I used to have to try to find the *Newsweek* . . . you know, go to the library – and sometimes it was so amazingly far-out, the way he would condense the whole sense of an article. I wasn't close to him at all, but I did meet him some. A remarkable person.

When the Dead started out, did you have a sense that it would last this long?

We had big ideas. I mean, as far as we were concerned, we were going to be the next Beatles or something – we were on a trip, definitely. We had enough of that kind of crazy faith in ourselves.

We were always motivated by the possibility that we could have fun. *Big fun.* I was reacting, in a way, to my bluegrass background, which was maybe a little overserious. I was up for the idea of breaking out. You know – "Give me that electric guitar – *fuckin' A!*" When we were in the Warlocks, the first time we played in public, we had a huge crowd of people from the local high school, and they went fuckin' *nuts!* The next time we played, it was packed to the rafters. It was a pizza place. We said, "Hey, can we play in here on Wednesday night? We won't bother anybody. Just let us set up in the corner." It was *pandemonium,* immediately.

I don't remember ever thinking, "Now, am I going to be doing this in twenty years?" But it never occurred to me that I *wouldn't* be doing it. And as things went on, we went past my own personal – what? – goals, visions, my own *imagining* "This is how far we could go." So we're way over in the land of pure gravy, so to speak. Now it's, like, stuff that I might idly have wished for one day in 1957 is coming up.

One thing that's coming up is a new Dead studio album that you're writing songs for. How does your relationship with Robert Hunter work? Do you say to him, "These are the things that are on my mind," or does he just give you lyrics?

I don't usually discuss content with Hunter – I discuss stuff like energy. Like I say, "We really need something that's like a strong medium-tempo rock & roll feeling; a big idea." Or sometimes I'll say, "I'd like to do something that's very intimate and personal." Hunter knows me well enough that he can write me as good as I could ever hope to write myself. He knows the way my mind works. He knows what I'll accept, that I have thresholds – like, "This lyric is too silly, I can't sing it."

You'll flat-out say that?

Yeah, or, "This lyric exposes too much of something, and I don't feel I can do that."

Exposes a fact or an emotion?

For me, it's always emotional – can I live with this song? I'm going to have to get onstage and *be* this song. I'm going to have to represent this point of view, this idea. And if it doesn't work for me, I can't do it. I can't act, you know? So there has to be something authentic about it. Hunter knows that, and he's very good at pulling things out that are both specific enough and diffuse enough for me to feel comfortable. It's very intimate, really, our relationship as cowriters. I feel like I can discuss anything with Hunter, any idea, without any difficulty at all. And we're both very comfortable with each other on the level of changing stuff. Sometimes I insist that he do something over and over.

Could you give me an example?

One of the songs we wrote recently is "The Days Between." I had an idea there: It had to do with the length of the phrases and how I wanted the phrases to work. I had a hard time communicating it. But with Hunter, it's a matter of finding the key. I'll sort of scat-sing the way I want it to work . . .

Like a melody?

Yeah. I always have the melody first. Well, that's not true, but the melody is the first thing I try to evolve. Sometimes it starts with the lyrics. I'll say, "I want these lines to rhyme and these lines not to rhyme." I tell him where I want the stresses to be, where I want vowels to be, and so forth.

It's that technical?

You can't hold a note if it's a consonant, so if you're going to have this long note in the melody, it has to be a vowel. You have to be that specific. Hunter and I have been doing this for a long time. We've discovered that – in the first three years – we wrote a lot of songs that you can't sing [*laughs*]. They were too rangy, and there was no room to breathe in them. And sometimes you accent things in a way that's *non-English*, you know what I mean? Part of it is making it so that the musical syntax is the same as the linguistic syntax.

In "The Days Between," there's a lot of repetition of words – like "phantom" and "days" – that adds to the song's spooky, melancholic feel.

The *phantom* thing was funny, because first that line went, "When ships with phantom sails set to sea on phantom tides." I said, "I want it to be, 'When something ships with phantom sails set to sea on phantom tides' – I want another two syllables." So Hunter came up with a bunch of things, but then he said, "What about *phantom*? Use *phantom* again." Yeah, *right*: "When *phantom* ships with phantom sails set to sea on phantom tides." It worked perfectly. It has this ghostly, hollow quality – it's skeletal. So singing that song is like, *oooh*, it *works* for me. I get chills. It's that happy marriage of setting and sense. Hunter – he's so good at that. We're really hitting some nice spaces lately.

The other two new songs you've been playing, "Lazy River Road" and "Liberty," both also have a real distinctive feel.

We have a few more on the rails that are not ready to be performed. I'd like to spit out another five or six tunes this year, and hopefully that'll happen. Really, it's pretty easy: All Hunter and I have to do is get together. I find it hard to write without being in his presence, but when we're together, it starts snapping. But it's also the hardest thing to do, because writing music is probably my least favorite thing in the world. I mean, I'd rather . . . you know, throw cards in a hat. Anything. Anything is more interesting than the idea of writing.

It's surprising to hear you say that. You're obviously literate and interested in words. Have you ever felt the impulse to write your own lyrics?

I never have. I've never felt that I have something to say that wasn't being said. I don't feel I have whatever it takes to be a writer. I've never been able to sustain an idea and get it down. It's hard for me to do it with music, too, as far as that goes. I feel like I'm swimming upstream; my own preferences are for improvisation, for making it up as I go along. The idea of *picking*, of eliminating possibilities by deciding, that's difficult for me.

So what does a studio album mean for the band now?

I can't encompass it with my point of view, because it usually isn't made up of just my material – it's made up of all of our material. The material has to speak to us, you know: "This album seems to be going in this direction, or it contains these elements," and then you try to see if you can sew it together. The basic odyssey format or variety show, you know. Something rubbery like that usually is best because it's tough to get everything under the same umbrella. Sometimes the sound of it will be the unifying feature. Sometimes it's not there at all.

Are all of you in compatible spaces as far as this upcoming particular album is concerned?

I think so. It used to be *wildly* different. If you checked on each of us about what our version of Grateful Dead music was, it used to be way different from each other. We're all sort of looking at the same thing now – kind of. I mean, each person still sees it through his own frame of reference, but that's what Grateful Dead music is, you know: Grateful Dead music is a holographic experience. It's made up of the points of view of all of the members of the band; consequently, every angle that you look at it from, it's different.

And a lot of times, it's unpredictable. That's one of the things that makes it interesting to keep doing.

The way we're approaching this album, and we've done it in the past, too, with our better albums, is to let the material live onstage for about a year. It starts to evolve into something different. I mean, it's probably a way of saying, "This is a collaborative effort." Even though, say, Hunter and I write some of the actual songs, the way they end up and the whole presentation is really a collaborative effort. The whole Grateful Dead makes the music, you know. The writers don't do arrangements. The Grateful Dead is kind of an arrangement machine, and the arrangements are, by their nature, surprising. I almost never can predict what the band's going to do in any given situation. And it took a long, long time to realize that I'm not always *right,* you know [*laughs*].

Is this possible?

It's a tough thing to admit. My point of view really is, musically speaking, sort of *conservative.* I'm like a little on the . . . maybe a little stodgy, you know. Slightly.

How do you mean?

Well, I don't think of my ideas as being very far-out, musically. The thing that works for me in music is the emotional component, not the technical side. I am fascinated by musical weirdness – like *Blues for Allah,* for example. But really, the thing that propels me through music is the emotional reality of it. And as I get older, I surrender more to that. I trust that intuition.

How do you perceive your various musical relationships: the Dead, your band, your projects with David Grisman? Do they merge, or are they clearly compartmentalized in your mind?

They do bleed into each other, but that's okay. I don't prevent that from happening. But I do try to keep them separate, because I love them for reasons of their own. I like their identities to be clear.

What are the differences?

The Garcia Band really reflects my musical personality. The people in that band think – musically, conceptually – the way I do. Their notion of the way the instruments should speak to each other – I don't have to show anybody anything. When we work out a tune, all I have to do is say, "Here's the tune, here's the changes, here's the chords" – and it just happens. And it happens *perfectly.* It happens better than if I told everybody, "This is *exactly* what I want you to play." I mean, that band, to me, is total resonance. It's consonance. It's like, yes, yes, that's *my* version of music! The Grateful Dead has more dissonance in it. It has more variables and more wild cards and more oddness. And it has more tension, too. I mean, to Grateful

Dead fans, my band might be a little bit too agreeable.

Grisman is a very rigorous musician. He likes to rehearse and get things down perfectly. He's a master of detail. I'm *not* those things, but we balance each other out. I'm loose enough to loosen him up, and he's tight enough to tighten me up. We also share a love for American traditional music, for bluegrass and for acoustic music. And for swing. Me and David are working on a children's album right now. It's something I never would have thought to do. It's kind of a reaction to the revisionist approach to children's songs.

Like what?

There are these shows that have the old children's songs, but they've rewritten the lyrics to make them tamer or

more gentle. It's infuriating, because these songs are part of the oral tradition of America. A lot of them are perfectly lovely. Some of them have teeth, but, hey, so what? I mean, kids get enough mindless, senseless stuff. So we've gone poking around in some mountain music and traditional stuff for children's songs that don't *want* to be changed. We'd like to introduce them to the kids the way they are and let them be. We've been taking a real simple and spontaneous approach – just picking and singing, you know. This music should be heard. It's part of our heritage.

One of your goals seems to be to explore every genre of American music.

Oh, definitely. If I live long enough, I hope to do exactly that. I missed out on a lot of legitimate music by not being a music student. I didn't play a band instrument; I didn't have that background. But I've been learning about these other worlds. I would love to be able to play, like, *Gershwin* tunes. And I will do it. There's a lot of great music in the American experience, and I hope to be able to touch as much of it as I can. I feel that I can honestly contribute something.

A friend mentioned to me that he had discovered Merle Haggard through the Dead, and on your solo albums you'll cover everyone from Smokey Robinson to Irving Berlin.

It's all good shit. I believe that a good song is a good song. My great experience in these last couple of years was Steve Parish, my road guy; his second cousin was Mitchell Parish, the guy that wrote the lyrics to "Stardust." I | *Above: Eric Clapton and Jerry Garcia, 1967. At right: Twenty years later, the Dead with inspiration and collaborator, Bob Dylan, 1987.*

got to hang out with him, ninety-two years old. I hung out with him, like, five or six times – good hangouts, you know. He was so fun. He was, like, the *book,* you know. He wrote "Deep Purple," "Sweet Lorraine"; some of the most incredible songs that were written in this century. *"Stardust,"* for Christ's sake! "Sophisticated Lady." I mean, God, what a guy. Getting to know him was an incredible experience. When he died last year, it was a crusher. I really wanted to write a song with him.

With your health problems, were you concerned that you might never get to do the things you've been talking about wanting to do?

Absolutely. I was getting to the place where I had a hard time playing a show. I was in terrible fucking shape. I mean, I was just *exhausted,* totally exhausted. I could barely walk up a flight of stairs without panting and wheezing. I just let my physical self slide as far as I possibly could.

Did you deny to yourself what was happening?

Oh, yeah, because I'm basically a lazy fuck. Things have to get to the point where they're screaming before I'll do anything. I could see it coming, and I kept saying to myself: "Well, as soon as I get myself together, I'm going to start working out. I'm going on that diet." Quit smoking – *ayiiiiii* [*waves lit cigarette*].

In a way I was lucky, insofar as I had an iron constitution. But time naturally gets you, and finally your body just doesn't spring back the way it did. I think it had to get as bad as it did before I would get serious about it. I mean, it's a powerful incentive, the possibility that, hey, if you keep going the way you are, in two years you're going to be dead. But I definitely have a component in my personality which is not exactly self-destructive, but it's certainly ornery. There's a part of me that has a *bad attitude.* It's like "*Fuck* you," you know? [*Laughs.*] "Try to get healthy" – "Fuck you, man." And, I mean, part of this whole process has been coming to terms with my bad-attitude self, trying to figure out "What does this part of me want?"

I don't know what it comes from. I've always clung to it, see, because I felt it's part of what makes me *me.* Being anarchic, having that anarchist streak, serves me on other levels – artistically, certainly. So I don't want to eliminate that aspect of my personality. But I see that on some levels it's working against me.

They're gifts, some of these aspects of your personality. They're helpful and useful and powerful, but they also have this other side. They're indiscriminate. They don't make judgments.

What about in terms of the Dead? Were there times when the band was discouraged about its future?

Well, there were times when we were really in chaotic spaces, but I don't think we've ever been totally discouraged. It just has never happened. There have been times everybody was off on their own trip to the extent that we barely communicated with each other. But it's pulses, you know? And right now everybody's relating pretty nicely to each

other, and everybody's feeling very good, too. There's a kind of healthy glow through the whole Grateful Dead scene. We're gearing up for the millennium.

Oh, yeah? What's the plan?

Well, our plan is to get *through* the millennium [*laughs*]. Apart from that, it's totally amorphous.

Historically, turns of the century have been really intriguing times. Does that date hold any real significance for you?

No, the date that holds significance for me is 2012. That's [*self-described expert in "the ethno-pharmacology of spiritual transformation"*] Terence McKenna's alpha moment, which is where the universe undergoes its most extraordinary transformations. He talks about these cycles, exponential cycles in which, in each epic, more happens than in all previous time. Like, he talks about novelty, the insertion of novelty into the time track. His first example of novelty is, say, the appearance of life. So the universe goes along, *brrrrmmmmm,* then all of a sudden, life appears: *bing!* So that's something new.

Then the next novelty is, like, vertebrates. Then the next novelty might be language, that sort of thing. They're transformations of a huge kind, gains in consciousness. So he's got us, like, in the last forty-year cycle now – it's running down, we're definitely tightening up – and during this period, more will happen than has happened in all previous time. This is going to peak in 2012. He's got a specific date for it, too; maybe December some time, I don't remember. But that moment, at the last 135th of a second or something like that, something like forty of these transformations will happen. Like *immortality,* you know [*laughs*]. It's an incredibly wonderful and totally transformational view of the universe. I love it, personally. It's my favorite ontology, my favorite endgame. It's much, much more visionary and sumptuous than . . . like, say, *Christ* is coming back [*laughs*]. "Oh, swell. That would be fun." McKenna's version is much more incredible.

Are you concerned about what you'd leave behind?

No. I'm hoping to leave a clean field – nothing, not a thing. I'm hoping they burn it all with me. I don't feel like there's this body of work that must exist. I'd just as soon take it all with me. There's enough stuff – who needs the clutter, you know? I'd rather have my immortality here while I'm alive. I don't care if it lasts beyond me at all. I'd just as soon it didn't.

Maybe it will just scorch in 2012.

Yeah, I'm hoping that the transformations will make all that – *everything* – irrelevant. We'll all just go to the next universe as pure thought forms – *wowwwwnnnng.* Yeah.   ☾

I'M BASICALLY a lazy fuck. Things have to get to the point where they're screaming before I'll do anything. I could see it coming, and I kept saying to myself, Well, as soon as I get myself together, I'm going to go on that diet. Quit smoking – *ayiiiii [waves a lit cigarette].*

IN A WAY I was lucky insofar as I had an iron constitution. But time naturally gets you, and finally your body just doesn't spring back the way it did. I think it had to get as bad as it did before I would get serious about it. I mean, it's a powerful incentive, the possibility that, hey, if you keep going the way you are, in two years you're going to be dead.

~JERRY GARCIA, 1993

FUNERAL FOR A

FRIEND

BY ALEC FOEGE

ON AUGUST 9, 1995, Jerry Garcia died in his sleep at Serenity Knolls drug treatment center, in the Marin County community of Forest Knolls, north of San Francisco. He was fifty-three. In addition to his wife, Deborah Koons Garcia, Jerry Garcia is survived by four daughters: Heather, thirty-two; Annabelle, twenty-five; Teresa, twenty-one; and Keelin, seven.

A preliminary coroner's report concluded that Garcia died of natural causes, and longtime Grateful Dead spokesman Dennis McNally specified the cause as a heart attack. But it was the continuing battle to end his heroin addiction that brought Garcia to Serenity Knolls less than two days before his death. He was found in bed by a counselor at the center; subsequently a staff nurse and Marin County paramedics administered CPR but failed to revive him. A long-term drug problem had debilitated Garcia, who also suffered from diabetes and heart problems in recent years. Still, he struggled to stay clean. Doctors at the Haight Ashbury Free Clinic's detox unit had also been treating him for several years, and he had entered the Betty Ford Center, in Rancho Mirage, California, after the July 9 conclusion of the band's tour. According to Koons Garcia, he left that facility two weeks shy of the scheduled one-month stay.

For Jerry Garcia and, perhaps, the Grateful Dead, the last musical note came July 9 at Chicago's Soldier Field, the final stop on a problem-plagued summer tour. Whether the band will carry on remains unclear. The band held a meeting August 14, according to McNally; it announced only that its fall tour would be canceled. On the night of August 9, Dead guitarist Bob Weir went ahead with a scheduled solo show at the Casino Ballroom, in Hampton Beach, New Hampshire, where Deadheads massed in the parking lot before, during and after the show. "If our dear, departed friend proved anything to us," Weir told the capacity crowd, "he proved that great music can make sad times better."

A private funeral was held for family and friends August 11 at St. Stephen's Episcopal Church in Belvedere, an upscale suburb on a peninsula north of San Francisco.

Preceding pages: (From left) Babatunde Olatunji, Paul Kantner, two drummers, John Perry Barlow, Bob Weir and Deborah Koons Garcia at the Polo Field memorial.

McNally said that the church was chosen for its size and availability, not to invoke "St. Stephen," one of the Grateful Dead's most popular songs. At 3:00 p.m. vans shuttled more than two hundred mourners from a parking lot in nearby Tiburon to Belvedere. "They kept the location so secret that even the people who were going didn't know where it was," said attendee Joel Selvin, a pop-music critic at the *San Francisco Chronicle.*

The service began at 4:00 p.m. In attendance were band members Bob Weir, Phil Lesh, Bill Kreutzmann, Mickey Hart and Vince Welnick, as well as Garcia's widow, Deborah Koons Garcia. Garcia, dressed in a black T-shirt, sweat pants and a windbreaker, was displayed in an open casket. The Reverend Matthew Fox officiated. Fox, an Episcopal minister, married Garcia and Koons on Valentine's Day 1994, in Sausalito, California.

While the general mood at the funeral was solemn, there were moments of irreverence and laughter. Ken Kesey told the crowd, "This guy is going to kick our asses if we get up there and we haven't carried the torches." Kreutzmann capped off his humorous comments by adding dismissively, "Anyway, funerals are for people, not spirits." Others in attendance included Robert Hunter, Bob Dylan, Bruce Hornsby and basketball legend Bill Walton.

As the word of Garcia's death spread in the days before the funeral, the public mourned as though a president had passed away. The Internet and commercial computer networks were flooded with fans' online reminiscences and eulogies. Spontaneous memorial services and impromptu wakes sprang up in dozens of cities around the United States. Over the course of a week, the informal Garcia tributes around San Francisco took on increasingly messianic tones. By early afternoon on Wednesday, August 9, hundreds of well-wishers had begun gathering at the northeast corner of Haight and Ashbury streets, the intersection irrevocably associated with the birth of the Sixties counterculture. That evening a crowd of nearly two thousand mourners headed for the Polo Field in Golden Gate Park – the site of a Dead performance at the Human Be-In twenty-eight years ago – where they kneeled at a makeshift shrine and danced into the night to bootleg tapes of Grateful Dead concerts.

On Thursday afternoon in Golden Gate Park, the constant beat of a drum circle mesmerized a group of dancers, who invariably danced the loose-limbed shimmy shake traditionally reserved for Dead concerts. Fans of all stripes comforted each other, as when a twentysomething Hare Krishna approached a quiet group of mourners who were genuflecting before a shrine built atop a traffic pylon. "I just want you guys to know that Jerry's going to have a good death," he said. "He once met with our leader."

"Whatever you believe, man," responded a reclining young woman in a granny dress without ever averting her gaze from a photo of Garcia that leaned on the shrine.

Joel Selvin, who had interviewed Garcia more than once over the years, professed that the humble guitarist would have been dismayed by the more extreme displays of devotion. "Fame was a real onus to him," Selvin said. "It terrified him; it squashed him in a corner and probably contributed to the self-destructive behavior. His mission was to be a musician, to be an artist."

By late Friday evening, the numbers at the Polo Field had grown. Sleeping bags dotted the lawn, and fleets of microbuses lurked in the woods surrounding the field.

"I didn't even come here expecting a big tribute," said Jennifer, twenty-three, a fan who flew in from Boston on Thursday with little clothing and not even a blanket to ward off the night's chill. "I just came here because this is where it all began." The manager of a Ben and Jerry's in Boston, Jennifer simply assigned her duties to other employees and left, uncertain when she might return. "I was coming here at any cost because Jerry gave us so much," she said.

At a brief press conference held Saturday afternoon at the downtown offices of Bill Graham Presents, concerned-looking representatives from the offices of the Grateful Dead, the city of San Francisco and BGP announced an official memo-

guru Wavy Gravy and Deborah Koons Garcia. Jerry Garcia's twenty-five-year-old daughter, Annabelle, referring to herself and her three siblings, said, "We love each and every one of you because you put us through college – and we didn't have to work at Dairy Queen."

Afterward the memorial service transformed into a festive, open-air Grateful Dead theme park. Self-deputized vendors sat on blankets, hawking T-shirts, beaded necklaces and face paintings. Deadheads were invited to write tribute messages on large poster boards ("Thanks for all the killer shows," one wrote) and splash paint on a swath of canvas hung from a goalpost. Major-league games of the unofficial Dead-head sport Hacky Sack, played with a small, saggy leather ball, erupted spontaneously.

In the middle of the approximately twenty thousand Deadheads who joined together to pay homage to Garcia stood a tall metal rod topped by a large cutout of the number seven.

rial gathering to be held from 10:00 a.m. to 3:00 p.m. the following day at the Polo Field. In a statement apparently meant to placate the millions of Deadheads rumored to be heading for San Francisco from around the country and the world, Dennis McNally insisted that there would be "no specific ceremony" and "no live music of any sort by the Grateful Dead or anybody else."

The faithful knew better. Orchestrated by BGP, the memorial took place on Sunday, August 13, at the Polo Field. Beginning at 10:00 a.m., members of a local group called the Art Police led a Mardi Gras–style funeral procession around the lawn in the shadow of an altar arranged around a gargantuan portrait of Garcia. The parade included a tie-dye flag, a Chinese New Year dragon and a Dixieland jazz band.

At the dais the marchers were met by a drum circle comprising the surviving members of the Grateful Dead and Nigerian drummer Babatunde Olatunji. When the drummers started pounding a familiar Bo Diddley beat, the tie-dye crowd broke into a spontaneous "Not Fade Away."

"If the Grateful Dead did anything, we gave you the power," said drummer Mickey Hart from the podium. "You have the groove, you have the feeling . . . You take it home and do something with it."

In addition to the members of the Grateful Dead, speakers included Jefferson Airplane's Paul Kantner, Woodstock

"We used to arrange on the Well to meet at Dead shows," said Freddy Hahne, forty-five, who sat next to his eighty-year-old mother, Grace. "And somebody once suggested to meet at light pole number seven – but when we got there, all the light poles ended at number six. There was no light pole number seven, so we made one."

As the waft of marijuana and incense intensified, fans gathered at the altar and danced, some raising their arms and crying. A concert-quality sound system blared tapes of vintage Dead shows as a patient line of fans waited in the midday sun to add bouquets, pictures and candles to the shrine, which consisted of multiple flower arrangements and smaller Garcia portraits arranged on a set of wooden bleachers.

Above: Barlow, Hart, Vince Welnick, Koons Garcia and Weir. Following pages: Garcia, June 30, 1995, in Pittsburgh; Polo Field shrine; Phil Lesh at the memorial; two mourners in San Francisco.

Living up to their reputation for rising to life's more rapturous moments, the Deadheads in attendance appeared to be, by and large, satisfied with the day's scope and mood. "I'm not going to be able to hear these crystal-clear tapes this loud ever again," said a beatific Josiah Sieber, thirty-six.

When a flock of white doves was set free at the foot of the shrine at noon, the crowd oohed and aahed at the circling birds as if marveling at a miracle. The police later reported only a few minor incidents and no arrests. ℰ

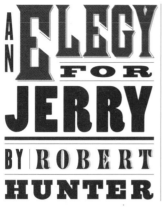

AN ELEGY FOR JERRY
BY ROBERT HUNTER

Jerry, my friend,
you've done it again,
even in your silence
the familiar pressure
comes to bear, demanding
I pull words from the air
with only this morning
and part of the afternoon
to compose an ode worthy
of one so particular
about every turn of phrase,
demanding it hit home
in a thousand ways
before making it his own,
and this I can't do alone.
Now that the singer is gone,
where shall I go for the song?

Without your melody and taste
to lend an attitude of grace
a lyric is an orphan thing,
a hive with neither honey's taste
nor power to truly sting.

What choice have I but to dare and
call your music who thought to rest
out of the thin blue air,
that out of the field of shared time,
a line or two might chance to shine –

As ever when we called,
in hope if not in words,
the muse descends.

How should she desert us now?
Scars of battle on her brow,
bedraggled feathers on her wings,
yet she sings, she sings!

May she bear thee to thy rest,
the ancient bower of flowers
beyond the solitude of days,
the tyranny of hours –
the wreath of shining laurel lie
upon your shaggy head,
bestowing power to play the lyre
to legions of the dead.

If some part of that music
is heard in deepest dream,
or on some breeze of Summer
a snatch of golden theme,
we'll know you live inside us
with love that never parts
our good old Jack O'Diamonds
become the King of Hearts.

I feel your silent laughter
at sentiments so bold
that dare to step across the line
to tell what must be told,
so I'll just say I love you
which I never said before
and let it go at that old friend,
the rest you may ignore.

*Read by Hunter at Jerry Garcia's funeral
on August 11, 1995, in Belvedere, California.*

HE HAD FACED HIS DEMONS
DEBORAH KOONS GARCIA ON JERRY BY DAVID FRICKE

O N AUGUST 16, 1995, a week after Jerry Garcia's death, his widow, Deborah Koons Garcia, spoke about his last days to ROLLING STONE's David Fricke. This is an expanded version of the interview that originally ran in the magazine's Garcia tribute issue.

* * *

Why did you want to do this interview?

Jerry had a lot of admirers and fans who are affected by his death and by his life, and I want them to know what his situation was because I want them to feel good about his life. He had a rich, full life, and the last years were the happiest. He told me that many times. He was growing in many ways.

I was involved with Jerry back in the Seventies for a few years. We spent nearly four years practically glued together. He was a great guy, but he had this kind of edge to him. He was working all the time. So I ended up not seeing him for fifteen years.

What do you mean by "edge"?

In terms of having a personal life. He didn't really have one. I don't think people realized how hard he worked. Sometimes he would be playing with three bands at a time. We went to the Fillmore to hear Eric Clapton a few months ago, and he was saying that back in the mid-Sixties he'd go there *all* the time, even when he wasn't playing. When the sound was really good at a show there, he'd go up, after the set, onto the stage and see exactly what equipment people were using. He was a very serious and hardworking musician.

He loved his work. And the Dead were on the road all the time. There was a part of him that was afraid that he didn't have enough left for a personal life. He wanted one but didn't have one. People were very possessive of Jerry at that time and were constantly promoting the idea that the Grateful Dead was more important than any relationship. The "loyalty test."

That gang mentality.

There was some of that. And there was his childhood. He'd watched his father drown, and then his mother was in despair for years. Then he got asthma. So it was a scary time for him. He had a lot of fear about loving someone, because of fear of loss and all this stuff.

It's funny, because when we got married a year and a half ago, a friend of ours who is a wonderful cinematographer interviewed both of us separately on our wedding day. She sent us the transcript several months ago, and what he had said was that one of the reasons he turned to drugs in the late Seventies was because of a lot of that fear, the conflict. How full a life could he have? Can you have the kind of life he had with his work and still have a fulfilling personal life?

How did the two of you get together the second time?

We ran into each other in a health food store two and a half years ago. He'd already had his second warning to get himself healthy. By that time, he'd already lost about sixty pounds. He was exercising and eating health food. We fell in love and had a very happy and fulfilling personal life. We were both more mature, and Jerry was determined to make me happy, and he never let me down, not once. He loved the Grateful Dead and the Garcia Band and all the adventures being in those bands threw his way. This time around, everyone was so pleased that Jerry was finally happy; they were totally supportive of our marriage.

How did Jerry's drug use affect your relationship?

Drugs were not part of our relationship. I discovered he was doing heroin a few months ago when I found it. He'd left it out, and I think he probably wanted me to confront him about it, to help him get help. The thing about Jerry's heroin use was that there were three stages. There was no drugs at all; then there was just him doing a little bit, when he was managing it, so that I couldn't even tell that he was on anything. And then there would be the times when he'd obviously be on something. It wasn't like this TV-movie version of a mad junkie going around, going crazy. I was more worried about his smoking cigarettes than his drug habit.

When I realized a couple of months ago that he had gotten strung out again, I said to him, "I know you're doing drugs. I want to tell you that if you want to keep doing drugs for the rest of your life, I will love you anyway. We will deal with it, and at least it won't be something that you have to hide and be afraid of. But do you want to stay on them?"

And he said, "No, I don't. It's a pain in the butt." That's exactly what he said. "I don't want to do it for the rest of my life." It was right before the [1995] summer tour. We decided it would be better for him to go to a treatment place.

It was a hard tour because of all the people breaking into the shows. Then he had a death threat against him in Indianapolis. The FBI talked to him about it. That really alarmed him. Because when he went onstage after he heard about it, he was afraid, and he'd never been afraid going onstage before. So that was new for him to deal with. It really upset him.

What happened after he returned from that tour?

When he got back, Jerry and I spent a week together. Then Steve Parish [Garcia's personal manager] and I took him down to the Betty Ford clinic. He'd told people close to him that he was going. He was open about it, that he needed to go someplace to deal with this.

The first week he was there, he called and said he really liked all the people there and that he was really sick – he had a pretty serious jones going. But he was very committed to getting off [heroin], and he did – the hard way. He suffered physically.

Then, after two weeks, he called me and said it was really hot, he hated the food, he wanted to come home. So Parish and I went down. Jerry came out, and he looked just great. He'd lost weight, and he was smiling. He was doing really well, and he was strong. He was clean. You're supposed to stay in a whole month, but he wanted to come home. So I said, "You can come home if you continue in the recovery stuff."

And he really wanted to do that because he was feeling good about himself. He was facing his pain and his joy in a real way. When we got back home, we met with some holistic doctors, and they thought, "This guy's got another ten or fifteen years," because he had so much life force.

He had been very hard on his body for a long time. And he'd spent thirty years on the road. Bad air in hotel rooms, flying, backstage with all the smoke – it's grueling work. But he liked to play. He was a working man, and he took great pride in his work, in the fact that his work kept a lot of other people working. He felt a lot of responsibility for that, and that was a part of his life that he liked. He wanted to keep doing that.

* * *

AT WHAT POINT did Jerry decide to enter the Serenity Knolls drug treatment facility?

For the two weeks after he got out of Betty Ford, we were at home, doing all these health things. He went up to the Grateful Dead studio and saw some people there who said that he was just beaming. He went to AA meetings and found a couple of recovery psychiatrists that he really liked, who he felt understood him.

We had a wonderful time together. He was working on the book of drawings and paintings from his childhood [*Harrington Street*]. He was healing himself.

But I think he found himself drawn back, wanting to do drugs again because his body hurt so much. He made the decision to check himself into Serenity Knolls. He'd wanted to do it. He'd turned a corner.

Jerry had this condition: apnea. It's when you're sleeping and you can't breathe. You stop breathing, and then you snap out of it. He'd had it for thirty years. And I think he was too weakened to breathe through it. He just stopped breathing. They tried to revive him, and they couldn't.

How would you characterize his state of mind when he died? Did Jerry really feel he could beat his addiction?

I definitely know he didn't want to die. He did a lot of living in fifty-three years. But he was very happy and strong, and he had pulled all of his intelligent spirit back into his

body. For many years, back in the Eighties, I kind of had this fear for Jerry, that he was losing himself. I was concerned about him. But when he did die, there was a part of me that realized he had found himself. He had recovered his dignity and his sense of himself and what was important to him.

After he died, they moved his body to a funeral home, and I went over there right away. It's strange to say, but he looked so peaceful. And Jerry had this smile on his face. I said to the guy at the funeral home, "Look, he's smiling. Did you do that to him?" And he said, "No, that's exactly the way I found him." His face was so at peace. At the funeral we decided to have an open casket because he looked so good.

It was like I said in Golden Gate Park [at the memorial service]: Jerry was purifying himself. We thought it was for a long life, but it was for a different journey. And I really feel that way. He had so much pain in his body, and he struggled with it. I have no fear at all that his soul is in some weird place. I feel like he burned up a lot of karma for himself by turning the corner these last two years. The tabloid mentality about "oh, drug addict" – that doesn't even faze me. Because the people that knew him and knew his music – they know who he is. And whatever else people want to say, screw 'em.

Jerry was always very generous. Fans would come up to him, and he would treat them well and with consideration. He was never rude. The thing that people here in San Francisco remember about Jerry is that he was *fun*. He wasn't this tragic figure moping around, feeling sorry for himself. We all had hundreds of stories about the goofy, wild things he did. He loved having a good time, and he loved that his work playing music was about people coming to have a good time.

That was the core of it. As for death – his father died when Jerry was young. To him, death was just something you walk with.

Jerry's death was a great loss to many people. But the peaceful way in which he died seemed to soften the blow.

The night before he went in to Serenity Knolls, we went out and had this wonderful romantic dinner, with the lights over San Francisco Bay. He was working on his book, making plans. His mind was very full and optimistic. And he even said the week before he died, "You know, I discovered that I'm an optimist."

I want people to know that he faced this particular demon that had been after him. He died a happy man. He died in his sleep in a beautiful place, filled with love and confidence. He went out on a really high level. He went out with enough of his own energy that he can still be a help to all of us.

Jerry created a lot of really good energy on this planet, and that energy is still going on. And maybe it's even been freed up. People should take heart from his good life and how he redeemed himself. He loved his life up to the very end. And I think he would want people to be happy. He was about creating joy and bringing people together. And to bring people together in his death – in a way that they can celebrate his life – is what he would want. ☾

I HAD THE GOOD LUCK to meet Jerry Garcia at an odd time in his life – just after his fiftieth birthday, when he was busy taking stock of himself and was happy to do some talking. He was trying hard to be the kind of person he had never been before, someone not quite so restless or reckless, a man hoping to come to terms with middle age, get rid of his bad habits and conserve his energies to go the distance – "the whole ten rounds," as he put it, "like an old boxer." He had given up cigarettes, junk food and hard drugs, was exercising three times a week with a personal trainer and even made regular visits to a Deadhead doctor whom he praised for being nonjudgmental. His mood was upbeat and expansive. The health and sobriety regimen was new to him, and he hadn't realized yet just how tight the fit would be. Discipline wasn't natural to him, except when it came to music.

We had our first interview session together backstage at California's Oakland Coliseum in December 1992. Garcia was bright eyed, friendly and surprisingly unguarded. It was easy for him to be intimate with a stranger. He was a big man, but he had a grace about him along with an air of mischief. He told me that he respected writers – he could never

write a book himself. The compliment was backhanded, though. Writers pinned things down on paper, and Garcia could not bear to see anything pinned down. He wanted to live in a fluid, unpredictable universe where chance and improvisation were king. The Dead's touring schedule bugged him, for instance. He wished it could be more "aleatory" – he liked such academic words – with the concerts occurring spontaneously, in no fixed pattern. Maybe a Deadhead would figure out how to do it someday, he said.

Garcia was gentle and soft-spoken and had an immense capacity for wonder. His childlike side was much in evidence that evening, but it was complicated by the presence of a sophisticated adult intelligence. The two parts of him were at odds sometimes. The band had just been taking a break from performing, for example, and he bumped into Robert Hunter at the Dead's offices, in Marin County, and asked what Hunter had been up to. "Translating Rilke from the German," Hunter said. "And you?" Garcia claimed to be embarrassed. How could he cop to the fact that he'd spent his own vacation building remote-control model cars?

There was no better company than Garcia in his prime. He squeezed every waking moment for all it was worth and

DEAD RECKONING
BY | BILL | BARICH

constantly risked exhaustion. He loved to talk, but he also loved to listen. Our second conversation went on for almost four hours. He was so accustomed to performing in sets that he took a break exactly in the middle. We covered a multitude of topics, but two or three were paramount to him, including, for obvious reasons, his drug use. He had the reflective attitude of a battle-scarred veteran reminiscing. He looked back on his early psychedelic days with real fondness: LSD, mescaline and psilocybin had helped to form his character, he said, and were linked in his mind to being young and carefree. (Once, with nostalgia, I mentioned the pastoral photos from those days, with beautiful, nearly naked hippie women everywhere, and Garcia smiled and said, "Yeah! What were we doing up there playing music?") He never bragged about his tripping and understood its hazards. His approach would be tough to duplicate, anyhow. He went at it like a mad scientist who'd accidentally become the subject of his own research.

I asked Garcia why psychedelics were so potent for him. He said that they had allowed him to get beyond ordinary reality and into a reality he had "always thought existed but had never been able to find." Everything on the other side was really okay, he discovered, and even fun – he knew no greater term of praise. The LSD world was "shadowy, ambiguous and half-concealed," not rigid but mutable and flowing. He was sure he'd "received direct instruction" about his life while high and swore that once he had ridden up into the heavens and had been shown the face of God, "close enough to see the pimples." The encounter shook him up plenty and left him with a stammer that lasted for a while. His final "fat trip" took place in California in the late Sixties, courtesy of some white-lightning acid mixed with mescaline. He developed 360-degree vision, died a few thousand times and unraveled every strand of DNA in his body. The word ALL scrolled into the sky, and "Bringing in the Sheaves" was the soundtrack. In the end he turned into a field of wheat.

Garcia continued to use psychedelics after that, but he never had another transcendental experience. ("I just got those little demons that try to scare you but can't if you don't give in," he said.) His strict religious upbringing as a Catholic had made him especially susceptible to hallucinogens, he believed. The drugs gave him the same "spooky sense of mystery" he'd felt in church as a boy. He was still a deeply spiritual person who was troubled, it seemed, by more than his share of guilt, concerned about his mistakes in public and in relationships and particularly with how he'd been an absentee father while his daughters were growing up. He had immersed himself in Christian literature and could discourse at length about saints, mystics and the Bible. One afternoon we began talking about the concept of sin – we were both experts – and Garcia suggested a new framework for examining what constituted ethical behavior. People should forget about trying to be good, he said. History had proved that human beings were incapable of it, but what if we tried not to behave so badly? In any case, that was how he measured the Dead's activities. The band tried to put something positive into the world and to satisfy a need for joy, ritual and celebration. Simple kindness, he thought, really mattered.

Garcia, of course, was far from perfect and knew it. Nobody could list his faults faster than he could. A taste for heroin was chief among them. It was a drug he said he regretted using. He was a proud, smart, talented man, and it had shamed him to be a junkie. He'd been a maintenance addict, he admitted ruefully, able to function after a fashion but unable to feel very much of anything. That had been the point, really, to block his emotions and anesthetize himself. "But the jones was terrible," Garcia said, shaking his head. "It wasn't worth it." He intended to take more responsibility for himself in the future – that was his goal, at least. In the past, he said, he'd been slow to deal with problems in his personal life, repressing his emotions instead and causing more pain in the long run. It was clear that he had a struggle ahead of him. He held himself to impossible standards. "I've been that way since I was a kid," he told me. "It's there on my first report card: 'Jerry's too critical of himself.' "

Still, Garcia appeared to be ready for the challenge. He was in excellent spirits and projected warmth, enthusiasm and energy. He got a kick out of all the unfamiliar oxygen pumping through his system. It made him high in a new way. He and Hunter had written some new songs they liked, and he thought the Jerry Garcia Band was in an ideal "jewel box" phase, with all the musicians meshing perfectly. Garcia had offers to direct a play, compose a soundtrack and collaborate on a movie. The creative options available to him were unlimited. His life was more tranquil and domestic than it had been for a long while, and anyone who cared about him had grounds to be optimistic about his survival. Yet I saw his cheerful manner collapse briefly into sadness once or twice. "I have no fantasies left," he said wistfully one day, looking tired. That wasn't true, but I knew what he meant. He'd packed a lot of experience into fifty years.

I talked with Garcia for the last time in April 1993. He burst into the Dead's headquarters, grinned his manic grin and announced in a supercharged way, "My life has changed totally!" I'd never seen him so excited before. He went on to tell me what had happened to him. He'd walked into a party the other day, he said, and his eyes had locked onto a woman across the room, someone he'd been involved with eighteen years earlier (and the person he would ultimately marry). A jolt of electricity went through him – their relationship had always been intense – and he had managed to rekindle the romance. He was very pleased with himself and obviously delighted to be in love. He'd decided to live for the moment, he said, and just deal with the consequences. The remark seemed harmless then, but I think now he was speaking in a broader way than I could fathom. I think he missed the old Jerry, blemishes and all. In his youth he embarked on a heroic journey of fulfillment and self-discovery. Maybe it was too late for him to turn back.

"It seemed that for him, the existential dilemma would always be the same," I wrote at the time. "How do you get to the edge of things without going over the edge?" I wish he had solved that riddle. His humility was genuine, his presence was soulful, and the world today feels smaller for his absence. ☾

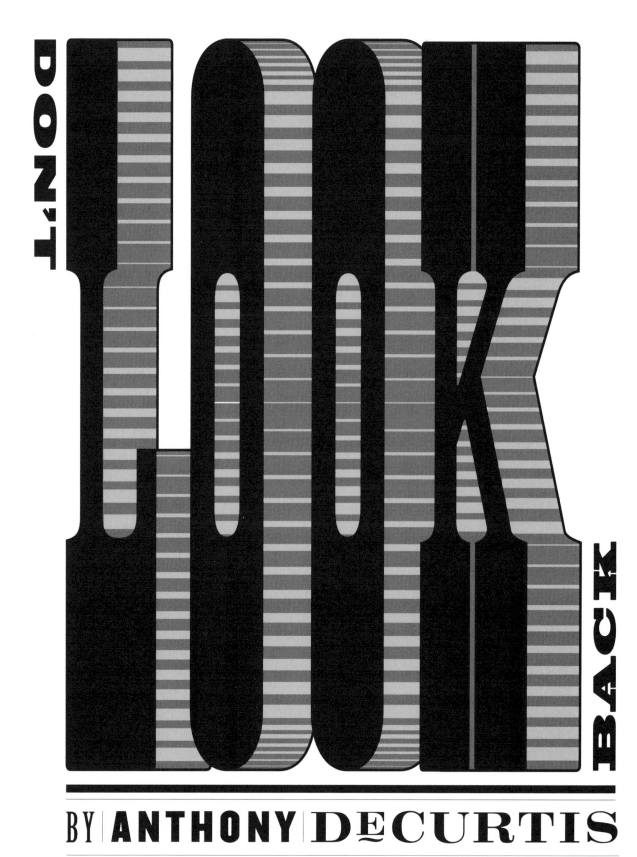

DON'T LOOK BACK

BY ANTHONY DeCURTIS

I FIRST SAW the Grateful Dead in June of 1967 at a free concert in New York City's Central Park, and I was disappointed. I was fifteen years old and was there to see the Jefferson Airplane, who, for reasons I couldn't fathom at the time, had opened for the Dead. I was confused. Why would the Jefferson Airplane – who had hits, who had a certifiable star in Grace Slick – open for a band I had barely heard of and whose six members seemed no closer to star charisma than I or any of my friends? I wish I could say that my eyes were opened that day, that the wonders of the Dead were forever manifested to me. But that's not what happened. After twenty minutes or so, I left.

The wonders of the Dead would finally manifest themselves to me a couple of years later – appropriately, through the efforts of a group of friends. I had started college, the counterculture was in full swing, I was still star-addled, and my new college friends couldn't believe I wasn't into the Dead. A group decision was made: The next time the Dead came to New York, my friends would buy me a ticket.

This time I got it – and the next time and the next time and the next time. The shows I saw over the next few years were mostly at the Fillmore East, where the late sets began at 11:30. With the Dead that often meant that I would re-enter the grimy streets of the East Village near dawn, humming with good vibrations. Those shows, as I at long last came to understand were not about star tripping or even, in many ways, about music – though musically they were transporting. They seemed primarily about ecstasy and community, about my relationship with my friends, about our relationship to the larger audience around us, about the deep bond between that entire audience and the Dead.

In my memory, those shows were also about redefining time and the meaning of performance. The band's sets evolved in ways that dissolved even the loosest, most progressive expectations. Extended jams that melted the boundaries between songs and improvisation, between structure and chaos, were followed by interminable breaks, during which the band seemed simultaneously to be relaxing, re-collecting itself, freeing the audience to its own devices and determining the next stage of the night's musical journey.

In a way that was remarkable even in those remarkable times, the Dead resisted being elevated above their audience. During one of those interminable breaks between songs, Bob Weir – sensing a discomfort in the crowd, an impatience, a hint that the audience was passively expecting the Dead merely to provide the evening's entertainment – stepped to the mike and suggested that we find ways to amuse ourselves. In the future, he said, the utopian future we all fully believed would soon arrive, there would be no distinctions between musicians and audiences. We would all create for each other. To force the band into a prescribed role would be to deny our own responsibility for bringing that future about.

But if the Dead refused the easy appeal of stardom, one man still stood at the center of the Dead experience, first among equals: Jerry Garcia. Not that he sought the spot-

light. Instead, the light emanated from him. That light helped guide the Dead through their most extravagant musical excursions, when they would wander far into places from which it would seem impossible to return. Suddenly, Garcia, with his Cheshire Cat grin, would reach into his bag of tricks for the move that would light the road home.

Maybe it's a cliché at this point to compare music to a drug experience, but the Dead's music always seemed an extraordinary rendering of what it's like to take LSD – and Garcia was a big reason why. That wasn't because of any self-conscious "psychedelic" effects, though Garcia could occasionally indulge in those. Mainly, it was because Garcia's consciousness was genuinely expanded: He saw vistas where others could see only barriers, windows where others saw walls.

He was endlessly curious. For him, every musical possibility, every variation, was worth exploring. The moment was everything. There could be no such thing as a mistake; every direction pulsed with potential revelation. No song structure was ultimately firm, everything solid would melt into air, disintegrate, yielding a freedom that was both spiritually transformative and a little frightening. Who would I be if I were to lose myself this completely? At those instants, everyone – the band, the audience – looked to Garcia for deliverance.

We looked to him and he looked into himself. Then, magically, form would return from formlessness, and you would be wildly exhilarated, yourself again but changed. Garcia's playing – that thrilling sorcerer's brew of casualness and wit, intelligence and complete openness, daring and ease, playfulness and desire for beauty – contained all that. And the sweet yearning of his voice, the way he loved to sing at the very top of his register, as if he were always reaching for something just beyond his range.

The only time I met Garcia was when I interviewed him for ROLLING STONE. I was struck by how totally his personality and talk recalled the manner of his playing. Ideas suggested ideas, which led to more ideas and eventually wound back to the first idea – it was no surprise when he told me that he learned about "musical things . . . rhythm . . . motion, timing" from Neal Cassady. He talked about hating to make choices as a songwriter, hating to eliminate possibilities in favor of one decision, preferring to "make it up as I go along." That made it hard to write songs. Closure did not come naturally to him. Improvisation and discovery, optimism and vision, those were Garcia's instinctive virtues.

At right: Garcia and concert impresario Bill Graham, circa 1971.

Now, the deal's gone down. It's hard to stand Garcia's loss and it's hard to mourn him. For one thing, like all people who feel truly and deeply, he despised sentimentality. So what is the best way to keep him present in our hearts? Garcia, of course, loved Dylan and these Dylan lines have been running through my head: "You must leave now / Take what you need, you think will last." Garcia gave us a lot. "Take what you have gathered from coincidence," take what you need, share it with friends, leave the rest for others, kiss the sky, don't look back. ☾

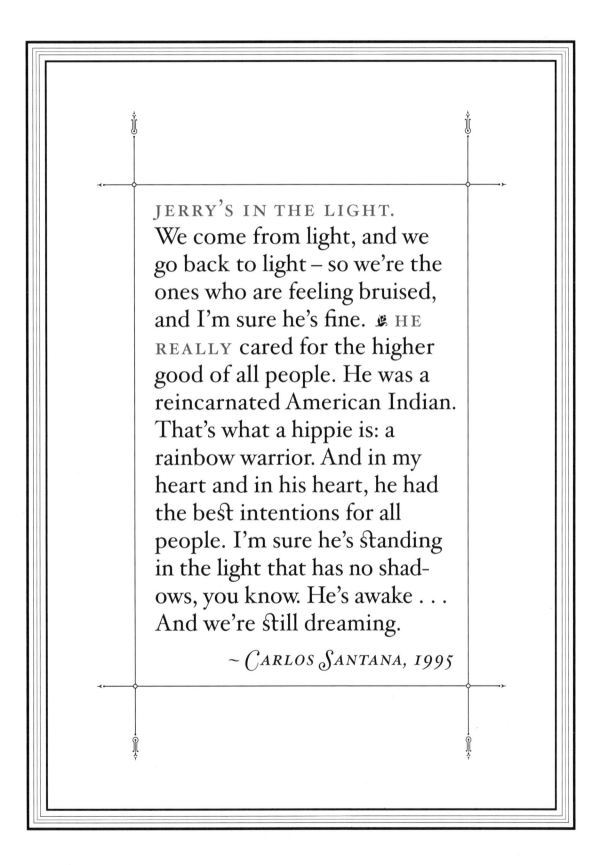

JERRY'S IN THE LIGHT.
We come from light, and we
go back to light – so we're the
ones who are feeling bruised,
and I'm sure he's fine. HE
REALLY cared for the higher
good of all people. He was a
reincarnated American Indian.
That's what a hippie is: a
rainbow warrior. And in my
heart and in his heart, he had
the best intentions for all
people. I'm sure he's standing
in the light that has no shad-
ows, you know. He's awake . . .
And we're still dreaming.

~ CARLOS SANTANA, 1995

THE GARCIA DISCOGRAPHY
BY ERIC FLAUM

THE GRATEFUL DEAD *(Warner Bros., 1967)*: Had the Dead produced only this one album and never developed a cult of followers, the two-minute "Golden Road (to Unlimited Devotion)" would have been a *Nuggets*-worthy artyfact from the "Spring" of Love. At the time of the album's release, though, its emphasis on short, amphetamine-quick songs was a disappointment. Only the album-closing, ten-minute workout of "Viola Lee Blues" hinted at the slow, spacey jams that had begun to exemplify the Dead live.

ANTHEM OF THE SUN *(Warner Bros., 1968)*: A fascinating, if dated, effort. The Dead tried to combine live performances with studio effects, expansions and gimmickry. Unlike most concept albums of its day, this one focused on aural constructions rather than topical subjects. Country rhythms give way to nitrous tempos; anti-establishment clichés yield to bluesy romps. It may be a relic, but its adventurous approach helped lay the groundwork for the band's next trip into the studio.

AOXOMOXOA *(Warner Bros., 1969)*: A muddled beauty, *Aoxomoxoa* is the trippiest of the Dead's studio efforts – trippy album art and trippy songs like "China Cat Sun-flower" and "St. Stephen." Some say that the original vinyl is superior to the '71 remix that superseded it. Regardless, this was their best album yet.

LIVE DEAD *(Warner Bros., 1969)*: What they really sounded like during the era some regard as their peak. This is a band on a roll. Pigpen's "Turn On Your Love Light" is one of his finest moments, and "Dark Star" is a cosmic musical adventure that stands among the best psychedelia ever recorded. A relic that still sounds very much alive.

WORKINGMAN'S DEAD *(Warner Bros., 1970)*: Their best collection of songs. Their best vocal harmonizing. Maybe the best slab of vinyl the Dead ever issued (its strongest competition being its successor). The lyrics' Old West/Americana imagery complemented the CS&N–style singing, and the instrumentation helped bring it all together on classics like "Uncle John's Band," "High Time" and "Dire Wolf." A drastic departure from anything the Dead had previously released, the LP signaled the start of the band's acoustic/folkier side, which would resurface over the years.

AMERICAN BEAUTY *(Warner Bros., 1970)*: "Truckin'," "Sugar Magnolia," "Friend of the Devil" – and those were just the "hits." Time has also shown "Ripple," "Box of Rain" and "Brokedown Palace" worthy of their better-known album mates. The harmonies are here, and the uptempo stuff coexists peaceably with the moodier numbers. The embodiment of the ethic the Dead would hearken back to forever after, it combines hippie sentimentality, self-referential fun and new blues in an old vein.

GRATEFUL DEAD [SKULL AND ROSES] *(Warner Bros., 1971)*: One of the best of the Dead's many live releases, Skull and Roses features a five-piece lineup as a result of Mickey Hart's temporary departure. Pigpen's role is as limited as it was on the previous two studio albums, and Garcia shines on "Bertha" and the slower-paced "Wharf Rat." Bob Weir's country infatuation peaks with covers of "Mama Tried," "Me and My Uncle" and "Me and Bobby McGee." Skull and Roses provides the definitive versions of a number of second-set favorites and ends with one of the band's signature pairings: "Not Fade Away"/"Goin' Down the Road Feeling Bad."

EUROPE '72 *(Warner Bros., 1972)*: Another great live offering, much of the album is even better than Skull and Roses. Only the third disc of *Europe '72*'s original vinyl configuration, with its extended jams, didn't get much wear. But the first two albums' worth were the only place to find Dead classics like "Jack Straw," "Brown-Eyed Woman," "Ramble On Rose" and "Tennessee Jed." At the time, this album set a standard for live recordings and established the Dead's norm by balancing the tally between live and studio releases. The only bad thing about *Europe '72* is the relegation of the ailing Pigpen to a secondary role with the addition of keyboardist Keith Godchaux and his wife, Donna, on backing vocals.

HISTORY OF THE GRATEFUL DEAD, VOL. 1 (BEAR'S CHOICE) *(Warner Bros., 1973)*: A relative obscurity in the Dead catalogue, *Bear's Choice* (the Bear being chemist extraordinaire Owsley Stanley) offers the highlights from two exceptional nights at the Fillmore East. Recorded in '70 but not released until the year of Pigpen's death, *Bear's Choice* was Pig's farewell. Side one further establishes the Dead's inclination for

introducing new material and new covers on live releases. Side two is all Pigpen on "Smokestack Lightnin" and "Hard to Handle."

WAKE OF THE FLOOD *(Grateful Dead, 1973)*: The Dead's first studio LP in three years, *Wake* is also the first created with Keith and Donna Godchaux's full involvement. Old-timey and traditionally structured, the songs sometimes carry similarly anachronistic, *Workingman's*-style lyrics, while "Eyes of the World" and "Weather Report Suite" return to the band's hippier, introspective aesthetic. Keith Godchaux's spare piano style signals a drastic change from the late Pigpen's fat, aggressive organ sound.

SKELETONS FROM THE CLOSET *(Warner Bros., 1974)*: A greatest-hits collection from a band that had barely dented radio? A singles compilation from a band that thrived on improvised jams? Deadheads knew it was bogus, but fledgling enthusiasts could find the "basics" here.

FROM THE MARS HOTEL *(Grateful Dead, 1974)*: The cold, sterile production of *Mars Hotel* belies the warmth of the songs themselves. Garcia is in fine fettle, tackling both fun, upbeat rock & rollers ("U.S. Blues,"

"Scarlet Begonias") and slow ballads ("China Doll," "Ship of Fools"). The normally reticent Phil Lesh unleashes a burst of creativity with two songs ("Pride of Cucamonga" and "Unbroken Chain") that became cult favorites.

BLUES FOR ALLAH *(Grateful Dead,1975)*: The peak of the Dead's Egyptian fascination, *Blues for Allah* originally struck Deadheads as some kind of aberration. But with the passage of time, it has proven itself to be a source of some of the best songs the Dead recorded following their 1970 peak. Garcia's lean, dry guitar playing may be among his most inspired, and "Franklin's Tower," "The Music Never Stopped" and "Crazy Fingers" were all live favorites throughout the Eighties and into the Nineties. The second side's musical and cultural hybrids may not be completely successful, but *Blues'* strengths far outweigh its weaknesses.

STEAL YOUR FACE *(Grateful Dead/ United Artists, 1976)*: A vague companion piece to the concerts featured in *The Grateful Dead Movie*, *Steal Your Face* has been rightfully scorned for its poor sound quality and lackluster performances.

WHAT A LONG STRANGE TRIP IT'S BEEN *(Warner Bros., 1977)*: A more representative compilation than *Skeletons*, *Trip* emphasizes the live gems (*Europe '72*'s "Jack Straw" and "Brown-Eyed Woman"), but what really makes this worthwhile are the studio "single" versions of "Born Cross-Eyed" and "Dark Star." The purging of Pigpen's contributions is disturbing, though. And too bad they couldn't have included the band's original '66 single on the Scorpio label.

TERRAPIN STATION *(Arista, 1977)*: The first side has a couple of good songs, but the album mostly continues the Dead's trend toward production so clean that it's practically passionless. "Estimated Prophet" and "Passenger" would become concert staples, but the real highlight here is the title track. Robert Hunter's classic tale-within-a-tale, love/sea story embodies much of the Dead's strengths, and Paul Buckmaster's orchestral arrangement helps "Terrapin" build to a stunning climax.

SHAKEDOWN STREET *(Arista, 1978)*: The Dead were on a studio roll, rushing back in with Little Feat's Lowell George producing. *Shakedown* invited references to a new, "DiscoDead" sound, particularly due to the

title track's steady beat. Weir's high-spirited "I Need a Miracle" spent the next couple of years as part of a cluster of second-set songs along with the band's cover of the Young Rascals' "Good Lovin'" (another of *Shakedown*'s highlights). Best of all was the appearance of "Fire on the Mountain," which had evolved from the rhythmic instrumental "Happiness Is Drumming" on Mickey Hart's 1976 Diga Rhythm Band album.

GO TO HEAVEN *(Arista, 1980)*: The end of the Dead's last burst of studio activity, *Go to Heaven* was the first album with new keyboardist Brent Mydland. Although some Heads decried his "DoobieDead" sound, Mydland's "Far From Me" is a catchy album opener that then gave way to strong contributions from all. Garcia's "Althea" was a classic, slow Dead blues, and his upbeat "Alabama Getaway" became the band's then-second-highest-charting single. *Heaven* includes a tandem of Weir songs, "Lost Sailor" and "Saint of Circumstance" that quickly became second-set favorites.

RECKONING *(Arista, 1981)*: This live album features acoustic highlights from shows in New York and San Francisco that were the basis for the band's *Dead Ahead* video. As in the early Seventies, the Dead played an acoustic set before their standard two-set format. There's a combination of old, traditional numbers, fun covers and folkier elements from the Dead's catalogue, making it the band's best Eighties release.

DEAD SET *(Arista, 1981)*: An inferior companion piece to *Reckoning*, *Dead Set* offers the highlights from the electric portions of the

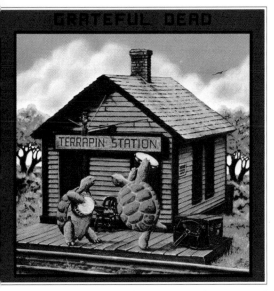

Dead Ahead shows. "Fire on the Mountain," "Brokedown Palace" and the slow version of "Friend of the Devil" were all long overdue for official live release, but the CD unfortunately omits side three's "Space."

IN THE DARK *(Arista, 1987)*: The Top Ten "Touch of Grey" revitalized interest in a band that hadn't released a studio album in seven years. The Garcia/Hunter songs dominate the proceedings, while Mydland is relegated to a single lead vocal and Weir to two. Given the paucity of Garcia's contributions to 1989's *Built to Last, In the Dark* represents his last strong studio work with the Dead.

DYLAN & THE DEAD *(CBS, 1989)*: The Dead's late-Eighties slow and plodding mode accompanies Dylan's straightforward, if inarticulate, performances on this live LP.

BUILT TO LAST *(Arista, 1989)*: A return to the studio, *Built to Last* features Brent Mydland in his most prominent role, and his and Garcia's last studio efforts with the band. Dominating the album, Mydland seems most at home in the lifeless production style the Dead used in the Eighties.

WITHOUT A NET *(Arista, 1990)*: The pity here is that the Dead chose this lackluster tour to release yet another live double disc when the very next tour was a revitalized outing with Bruce Hornsby assisting on keyboards. Of all the Dead's live releases, this may well be the least necessary. Branford Marsalis sits in on "Eyes of the World" with minimal impact.

ONE FROM THE VAULT *(Grateful Dead, 1991)*: The first foray into the Dead's live past, *One From the Vault* documents a 1975 show from San Francisco's Great American Music Hall. The performance highlighted material from the then-soon-to-be-released *Blues for Allah*, and it quickly became a tape-traders' favorite. This official release offers first-rate sound quality and enough great music to make it another of the band's best live releases.

INFRARED ROSES *(Grateful Dead, 1991)*: The Dead have always explored the outer reaches of improvisation, which *Infrared Roses* captures, creating a collage from the "Space" portion of the Dead's traditional mid-second-set improvs. Producer Bob Bralove has intertwined a wide range of sounds – some musical, some otherworldly – into a fascinating work that's almost as colorful as the titles he's given to "songs" like "Silver Apples of the Moon," "Magnesium Night Light" and "Post-Modern Highrise Table Top Stomp."

TWO FROM THE VAULT *(Grateful Dead, 1992)*: Another oldie from the archives, the second *Vault* release offers up a pair of concerts at L.A.'s Shrine Auditorium from '68. These shows are very similar to the ones incorporated into *Anthem of the Sun*, with the added bonus of Pigpen opening things with the best officially released "Good Morning, Little Schoolgirl" and a rousing "Love Light." Almost a cross between *Anthem* and *Live Dead, Two* has very little new to offer.

DICK'S PICKS, VOL. ONE *(Grateful Dead, 1993)*: The *Dick's Picks* series was introduced as an alternative to the *Vault* releases. Unfortunately, Dick has weird taste. Given the breadth of the Dead's touring existence, Florida '73 seems a strange place to start, chronologically and geographically. What's most interesting is that this is a band in transition: Hart-less and still working in the Godchauxs via slow, meandering jams. Though quite strong versions of these songs, the choice of material leaves much to be desired, drawing heavily from *Wake of the Flood* and what's available on other live LPs.

GRAYFOLDED *(Swell/Artifact, 1994)*: This is a collaborative effort between the Dead and producer John Oswald, whose "plunderphonics" approach to sound collage is applied to "Dark Star" performances dating from '68 to '93. Oswald includes every band member past and present, as well as a chorus consisting of several years' worth of Garcias. *Grayfolded* is as interesting in its use of sound collage as are the performances themselves. A sequel, *Part Two: Mirror Ashes*, was released in 1995.

DICK'S PICKS, VOL. TWO *(Grateful Dead, 1995)*: Unlike Dick's first pick, *Vol. Two* (Ohio, Halloween '73) is a single disc featuring an early Keith Godchaux appearance on keyboards, sans Donna. With extended experimental excerpts, it is slower, maybe even spacier, than *Live Dead.*

HUNDRED YEAR HALL *(Grateful Dead/Arista, 1995)*: Culled from a German show of the fabled Europe '72 tour, much of this "feels like we've been here before." ("The Other One" makes its sixth live appearance!) "Bertha" is at least as good as the Skull and Roses version, but only "Comes a Time" and the long-overdue "Next Time You See Me" are Dead debuts. The sound quality is superb, but some of the material included seems pretty redundant at this point.

HOOTEROLL? Jerry Garcia and Howard Wales *(Douglas, 1971)*: Garcia's first extra-curricular outing, *Hooteroll?* is a jazz/funk instrumental album with keyboardist Howard Wales, who appeared on *American Beauty.* The music is loose and loopy (and dated).

GARCIA Jerry Garcia *(Grateful Dead, 1972)*: *Garcia* is perhaps the best side project any member of the Dead has ever released. "Deal," "Sugaree," "Loser," "The Wheel" and "Bird Song" were consistently performed live by the Dead over the next twenty years, and the aural collage on side two has aged surprisingly well.

LIVE AT KEYSTONE Saunders/Garcia/Kahn/Vitt *(Fantasy, 1973)*: In July '73 Garcia teamed with keyboardist Merl Saunders, bassist John Kahn – who accompanied Garcia on nearly all his solo outings – and drummer Bill Vitt, another frequent collaborator. Covers of "The Harder They Come," "My Funny Valentine" and "I Second That Emotion" illustrate Garcia's eclecticism. Garcia's guitar playing is impressive, but the jams tend to wander.

COMPLIMENTS OF GARCIA Jerry Garcia *(Grateful Dead, 1974)*: This is Garcia's homage to personal favorites, including Van Morrison, Smokey Robinson and Irving Berlin. There is no defense, however, for the flaccid covers of "Let It Rock" or "Let's Spend the Night Together." Imminently forgettable.

OLD & IN THE WAY *(Round, 1975)*: An all-star lineup of bluegrass virtuosos who were so good that Garcia might actually have been the weakest musician here, working hard on banjo to keep up with Vassar Clements' fiddle and David Grisman's mandolin. This ranks as one of Garcia's best efforts, though.

REFLECTIONS Jerry Garcia *(Round, 1976)*: A "solo" outing in which half of the songs are essentially performed by the Dead. As a result, many of these tunes became part of the Dead's repertoire, and with the exception of *Garcia*, *Reflections* has some of the strongest material to be found on any of Garcia's solo albums. "Mission in the Rain" would have been one of Hunter's strongest lyrics from this era were it not for the even more beautiful "It Must Have Been the Roses."

CATS UNDER THE STARS Jerry Garcia Band *(Arista, 1978)*: Adopting the cold, over-produced studio sound the Dead had settled upon by this time, *Cats Under the Stars* could have used a softer touch. Songs like "Rubin and Cherise" and the title track are nearly smothered by synthesizers but remain some of the Garcia Band's best work.

RUN FOR THE ROSES Jerry Garcia Band *(Arista, 1982)*: The title track of the Garcia Band's last studio outing is an upbeat ditty in the spirit of "Alabama Getaway" and "Touch of Grey." And there's a cover of "I Saw Her Standing There" so earnestly goofy it works. Unfortunately, there's little else to recommend this inconsequential effort.

ALMOST ACOUSTIC Jerry Garcia Acoustic Band *(Grateful Dead, 1988)*: Culled from a series of Fall 1987 shows, *Almost Acoustic* returns to Garcia's early days of playing coffeehouse folk and blues. Garcia reunites friends from those early days, including Kahn and New Rider Dave Nelson. The sound quality is crystal clear and worthy of Garcia's sharp leads and the subtle interplay of strings.

JERRY GARCIA/DAVID GRISMAN *(Acoustic Disc, 1991)*: A long-overdue reunion between the two, this is another product of Garcia's lifelong commitment to acoustic music. Instrumental frolics are mixed with Irving Berlin and Hoagy Carmichael standards and a nice reworking of "Friend of the Devil."

JERRY GARCIA BAND *(Arista, 1991)*: A perfect representative of what latter-day Garcia Band tours were like, this live two-disc collection includes material from Garcia's solo albums as well as a couple of Dylan covers and a Motown romp ("The Way You Do the Things You Do"). But who could've guessed that covers of "Stop That Train" or "Dear Prudence" would be here unless you'd seen the shows or heard the tapes. A wonderful souvenir from an era when Garcia's solo shows were still something special.

NOT FOR KIDS ONLY Jerry Garcia and David Grisman *(Acoustic Disc, 1993)*: A fun project for two old friends that features childish ditties, corny jokes and some real fine playing. It's hard to say whether *Not for Kids Only* really works as either a children's record or an adult one, but it's great for family road trips.

CAMEOS

[Selective]

ZABRISKIE POINT [soundtrack] *(MGM, 1970)*: Garcia's very first solo credit was the gorgeous instrumental "Love Scene," a mesmerizingly delicate multitracked guitar piece. There's also an excerpt of the *Live Dead* version of "Dark Star."

DÉJÀ VU Crosby, Stills, Nash and Young *(Atlantic, 1970)*: That's Garcia's lovely pedal-steel playing on "Teach Your Children."

BLOWS AGAINST THE EMPIRE Paul Kantner and Jefferson Starship *(RCA, 1970)*: Before it became an arena-rock act, this aggregation prominently featured Garcia, who made lots of cool sounds behind Kantner and Slick's conceptual psychedelia.

NEW RIDERS OF THE PURPLE SAGE *(Columbia, 1971)*: Garcia helped guide the NRPS debut and adds great pedal steel.

IF I COULD ONLY REMEMBER MY NAME David Crosby *(Atlantic, 1971)*: Garcia is one of a host of notables to lend a hand on this underrated relic. In addition to providing guitars, Garcia is credited as coauthor of one rambling jam.

FIRE UP Merl Saunders *(Fantasy, 1973)*: The highlight: Garcia belting out "Expressway (to Your Heart)." The '92 CD also included his vocals on "The Night They Drove Old Dixie Down" from Saunders' *Heavy Turbulence*.

WANTED DEAD OR ALIVE David Bromberg *(Columbia, 1974)*: Garcia's acoustic and electric guitars ride shotgun on Bromberg's wild and exhilarating cruise.

DIGA RHYTHM BAND *(Round, 1976)*: Hart's international percussion ensemble features Garcia's loopy guitar playing.

BLUES FROM THE RAINFOREST Merl Saunders *(Summertone, 1990)*: Not only is this Saunders' best LP, it may also be Garcia's best extracurricular outing: a glorious blend of world music, jazz, nature recordings and ethereal instrumentals, featuring Garcia's indescribable guitar work.

SMOKE [soundtrack] *(Hollywood, 1995)*: The Jerry Garcia Band's final studio work brought Garcia full circle with covers of "Cigarettes and Coffee" and Jerome Kern's "Smoke Gets in Your Eyes."

BILL BARICH is the author of *Laughing in the Hills, Traveling Light, Hard to Be Good* and *Big Dreams: Into the Heart of California.* His writing has appeared frequently in *The New Yorker.*

* * *

ANTHONY DECURTIS is a contributing editor to ROLLING STONE. He is the author of *Rocking My Life Away* and coeditor of *The ROLLING STONE Album Guide.*

* * *

ERIC FLAUM was a freelance writer and ROLLING STONE's production manager. He attended thirty-eight Dead concerts and eight Garcia performances and took his six-year-old daughter, Casey, to her first Dead show in June 1995.

* * *

ALEC FOEGE is the author of *Confusion Is Next: The Sonic Youth Story.* He is a regular contributor to ROLLING STONE and various other publications.

* * *

BEN FONG-TORRES began writing for ROLLING STONE in 1968 and served as senior editor until 1981. He has written for numerous magazines, and his books include *The Motown Album, Hickory Wind* and his memoirs, *The Rice Room.*

* * *

DAVID FRICKE is a senior editor of ROLLING STONE, having joined the magazine in 1985. He is also the American correspondent for *Melody Maker* and the author of *Animal Instinct,* a biography of Def Leppard, and has written liner notes for CD reissues of the Byrds, Moby Grape, John Prine, Led Zeppelin and the Velvet Underground.

* * *

DAVID GANS has been a Deadhead since 1972. He is the author of *Playing in the Band* and *Conversations With the Dead.* Gans has also served as host of the syndicated radio show *The Grateful Dead Hour* and edited *Not Fade Away: The Online World Remembers Jerry Garcia.*

* * *

MIKAL GILMORE is a ROLLING STONE contributing editor and the author of *Shot in the Heart.*

* * *

FRED GOODMAN, a freelance journalist and contributing editor to ROLLING STONE, is the author of *The Mansion on the Hill,* a forthcoming history of the rock & roll business.

* * *

JOHN GRISSIM cut his journalistic teeth freelancing for ROLLING STONE until the mid-Seventies, when his interests turned to the ocean. The author of seven books, he is publisher and editor of the quarterly journal *Marine Watch.*

* * *

JAMES HENKE is the chief curator of the Rock and Roll Hall of Fame and Museum in Cleveland, Ohio. He spent fifteen years on the staff of ROLLING STONE, including ten as music editor. He is the coeditor of *The ROLLING STONE Album Guide* and the third edition of *The ROLLING STONE Illustrated History of Rock & Roll.*

* * *

JERRY HOPKINS is a former correspondent and contributing editor of ROLLING STONE and the author of twenty-six books, including the Jim Morrison biography *No One Here Gets Out Alive.*

* * *

ROBERT HUNTER has been the primary lyricist for the Grateful Dead for thirty years. His lyrics are collected in *A Box of Rain: Lyrics 1965–1993.* Other works include translations of Rilke and several collections of his own poetry, including *Night Cadre* and *Sentinel.*

* * *

BLAIR JACKSON has been writing about the Grateful Dead for twenty-five years. From 1984 to 1993 he published the Dead fanzine *The Golden Road,* and he is the author of *The Music Never Stopped* and *Goin' Down the Road.* The executive editor of *Mix,* a trade magazine for the sound and recording industries, Jackson is currently at work on an oral biography of Jerry Garcia.

* * *

LENNY KAYE is best known for his guitar work with Patti Smith; he has also played with Jim Carroll and with his own band, Dog-A-Bone. As a producer, he has worked with Suzanne Vega, Soul Asylum and Kristin Hersh, among others, as well as assembling the garage-band anthology, *Nuggets.*

* * *

KEN KESEY is the author of *One Flew Over the Cuckoo's Nest, Sometimes a Great Notion, Kesey's Garage Sale, Demon Box,* *Caverns* (with O.U. Levon), *The Further Inquiry, Sailor Song* and *Last Go Round* (with Ken Babbs). His children's books include *Little Tricker the Squirrel Meets Big Double the Bear* and *The Sea Lion.*

* * *

MICHAEL LYDON, a founding editor of ROLLING STONE, is the author of *Rock Folk, Boogie Lightning, Writing and Life* and *How to Succeed in Show Business by Really Trying.* He is also a musician and a songwriter and, with Ellen Mandel, has composed an opera, *Passion in Pigskin.* Lydon is currently at work on a biography of Ray Charles.

* * *

CHARLES PERRY worked for ROLLING STONE in San Francisco; he then became a freelance writer specializing in food and food history and moved to Los Angeles. He is the author of *The Haight-Ashbury: A History.* Today he is a staff writer at the *Los Angeles Times* and a contributor to the *Oxford Companion to Food.*

* * *

CHARLES REICH is a visiting professor at the Yale Law School. He is the author of *The Greening of America* and *The Sorcerer of Bollnas Reef* and the coauthor (with Jerry Garcia and Jann S. Wenner) of *Garcia: A Signpost to New Space.*

* * *

ROBERT STONE is the author of five novels, including *Dog Soldiers* and *Outerbridge Reach.*

* * *

STEVE WEITZMAN has written for ROLLING STONE, *Playboy, Sports Illustrated, Billboard* and other publications. He is currently the talent buyer for the New York City club Tramps.

* * *

JANN S. WENNER has been the editor-in-chief of ROLLING STONE since he founded the magazine in 1967. The chairman of Wenner Media, he is also devoted to several causes, including the Rock and Roll Hall of Fame Foundation, of which he is vice chairman, and the Robin Hood Foundation, a philanthropic enterprise that funds New York City community-based organizations.

* * *

CHARLES M. YOUNG is a former associate editor of ROLLING STONE and is currently a freelance writer.

GENE ANTHONY [21, 22, 23, 60, 62-63, 68-69, 88-89, 96-97]; AP/WIDE WORLD PHOTOS [209]; ARKIVES © [186-187]; DAVID BERKWITZ/Sipa Press [210-211]; RON BEVIRT [6-7; 7 bot. r. courtesy Viking Penguin]; JAY BLAKESBERG [31, 158, 163, 174-175, 202-203, 205, 208]; ADRIAN BOOT/Retna [130, 132, 134, 136-137, 138-139]; MARY KAY BROWN [116 bot. l.]; PHILIP BURKE [168-169]; WILLIAM COUPON/Onyx [171]; R. CRUMB/Shanachie Entertainment [120, 121, 122, 123]; STEPHEN DANELIAN [105]; MICHAEL DOBO/Michael Ochs Archives [98, 100-101]; ALLEN GINSBERG [178-179]; MILTON GLASER [201]; HERBI GREENE [9, 11, 29, 42, 43, 47, 56, 73, 83, 84, 102, 141, 167, 197]; RICK GRIFFIN [115 top r., 115 bot. l., 117 ©1967 Family Dog 54]; ROBERT GROSSMAN [239]; AL HIRSCHFELD/Margo Feiden Galleries Ltd. [190-191]; ALTON KELLEY [114 top l., 114 bot.]; JEFF KRAVITZ [207]; ANITA KUNZ [i]; ANNIE LEIBOVITZ/Contact Press Images [221, 223, 224-225, 226-227, 228-229, 230-231, 232]; MALCOM LUBLINER [65]; JIM MARSHALL [33, 35, 37, 44-45, 50, 51, 71, 81, 92, 126, 127, 128-129, 146, 194, 196, 198-199]; STANLEY MOUSE/ALTON KELLEY [113 ©1966 Family Dog 26, 116 top r. ©1978 Bill Graham/Stanley Mouse/Alton Kelley #WIN781231]; DENNIS NOLAN [115 top l. ©1967 Family Dog 82/03]; MICHAEL OCHS ARCHIVES [124-125, 193]; JOSÉ GUADALUPE POSADA [240]; EDWARD RIEKER [206]; EBET ROBERTS [151]; JONATHON ROSEN [end]; Courtesy of Lenore Ross [15, 18]; BOB SEIDEMANN [40-41, 79]; MARK SELIGER [16, 181, 184, 213, 215, 216-217, 218]; DAVID SINGER [116 top l. ©1970 Bill Graham #263]; JON SIVERT/Michael Ochs Archives [103]; THOMAS WEIR [107]; WES WILSON [114 top r. ©1966 Wes Wilson/Bill Graham #22, 115 bot. r. ©1967 Wes Wilson/Bill Graham #51, 116 bot. r. ©1966 Wes Wilson/Bill Graham #41]; BARON WOLMAN [2-3, 27, 48-49, 53, 54-55, 74, 75, 76, 77]; JANET WOOLLEY [153].